POETRY, POLITICS & CULTURE

POETRY, POLITICS & CULTURE

Argument
in the
Work of
Eliot,
Pound,
Stevens
& Williams

Harold Kaplan

Transaction Publishers
New Brunswick (U.S.A.) and London (U.K.)

Library of Congress Catalog Number: 2006040384
ISBN: 0-7658-0303-8
Printed in the United States of America

Library of Congress Cataloging-in-Publication Data

Kaplan, Harold, 1916-
    Poetry, politics, and culture : argument in the work of Eliot, Pound, Stevens, and Williams / Harold Kaplan.
        p. cm.
    Includes bibliographical references and index.
    ISBN 0-7658-0303-8 (alk. paper)
        1. American poetry—20th century—History and criticism. 2. Politics in literature. 3. Culture in literature.   4. Politics and literature—United States—History—20th century. 5. Eliot, T. S. (Thomas Stearns), 1888-1965—Criticism and interpretation. 6. Pound, Ezra, 1885-1972—Criticism and interpretation. 7. Stevens, Wallace, 1879-1955—Criticism and interpretation. 8. Williams, William Carlos, 1883-1963—Criticism and interpretation. 1. Title.

PS310.P6K37 2006
811'.5209358—dc22   2006040384

In dedication to Wallace Stevens and Emmanuel Levinas:

I wish to express my debt to a poet and a philosopher who inspired and instructed me during the years in which this book was in progress. My deepest wish is that it does them full justice and honor.

> Though an heroic part, of the commonal.
> The major abstraction is the commonal,
> The inanimate, difficult visage. Who is it?
>
> What rabbi, grown furious with human wish,
> What chieftain, walking by himself, crying
> Most miserable, most victorious,
>
> Does not see these separate figures one by one,
> And yet see only one, in his old coat,
> His slouching pantaloons, beyond the town,
>
> Looking for what was, where it used to be?
> Cloudless the morning. It is he. The man
> In that old coat, those sagging pantaloons,
>
> It is of him, ephebe, to make, to confect
> The final elegance, not to console
> Nor sanctify, but plainly to propound.
>   "Notes Toward a Supreme Fiction"

* * *

"I think that across all literature the human face speaks-or stammers, or gives itself a countenance, or struggles with its caricature. Despite the end of Europo-centrism, disqualified by so many horrors, I believe in the eminence of the human face expressed in Greek letters and in our own, which owe the Greeks everything. It is thanks to them that our history makes us ashamed. There is a participation in Holy Scripture in the national literatures, in Homer and Plato, in Racine and Victor Hugo, as in Pushkin, Dostoyevsky or Goethe, as of course in Tolstoy or in Agnon. But I am sure of the incomparable prophetic excellence of the Book of Books, which all the Letters of the world awaited or upon which they comment. The Holy Scriptures do not signify through the dogmatic tale of their supernatural or sacred origin, but through the expression of the face of the other man that they illuminate, before he gives himself a countenance or a pose." (Ethics and Infinity)

Contents

Prefatory Note

In writing this book I recognized the difficulty of writing a comparative study of four major and distinctively original poets. Knowing the risk I pressed on, but I decided to work inductively and closely as possible from their texts so that theoretically tendentious reading would be at a minimum. Thus the first sixteen relatively short chapters of the book undertake to stay with the verse texts as much as possible in order to see the actual texture and quality of political and cultural interest one may find. The theoretical and comparative aspects are stressed in the last two chapters with support from the concluding appendices. What makes all this easier for structure is the principle I cite for myself and the reader, that a profoundly significant debate was going on among the four poets, explicitly or implicitly, on the themes which have most interest.

The discussion leads to the topic of modern poetics in its direct connection with cultural history and politics. It faces the fact that other large bodies of principle exist today which are most certainly strong rivals for the interest of students. The poetry and thinking about poetry found in the work of Stevens and Williams I call a "humanist poetics" deeply in harmony with liberal and democratic humanism. The contemporary interest in a poetics broadly comprehensive to include history, culture and politics and treated under the discipline and philosophy of linguistic analysis has been named "cultural poetics" (formerly the New Historicism and claiming to include both neo-Marxist and gender criticism)by its contemporary authors. Both terms are used by me for convenience and should not suggest doctrine in literary study. They are descriptive and analytic terms, not intended to be prescriptive even by their most loyal disciples, I believe. To do justice to the complexity and seriousness of these two bodies of thought and all the cross currents of problematic issues they contain, I suggest that some readers may find it helpful to review chapters 18-19 before reading the rest. Meanwhile I offer a brief précis of the theme.

Stevens, who I affirm at the start is at the focus of my discussion, provides essential terms for a study of a humanist poetics which both tallies and contrasts with cultural poetics and politics. To paraphrase my theme in this book and follow his lead, the "pressure of (modern) reality," forced efforts to retrieve or redeem the poet's vocation, the poet being now understood, explicitly or implicitly in the minds of at least three of the poets I have in view, to be the representative of a clerisy bound to create and defend a culture of values. Eliot would not have it this way for poetry, though he certainly evoked religion as the source and support of culture. On the other hand, Stevens would think of religion as the supreme of fictions or high poetries. Rather soberly and without romantic exaggeration Stevens studied the poetic imagination and universalized it as the source of value. Poems (which in this discussion represent the art or poetics of literature) are statements that assert "I poeticize," therefore I find value. If a culture constitutes acts and propositions that define meanings and valuations, poems are such exercises in basic miniature.

Inevitably the issues, as they are discussed today, become the fundamental issues of cultural politics. Stevens wrote his most urgent essay, "The Noble Rider and the Sound of Words," exactly in the mood of cultural and political crisis. In this country, that tone has become familiar and it is taken for granted that large cultural issues are at the forefront of political debate. But the same perspective on politics has great familiarity in the work of Pound and Eliot. One is surprised not to find them quoted on the side of the more extreme positions of either left or right.

As if it were a divided task, Williams wrote as if "things," the real world, needed redemption, and for Stevens, dominantly, the "imagination," needed redemption. That meant giving them central place in the name of culture, where the great enterprise of modernism would recruit Pound and Eliot. It is true that for Pound his esoteric economics and the whiphand of totalitarian politics would be the saving of culture, and for Eliot the Church and transcendent religion must perform that mission, but in the end culture and cultural politics gained their most active dedication, and to campaign for culture was to campaign for the normative imagination. These poets were engaged in what we call today the cultural wars, though they may seem either archaic or anachronistic in the belief that the imagination created value and that what happened in poetry could be the vitalizing source for ethics, politics, and culture. In Eliot's case this was a thesis he would overtly deny, but I suggest that his cultural criticism as well as his poetry contradict his denial, even as he draws in the defense of culture from the higher poetry of religion.

Much is said in the following discussion about value and its connection to poetry and the imagination that creates it. As much will be clear from Stevens' text and the attached commentary and analysis, but I should offer at the beginning that Stevens meant the power to discriminate among experiences and draw out their weight of meaning and illumination of quality. This has no limit on the grade or rank of goodness or badness, but it is the measure of the imagination to transform all appreciations through the excellence of the poetry. In effect poetry has the power to create or support the structure of values that define culture. What was at stake in Steven's mind was a cultural crisis in the faculties of valuation more than any specific set of values.

Finally, I wish to make acknowledgment to the Rockefeller Foundation, Northwestern University, and my colleagues at Northwestern and Bennington

College who together with my students helped this book in its long gestation and completion. My index will refer to only some of the several scholars and critics whose work in this rich field has helped form the resources for writing it. I must not omit thanks to the students and faculty of the Universities of Aix-en-Provence, Clermont-Ferrand, Poitiers in France, University of Bari in Italy, and Hebrew University in Israel who were of key importance in my study of American writing.

1

Introduction and Argument

A summary statement of mission was made by Wallace Stevens in 1946, just after the Second World War, when he called for "the highest poetry," at a time in modern history "that challenge(s) the poet as the appreciatory creator of values and beliefs."[1] It was a challenge William Carlos Williams could understand and voiced bluntly years earlier. There is this typically engaging passage from his letters: "There are not many things to believe, but the trouble is no one believes them. Modern verse forces belief."[2] He wrote this in a letter to Pound in 1932, who at that time was embarked on his own passage to belief. The issue, Williams wrote, was that of a modern poet in America, "the product of a new country." In an era discovering "the relativity of all knowledge" the world about him "still clung to the old measurements" [WLTRS,126]. In one way he was returning a message to his old mentor, Pound, who had taught him and their revolutionary generation to "make it new."

In brief essence Stevens and Williams eventually declared a premise they held in common with Eliot and Pound, that the imagination (in poetry) adds something to the world indispensable for living in it. The irreducible impulses of the poetic sensibility engaged the poets I study in sharply differing ways that point not only to their verse but to the political and cultural wars of the century. As a matter of poetic method they demonstrate the broad issues best in dramatizing the different tones of struggle and failure in the imagination. Whether idealized or reductive, the forming dialectic juxtaposed heroic myth and literary idealizations against quotidian and naturalist reality, or more definitively, both sides against the void. Poetic "reality" moved in constant cycles of a "Fall" between past and present, heaven and earth, god and man, man and animal, art and life, life and a dead universe. That was the psychic drama of classic modernism; "Gerontion" is explicit and so are "Prufrock" and "Mauberly" in expressing what Williams so straightforwardly described as "Not many things to believe..." and no one to believe them.

If I speak of mission it was Eliot who was most directly the missionary of culture and religion,(where "things to believe" had their source), at least in his

1

continuous prose writing and most ingeniously indirect in his poetry. It was a mark of Eliot's perception and his sense of a personal as well as general crisis that he should emphasize both transcendent religious experience and the Church in its most basic institutional loyalties. But it was specific that the binding support for imaginative belief and imaginative value was culture, with all the detail he approved in English cabbage dinners and the games of Epsom Downs. It seems certain he believed that if one pursued the ultimate order and substance of the secular imagination one would find culture- the product of the living thoughts and beliefs of the generations that make a tradition. The corollary for him was this: if one consulted human experience and natural reality without the support of culture and faith in the divine, one would reach only the place where Prufrock, Gerontion, Sweeney, and Bleistien make their lives—the place where the religious and poetic sensibility knows only loss and alienation. The extreme test of the imagination was in the modern cultural apocalypse. That fierce demand entered into the greatest of Eliot's verse and I think it defines the energy and encompassing vision of high modernism. Meanwhile the Church, with whatever its ordering metaphysics could provide, was a real and practical institution, that is, essentially political in its function.

The Reductive Imagination

The deepest relation of my four subjects came in the need they felt to theorize for poetry, that is, to consider the poetic imagination in its representation of human normative faculties at their highest. The time was urgent, what presented itself to all four poets was the apocalyptic crisis of culture embodied first in the Great War of Pound and Eliot's youth and the second wave of crisis in the Second World War with its long-lasting effects of political and cultural conflict.

For poets of the order of Stevens, Eliot, Pound, and Williams the chief threat was the loss of confidence in their own vocation, constantly subject to its negative dialectic in modern reductionist or scientist thinking and the pressures of quotidian reality. That was best expressed in these lines from Yeats' "The Circus Animals' Desertion."

> These masterful images because complete
> Grew in pure mind, but out of what began?
> A mound of refuse or the sweepings of a street,
> Old kettle, old bottles, and a broken can,
> Old iron, old bones, old rags, that raving slut
> Who keeps the till. Now that my ladder's gone,
> I must lie down where all the ladders start,
> In the foul rag and bone shop of the heart.

Searching for the source in "pure mind" or in the residue of all destructions could become a major task and obsession. As all ladders must have a start, the indices of imagination that arise from need and desire, pleasure and pain, order and beauty had to be linked with nature's truth and be capable of surviving disgust or the fiercest ostensible negation. Was poetry on the side of nature or of culture? Either way it was fated to be only half certain of its authenticity or source. One choice was to achieve perfect immediacy of perception. Red wheelbarrows, on which so much depend, wrote the poet, Williams, are at the beginning of everything, a "fact" in the empiricism of value. For Eliot, the deeper place to begin was with such things as a pair of claws on the sea floor. The Sweeney poems give us the poet's protagonist as ape, and what we might call the zoo or bestiary of modern poetry is brought to mind. Lawrence's snakes and tortoises, Marianne Moore's rare birds of exotic plumage, present a world both to humble and please the taste. In fiction, Hemingway's bulls and lions move on stage as if to simulate tragedy.

The large context is that of an impoverished world, even with the stoic or romantic compensations of vitalism. Beyond all is the void of being and against its blank background appear shadows that still charge response. Envisioned as blackbird or snowman in Stevens, for example, they call upon the imagination specifically as the will to order in a world deficient in its forms. Form is a force, the Vorticist Pound would say, channeled and controlled in a world of ultimately uncontrolled energies. The imagination responds to natural power, and the will which Stevens called the "rage for order" is the will to master force. The need to confront disorder is itself an order of the imagination. The first victim might be the established conventions of form but the poet or artist could survive destruction and make something out of "A mound of refuse or the sweepings of a street." The artist engages with the sordid, the ugly, the terrifying, the trivial, in order to transcend those limitations on terms outside their reach. Is this a perversion of the value consciousness or an effort to redeem it against, as Stevens would say, "the pressure of reality?" Or must all things descend before they ascend to the heaven of esthetic form?

The possibility that the universe and world have no intrinsic order is always a challenge to poets. Here the issues of modern normative discourse have their confrontation. One feels the esthetic heroism, a megalomania of talent and style in the writing and teaching of Pound. But while Pound reached for power immediately as the esthetician of order, tyrannical in the name of beauty, he contrasts with Eliot, who was first a tragedian of the spirit, and then, as in purgatory, begged for the discipline of tradition and the order of faith. If Eliot and Pound were poets whose imaginations occupied the center of modern spiritual and moral conflict, as much was true for my two other subjects, who, I believe, wrote with a native American temper and mind which made them loyal to reality beyond art and order, and made art from that loyalty. The thematic contrasts among the four poets I treat as poet-theorists can be observed from my chapter titles drawn from their words, "The Pressure of Reality," "The Lords Over Fact," "A Confidence in the World, " The Malady of the

Quotidian," "The Imagination as Value," "The City as a Man." These words have a ring, they memorialize a confrontation of ideas that do what Shelley proposed and Ezra Pound attempted, to connect the force of civilization with its poets as its "unacknowledged" legislators.

The Cultural Apocalypse

As I've noted culture became a totem word for a system of values, an attitude and way of life in the earliest youth of Eliot and Pound, and it also became a theme of conflict, a "clash of civilizations." One went to war or fought in revolutions to save civilization or change it. In an "age of disbelief," in Stevens' phrase, and of revolutionary imperatives, the principle of order could be distinguished among values to become the generalized value of civilization itself. "O blessed rage for order," Stevens wrote in one of his most resonant poems, and he might have spoken in ironically refined wisdom for his contemporaries, Pound and Eliot, as well as for himself.

That passion for order cannot be separated from as deep a call for disruption in modernist art and culture. To accept the fully subversive role, both within art and against the correlated conventions of value, was to imply strength in the ability to preside over chaos. To "seize the power from nature" (in Picasso's words) could mean to make art surrogate for an absent or moribund civilized order.[3] "I want a new civilization," Ezra Pound cried, and that accent is in all the manifestos of Futurists, Vorticists, Dadaists and Surrealists. Essentially their great theme, in the midst of revolt, was the power of the imagination in acts of creation. Stevens too was obeying the logic of the imagination and its power as he conceived it when he wrote the following in a time of crisis, the Second World War.

> We are confronting, therefore, a set of events, not only beyond our power to tranquillize them in the mind, beyond our power to reduce them and metamorphose them, but events that stir the emotions to violence, that engage us in what is direct and immediate and real, and events that involve the concepts and sanctions that are the order of our lives and may involve our very lives....(NA,22)

In writing this as a poet and on behalf of poetry Stevens was making a claim to rival Pound's in the interest of a "new civilization," and that of Eliot in the defense of a traditional culture. Such terms equate with "ideas of order" and "supreme fictions" that have their succinct definition in "the concepts and sanctions that are the order of our lives." Stevens was doing even more to define poetry in his mind, a power to reduce and tranquillize experience, and yet be directly engaged with what is immediate and real.

In Stevens' mind the message for poets was not to call them to arms but to explain the fundamental value of the art they achieved. Writing in the era of the earlier world war, with even more sense of the apocalypse, Pound could have well understood those words of Stevens, though voiced far from his temperament and very far from his specific goals. Eliot, too, despite his denial, acted as if he believed Shelley on the role of poetry in legislating a world, most openly in the strong avocation they held as cultural critics. The first of the great modernists, James Joyce, began fiction as if with the mock assumption of deity by the young Stephen Dedalus as an artist, and all three suggested that the dominant aspect of the Creation was perhaps its order and not its truth. Stevens himself implied the same presumption to direct the narrative of human creation when he wrote that "the fundamental glory" of the gods was "the fundamental glory of men and women, who being in need of it create it." This may sound sublimely casual, but he meant to describe the major work of the mythic, religious, and literary imagination and seriously claim that the universe we know is human.

In the obsession with the origin and fate of culture, Eliot led the way with a focused anxiety which had its direct descent from the nineteenth-century literary generations. Arnold, Carlyle, Ruskin, Pater, and Morris emerged significantly enough in the early Darwinian climax of naturalist thought which exposed the naked roots of culture, its vulnerability to temporal change and variant contexts. If the Darwinian simians could speak, they might claim that culture had been created esoterically, by human hands. That in itself was an idea with endless evolutionary implications. The cultural apocalypse, a standard theme in writings, manifestoes, and journals, meant that culture had to be created anew. In hope or anxiety the interest in the unmaking and remaking of culture was the natural partner of revolution in an age of revolutions; the active tradition fostered the certainty that culture itself was the byproduct of the deepest biological and economic forces. The surrounding effects color and heighten Eliot's strong countereffort to prove the dependence of culture on religious belief.

Cultural anxiety and cultural revolution became powerful themes in modern writing for the reason that they were both the logical outcome of modern naturalist thought and the main defense against its implications. They have their melodramatic and typical effects in Spengler, and strength for lasting influence in Marx. Among modern writers of greatest prestige, the examples of Yeats and Eliot suffice to stress cultural prepossession as a category of literary study. Yeats' *A Vision* is the ambitious project of a poet writing his own book of culture, matched by the more judicious effort of Eliot in his later life to bring preachment for the survival of Christian culture. Pound's *Cantos* might without exaggeration be seen as the large cultural epic he thought he found so powerfully abbreviated in Eliot's *The Waste Land* and masterfully enlarged in Joyce's *Ulysses*. It was art in its power over language and meaning that brought the theme and narrative of culture so far for the classic modernists. Today in the schools of postmodern thought and in their consequences for literary criticism and theory, culture and its contingent issues, (not surprisingly leading or following directly from social anthropology and politics), have almost wholly replaced the topics of traditional literary study for priority of interest.

The Modern Americans

The keynote of cultural exile marks the background in the lives and works of the Americans Eliot and Pound, and certainly both were American poets in a deeper sense than mere nativity. In fiction the classic American historian of culture must surely be Henry James, writing of cultures in confrontation on the cosmopolitan streets of Paris, London, Rome and Florence. "We are all a famished race," James has one of his culture starved Americans say in his fiction, and that hunger openly or insidiously expresses its force in modern American writing, in Stevens and Williams, in Eliot and Pound, and in Hemingway and Faulkner, a keenness of need which has everything to do with the strong response met by their writing.

The issue might have been described as that of the perennial quarrel between Europe and America. On crudely simple terms of life experience and politics, one might declare at the start that Williams and Stevens remained Americans while Pound and Eliot achieved vivid and complete forms of expatriation. On political terms, Pound introduced Fascism of the European model to oppose the traditional American system. Eliot seemed to go further in fact, since Pound's economics and politics had a clear American source in reactionary populism. To Williams it might have seemed as if Eliot had returned whole body and soul to the world of Thomas à Becket, with all its ideological and institutional loyalties made present in the context of twentieth century alienation from religion and culture. But what was tradition, what was modern, and what was American converge in my discussion on the issues for poetry and belief.

The questions quite overbearing in the American tradition itself were these: where is culture to be found, where does it begin, and what exists *beyond* culture? What did the words of poets, priests, and statesmen (among those representing "culture") have to demonstrate in order to make their account with reality and belief? In great historic contrast, when Thoreau wrote a climactic passage in Walden, which I quote, he could not believe that the "reality beyond" culture that he celebrated might be considered a void or mere animal reduction as in so many minds of a later generation. The passage is memorable for the positive zest that pertains to metaphors of reduction.

> Let us settle ourselves, and work and wedge our feet downward through the mud and slush of opinion, and prejudice, and tradition, and delusion, and appearance, that alluvion which covers the globe, through Paris and London, through New York and Boston and Concord, through church and state, through poetry and philosophy and religion, till we come to a hard bottom and rocks in place, which we can call reality, and say, This is, and no mistake; and then begin....[4]

This of course was really transcendence "downward" on behalf of nature and not reduction at all. "Reality is fabulous," he wrote, echoing his master, Emerson, who said, "God himself culminated in the present moment, and will never be more divine in the lapse of all the ages." But the matter was more complicated than that as Emerson himself explained in a passage from his essay "Experience."

> It is very unhappy, but too late to be helped, the discovery we have made that we exist. That discovery is called the Fall of Man. Ever afterwards we suspect our instruments. We have learned that we do not see directly but mediately, and that we have no means of correcting these colored and distorting lenses which we are, or of computing the amount of their errors. Perhaps these subject-lenses have a creative power; perhaps there are no objects. Once we lived in what we saw; now the rapaciousness of this new power, which threatens to absorb all things, engages us.

That "second" Fall of Man in Emersonian prophecy was from *trusted* knowledge, we "suspect our instruments." The theme of dissociation, which is at the center of both Eliot's poetry and his literary and cultural criticism, is expressed in a similar division between the world, reality, and the human instruments for living in it. The "rapacious new power" can be what you like, nineteenth-century new science, industrial technology and commerce, the ebb of religion in material goals and values, where all these were in conflict with the normative needs and beliefs of humans expressed in old fables dissociated from non-"fabulous reality." Primarily the divorce for poets was deep in "a dissociation of sensibility." "Tennyson and Browning are poets, and they think; but they do not feel their thought as immediately as the odour of a rose"(ESE, 247).

It is precisely the conjunction of a faith in "fabulous reality" with the possibility that it might reach mere solipsism or anarchic nature or a void, and the parallel passion for *creating* a human world in the promise held forth in Emerson's "The American Scholar" that marks the poignance of any study of the modern Americans in their work of creation or in what Stevens called decreation. Emerson is in fact a key figure in any conjunctive relationship which involves Eliot and Stevens as well as Eliot and Williams. Harold Bloom has called Emerson the "inventor for American poetry of the Optative Mood," which he defined in Emerson's words, "All writing must be in a degree exoteric, written to a human *should* or *would*, instead of to the fatal *is*." The special emphasis of this in respect to the modern poets is the search for their own function, that of the imagination in an age of empirical truth. The high focus on the American context, again furbishing Emerson, was given by John Dewey in *Art as Experience.*

> ...imagination is the chief instrument of the good...art is more moral than moralities. For the latter are, or tend to become, consecrations of the status quo... The moral prophets of humanity have always been poets even though they spoke in free verse or by parable." [5]

With Dewey and the Emersonian background in mind we may say that the poets of American modernism each made the effort to break the barriers of "dissociation" and reductive thought. A distinctly American and stoic view of reductive dissociation can be found in the verse of Robert Frost: In "The White-Tailed Hornet," he asks why we pay so much compliment to animal instincts, or the ordinary biologically reductive image of man. "To err is human, not to, animal," the poem says, and so we congratulate ourselves on being animal, a truly dubious, self-limiting compliment. It doesn't give but takes away, the poem says, and what is taken away is worship, humor, conscientiousness. The poem goes on:

> And served us right for having instituted
> Downward comparisons. As long on earth
> As our comparisons were stoutly upward
> With gods and angels, we were men at least,
> But little lower than the gods and angels.
> But once comparisons were yielded downward,
> Once we began to see our images
> Reflected in the mud and even dust,
> 'Twas disillusion upon disillusion.
> We were lost piecemeal to the animals,
> Like people thrown out to delay the wolves.
> Nothing but fallibility was left us,
> And this day's work made even that seem doubtful.

Those barriers marked the distance between language and reality and between normative judgment and its imputed references. The issues are immense that can support such terms as "the Fall of Man;" there is the project of knowledge and judgment to begin with in the need to name "reality" at all, the word's dubiety seemingly endorsed by the most influential of modern thinkers, namely Nietzsche and Heidegger.[6] The former proposed that factual truths disappear inside their interpretation, and the latter wrote to great effect that "we live in the house of language," to which some of his followers might add there are no doors or windows leading out. We cannot overestimate the effect of these pronouncements. In the context of my discussion the project for poets (as well as wisdom seekers) would be to affirm subjective consciousness and personal identity and still escape solipsism, to redeem tradition and history and escape mechanical determinism, to rediscover the power to name values and escape nihilism. The striving of the poets with those variations of a second "Fall" required wrestling with "reality" while giving full self-criticism to the "instruments" of consciousness under suspicion.

The Poetic Imagination and Politics

The reader of my book should be quite aware by now that I deal with a major quarrel among these poets whom I mark as archetypally influential figures on the cultural, political, and literary levels of the modern West. This may surprise many who would dismiss the pretensions of poetry as such on those levels, particularly the political, but it would not surprise my subjects themselves. The issues indeed bring up the project of creative freedom as it pertains to the imagination, versions of order and power in patterns of creation and de-creation, and ultimately, the foundational premises for culture and the normative imagination which affect politics. They interplay in a series of important distinctions to be made among the poets I study in the chapters that follow. The cultural debate in their time was definitely cultural politics, but closer to the edge of practical politics than even today with the strong emergence of post-modernism.[7]

At the center of the dramatic contrasts one finds between these two pairs of American poets, major in all respects, is the debate within democratic culture over the role of authority, the conflicting ideals of order, freedom, and equality, the sanctities and immunities protecting the lives of individuals, and the centrality of individuals in the democratic ethos. My focus on their writing that can be viewed as political in this sense can be illustrated in an example from the political conflict between two old literary friends, Williams and Pound.

The issues in Williams' own political thinking and his quarrel with Pound came to a head at the time Pound was taken prisoner during the war and accused of treason. In a letter written to Robert McAlmon, Williams committed himself to an explicit democratic humanism.

> What I wanted to say, of course, is that unless we have some moral code, based on our responsibility to our fellow-man to go by, based that is on the essential value of the individual, any individual,-then we have no right to judge as between two sides in any contest and there can be no objection to war and slaughter to our heart's content and one side is like another once it wins. (WSL,p. 222)

Contemporary readers may find that last reference curious; the taboo possibly refers to dominant sentiment in the intellectual and literary avant-garde during the long seduction by anti-humanist or anti-democratic ideologies in the thirties and forties. Williams' claim for individual rights to counter Pound's Fascism was extreme; "an absolute faith in man's value from an absolute standpoint" and would jar any modern sensibility which could not claim religious sanction for it, and the most acute religionists like Eliot would rather stress "fallen man" and the complex destinarian doctrines of "original sin." The faith, if it is one, is that of Whitman. In any case it was more than lip service to this creed, stated in the letter, that we find in his verse. He put his presence into the unredeemed world, without remaking it and begging no favors. His city, Paterson, was a "man," but the closer humanism is found in such shorter poems as "Tract," where the towns-people are commanded to recognize the absolute distinction between life and death, how to perform proper service at a funeral, without costume or ritual, without symbol of status or icon of belief.

> I will teach you, my townspeople
> how to perform a funeral
> for you have it over a troop
> of artists—
> unless one should scour the world—
> you have the ground sense necessary.

To believe in that "ground sense" it was necessary to practice anthropocentric democracy. More then ceremony and ornamentation was involved, a respect for reality as one found it as opposed to the immense superstructures of culture. Williams said he would write *Paterson* in attack or defense against "those principles of knowledge and culture which the universities and their cripples have cloistered and made a cult... (and he would make)...the keg-cracking assault upon the cults and the kind of thought that destroyed Pound and made what it has made of Eliot" (WSL, p 214). He assuredly means the "systems" of hierarchy and tradition, of totalist established culture with its codes and cults. The bigotries of secondary value systems, the prosody of established societies and cultures, rhyme schemes and metrical systems, became the surrogate target for him. In the same letter he wrote,

> If Stevens speaks of *Parts of a World* , this is definitely Parts of a Greater World- a looser, wider world where "order" is a servant not a master. Order is what is discovered after the fact, not a little piss pot for us all to urinate into- and call ourselves satisfied.

In his mind, the "order" that was "after the fact" might be found with intrinsic democracy. Williams would surely not object to being called defender and champion of a specifically American democratic culture. He made this role most explicit in his letters and his autobiography. To Horace Gregory he wrote,

> I have maintained from the first that Eliot and Pound by virtue of their hypersensitivity (which is their greatness) were too quick to find a culture (the English continental) ready made for their assertions. They ran from something else, something cruder but, at the same time, newer, more dangerous but heavy with rewards for the sensibility that could reap them.

He and Gregory were thinking of a project together studying the "forms" of culture, "a study of the formal resources of a new cultural concept (not to be narrowly designated American though perhaps first adequately perceived here)" (WSL, p. 228). However, the culture he spoke of was determinedly democratic. "The essential democracy upon which an attempt was made to found the U.S. has been the central shaft about which all the other movements and trends of thought have revolved...." In the end, he wrote in April, 1936, it would defeat both Marxism and Fascism (WSL, p.157).

These are specifics that describe the urgencies of political allegiance in the lives of my subjects. It was a time when Eliot felt it necessary to declare his politics to be monarchist and Tory, his church the High Anglican, and his literary allegiance, classicist. It was the period when the quasi-emperor of high literary culture was Ezra Pound who declared himself a Fascist in Italy. Such declarations very much make what I have quoted from Williams' letter sound mild spoken and the silence of Stevens glaring on the subject of political allegiance. Yet both in their work are intrinsically the heirs of Emerson and the classic American tradition of literary democratic humanism.[11]

Williams might have argued that Emersonian affirmations were indeed what Eliot said they were, explicitly the sharpest contrast with his vision of unredeemed man. If Sweeney's shadow haunts and mocks Emerson's pages, he also moves in argument with Williams as well as where Stevens' trope of "major man" has specific relevance. Again to sharpen the contrast with Eliot, when Stevens invokes the creative spirit in "Sunday Morning," "not as a god but as a god might be" we can hear clear echoes of Emerson in "The Poet," his invocation of the liberating gods of poetry. As for Eliot, if he had modeled a political and literary anti-self in every detail he could have chosen parts from Emerson's "The American Scholar" and "Self-Reliance."

With such perspectives I mind, it is not surprising to find how much the work of the poets in their implicit quarrel with each other, specifically engaged in the century's wars for and against liberal democracy. It is certainly true that in these generations the liberal humanism of Jefferson and Emerson found itself under siege on grievous terms hardly imagined by those two forebears. We gather important topics in this debate within the high culture of the democratic West— the nostalgia for the hero and for real and symbolic hierarchies of rank and value, the revulsion from quotidian humanity and mass culture in their variant spiritually depressing forms. It was inevitable that as Dewey suggests these themes for poets began to build an ethos, a poetics, and an expression of politics in harmony with the vivid history of their time.

Democracy and its byproducts understandably offended the esthetic sense, as Pound makes very clear, and if the esthetic sensibility could rebel by seizing power, as he also quixotically urged, artists by character and standard could plausibly become Fascists and Pound was by no means alone in that respect. But democracy, as with Eliot, also challenged the moral and religious sense. It is pertinent to say that Eliot most disliked the optimized state of secular grace implicit in the liberal ideal. His imagination moved in revulsion from "fallen" humanity, that is, average quotidian humanity; what was the second Fall then if not that into the universal indiscriminate animal, and so he pursued stark sacrifices of the body, of time, of fallen cities and decayed communities. Within all, the social anarchy threatened by the ethnic or racial stranger joined with the natural anarchy of the body, until the virtues of traditional hierarchies and a cultural order became manifest with absolute clarity.

Eliot's further rejection of humanism thus was entailed with his religious search and his campaign for an authoritarian Christian culture. The contrast with Williams appears most sharply here and accounts for much of Williams instinctive reaction against Eliot's creed in toto, including both his reverence for tradition and his cosmopolitanism in writing. In his own verse Williams moves as far as Eliot and further into the urban human waste land, bringing poetry out of anti-poetry in order to redeem "reality," a term for him that reflected an immanence of value in things and persons. The spirit of Whitman's democracy thrives in Williams' verse, distinctive as they both were in their forms of emotional rhetoric and verse display. Williams repeated one message: bring the world close enough and it will reveal itself without translation or interpretation, without spiritual or esthetic gloss.

In the work of Stevens one will find a more subtly extended response to Eliot. To Stevens the poetic imagination was linked or equivalent to the creative force in freedom; it represented, I believe, the ideal democratic intelligence, human autonomy by privilege of the imagination, not bound to doctrine nor authoritarian, not bound to abstract loyalties nor crushed under what most often represents "reality" though the latter was nevertheless and finally the more necessary "angel." There is a sober Emersonian creed in Stevens, an undefeated imagination that believes in itself more than its fallible creations. The democratic imagination is personal and individualistic in its work and in its essential humanism it speaks for adventure, open discourse, and consensus rather than fate, contingency and power. Perhaps Stevens' poetic concept of "the first idea" is that of the primordial franchise itself, the first step toward communication and discourse. The franchise, in this vein of idealization, gives first consideration to the immediacy of place, thing, and person, while invoking the ordering angel that guides the exercise of freedom. That was one "necessary angel"; the other supervised respect for "reality" conjoined with respect for language, a combination to fight off solipsism or the fatalist surrender to rule and conformity. Thus poetic theory could edge into cultural politics as Stevens called on the autonomous activity of the imagination to justify its freedom and explain its reward in a struggle against the "pressure of reality." In voicing this he must have considered another "pressure" reaching him from the equally strong poetic imaginations of Pound and Eliot.

Notes

1. *Letters of Wallace Stevens*, ed. Holly Stevens (New York: Alfred A. Knopf, 1966), p. 526. (Hereafter noted as SLTRS).
2. William Carlos Williams, *Selected Letters*, ed. John C. Thirlwall (New York: McDowell, Obolensky, 1957), p.126 (hereafter WLTRS).
3. The words are attributed to Picasso by Françoise Gilot. "Painting isn't a question of sensibility; it's a matter of seizing the power, taking over from nature, not expecting her to supply you with information and good advice....Once the painter takes it into his head to arrive at an arbitrary determination of color.... he will choose, for all the

rest, colors and relationships which burst out of nature's straitjacket. That's the way he asserts his freedom from nature. And that's what makes what he does interesting." (Francoise Gilot and Carlton Lake, *Life With Picasso* (New York: McGraw Hill, [1964], p. 59.)

4. *Walden* (Boston: Houghton Mifflin Co., 1960), p.67.

5. John Dewey, *Art as Experience* (New York: G.P. Putnam's Sons, 1958), p.348.

6. Martin Heidegger had his own view of the "second fall of man." "Dasein usually busies itself in quotidian affairs losing itself in the present, forgetting what is most its own: this is its *Verfallensein.*" See "Letter on Humanism," *Basic Writings,* ed. David F. Krell (New York: Harper & Row, 1975), pp., 212, 212n. and *Being and Time*, sectiions 25-27, 38 and 68C.

7. Their successors today, dominant in the humanities departments of many universities and in critical journals, are found in a third contemporary generation of scholars and critics who stress the relations of literature and cultural politics. An impatient friend once exclaimed that they might all be taken over as subsections of the departments of anthropology, archaeology and politics, "and a good thing, too."

Part 1

Eliot and Pound:
Dissociations of Sensibility and Power

2

Dissociations, Natural and Supernatural

One of the more famous of Pound's teaching aphorisms was the remark that poetry should be as well-written as prose. Eliot concurred in holding that "verse should have the virtues of prose," and by this both he and Pound clearly meant the constraint and detachment borrowed from dominantly realistic fiction, specifically that of Flaubert, Stendhal, and Henry James. In more direct support as a model there was Baudelaire who could teach poets how to write a modern poetry.

> From him [Baudelaire], as from LaForgue, I learned... that the source of new poetry might be found in what had been regarded hitherto as the impossible, the sterile, the intractably unpoetic. . . . that the poet, in fact, was committed by his profession to turn the unpoetical into poetry.[1]

Behind this thinking, important as it was in Eliot's program for his own poetry, there was a larger project than merely to convert to poetry the "intractably unpoetic" materials of modern urban life. Here he was facing and expressing in his poetry what Stevens memorably called "the malady of the quotidian" and in another reference, "antipoetry," like Stevens converting it to poetic use. The comprehensive ideal was Dante (with whom even Baudelaire compared as a "bungler") in "the adjustment of the natural to the spiritual, of the bestial to the human, and the human to the supernatural."[2] This was the high mission on whose scale Eliot's work must be understood, if not measured. But in the immediate case the issue was related to the embroilment with "Romanticism" in Eliot's generation, much of it stimulated by the vital literary quarrels of the French. Eliot called Baudelaire the "first counter-Romantic in poetry," and so approved of him. With a degree of simplification that suited his polemical needs, he liked to consider romanticism's chief failure a betrayal of reality leading to a cultivated solipsism. Like Pound, Eliot wished to defend the virility of poetry; it was necessary to rescue both the higher and lower vision from "the phantasmal imagination." How well defined this impulse was in both a psychological and metaphysical sense became clear in the later work, where to become "unreal," whether as person, city, or world, is the worst desolation of all. In *The Cocktail Party*, for instance, Harcourt-Reilly teaches his spiritual patients to avoid

> . . . .the final desolation
> Of solitude in the phantasmal world
> Of imagination, shuffling memories and desires.

Of course the latter is the lost world of Prufrock and Gerontion, a "shuffling" in the void that makes the razor scrape on Sweeney's leg, the scream of the epileptic on the bed, and all the movements of "ragged claws" and "silent vertebrates" in the early poems almost welcome in their aggressive shock.

The margin of a "final desolation" marks Eliot's work in its characteristic dramatic tension. "Reality" had its definition against the void and from there rapidly extended itself. The Dantesque vision was his support.

> . . .the great poet should not only perceive and distinguish more clearly than other men, the colours or sounds within the range of ordinary vision or hearing; he should perceive vibrations beyond the range of ordinary men, and be able to make men see and hear more at each end than they could ever see without his help.[3]

The way of perceiving was that of sharp juxtaposition in extreme range where the disparity itself rendered the completeness of vision. All of Eliot's dramatic violence in arraying the natural and supernatural worlds, the bestial and the human, the human and divine, was intensely serious, for these dualities, or dissociations, were charged with redemptive energy. The violence of juxtapositions worked toward its own relief, purging defective and blurred vision, cleansing the spirit of decayed legend, pious illusion, untested faith. Sweeney, Doris, and Grishkin had such cleansing work to do in "Mr. Eliot's Sunday Morning Service," "Whispers of Immortality," and "Sweeney Erect." It was a source of poetry for priestly metaphysicians, those "sable presbyters" to confront Sweeney, "shifting from ham to ham" in his bath. Nor had the American humanist and prophet of a normative naturalism, Emerson, seen "the silhouette of Sweeney straddled in the sun." This made for a triple level of dissociation with Sweeney as the shadow haunting all discourse that sublimated animal existence.

It is necessary to keep such pronouncements in mind when reviewing the familiar issues of Eliot's career as a critic. The polemic against "romanticism" and the heralded choice of "classicism" tended to obscure Eliot's allegiance to a neo•positivist esthetic different from both. It is usually clear that Eliot's literary choices were based on issues that went deeper than ostensible literary values, and in this respect we don't need to review here the roles of Bradley, Babbitt, Maurras, and Hulme in the intellectual debates that did so much to form Eliot's mind. Generalized far enough, the issue for Hulme as for Maurras was a distinction between liberal and conservative in politics and religion.

This "realism" was power and classicism meant authority, and both were identified with process, time, and the force in things. The classical was not a choice of mere style, hard and dry, understated and lucid, but a whole world of values and judgment on issues for which men might well fight.

Eliot saw the theme even more succinctly in a note prepared for his early lectures on French literature while he was still a post-graduate student in England.

> Romanticism stands for *excess* in any direction. It splits up into two directions: escape from the world of fact, and devotion to brute fact. The two great currents of the nineteenth century—vague emotionality and the apotheosis of science (realism) alike spring from Rousseau.[4]

This is characteristically sharp in the posing of alternatives. One revulsion fed upon the other in his poetry, a reaction from self-indulgent emotion in a world dominated by brute fact. Despite Eliot's presumed respect for science, its gospel of fact could be hopelessly reductive; perhaps it would permit the brutalization of all human culture. Yet the romantic escape from reductive truths was an even greater divorce of spirit where it lived on private ground. In that respect Eliot himself cultivated an account in his early verse which was strong enough to shock genteel sentiment, purge false consciousness, and seize the vantage ground of realism. But the reaction was directed to become a part of spiritual discipline; the violence of nature was to be the resource for the ultimate transcendence of both fact and fantasy.

Even in the deepest Prufrockian stalemate of his poetry there is an energy that leads to the strong resolutions of politics and religion in his later career. The polemic against "romanticism" for its moral vagueness and irresponsibility helped him, as did dealing with "brute fact" in his own vein. The interesting aspect of this debate is the way in which the party of Hulme and Eliot, calling themselves classicists, were expressing themselves as stoic naturalists, as emphatic upon the animal nature of man as anyone could be in the post-Darwinian era in which they wrote. But this had inverse response to what they considered the romantic premise. Hulme wrote, "Man is an extraordinarily fixed and limited animal.... It is only by tradition and organization that anything decent can be got out of him."[5] In so many words, a reductive naturalism could give ground for an appeal to authoritarian hierarchies of order.

The remark illustrates how the view of man as an "extraordinarily fixed and limited animal" would vie with spiritual transcendence. It suggests how Eliot, too, in his cultural criticism and his politics would place the value of order and tradition into priority very close to the actual illuminations of personal religious experience. Above all it could demonstrate for himself how he could traverse a reductive procedure in order to pierce below the natural and the human and beyond time and mortal substance to find the hints of redemptive grace. Paradoxically, the process of naturalization became an act of spirit.

A Mechanism of Sensibility

In his important essay on Blake, Eliot remarks for contrast that Tennyson was the poet "almost wholly encrusted with opinions, almost wholly merged into his environment." Such a mind and temperament could stand for the accommodating spirit of the middle way, a man dressed for the everyday conciliatory world. But Blake "was naked, and saw man naked, and from the centre of his own crystal....He approached everything with a mind unclouded by current opinions.... This makes him terrifying" (ESE, 277). In the same essay, Eliot went on to observe that Blake was only a genius whereas Dante, as an example, was a classic who subsumed in his work the same ferociously naked "honesty" of genius and then rose from the fearful confrontation toward an ultimate harmony of vision with the help of a "framework of accepted and traditional ideas." The classic was a conception of the highest poetry, bridging the dichotomy in Eliot's own mind between the incrustations of tradition and the nakedness of Blakean honesty.

However, the preoccupation with honesty was most supported in another context, the disinterestedness of the scientist. Eliot writes in "The Perfect Critic" that the aim of art, like the aim of scientific knowledge, was to transcend mere emotional states or the accidental stimuli to the emotions that may come from poetry. "The end of the enjoyment of poetry is a pure contemplation from which all the accidents of personal emotion are removed; thus we aim at the object as it really is..."[6] Aristotle was the "perfect critic" in this respect, for he "had what is called the scientific mind..." though Eliot conditioned this by saying it was a mind "rarely found among scientists except in fragments" (SW, 13). Two literary critics Eliot particularly admired, Sainte-Beuve and Remy de Gourmont, were he points out trained in physiology.

For a modern poet science meant one thing enviable in the end, it brought true dignity to acts of intellectual imagination. It had authenticity that even "sable presbyters" could not question and made "romantics" seem veritable children. Eliot's almost casually delivered critical programs for the "objective correlative" and "dissociated sensibility" reveal an obsession not with science but with its psycho-cultural effects on the integration of knowledge and experience. There was a notable prejudice working in the "anti-romanticism" of Eliot's youth, directed against a subjectivity without bounds. As if to punish sensibility, his language in the essay on Hamlet imitates the style of science, its severe ideal of exactitude even offering a rather simplistic view of psychological stimulus and response.

> The only way of expressing emotion in the form of art is by finding an "objective correlative"; in other words, a set of objects, a situation, a chain of events which shall be the formula of that *particular* emotion; such that when the external facts, which must terminate in sensory experience, are given, the emotion is immediately evoked. (ESE, 125)

The words almost exactly resemble Pound's own definition of the image, suggesting a radical distrust of personal subjectivity and a need to reassert the authority of art and its power. Upon reflection, however, this thinking might seem rather absurd. Objectivism, even in art, would be strained to find formulae certain to evoke "a particular emotion" or response. "Hamlet (the man) is dominated by an emotion which is inexpressible, because it is in excess of the facts as they appear." Eliot suggested "a study for pathologists;" however, in his criticism Eliot was actually engendering a very good analysis of the interest which Hamlet's character has for the audience. Hamlet has, he says, "a feeling he cannot understand; he cannot objectify it, and it therefore remains to poison life and obstruct action."

The issue was not chiefly Hamlet but an almost morbid care for the intellectual seriousness of literature. His friend and mentor, Pound, and other modernists were campaigning to liberate art from its specialization in personal emotions, and, defying solipsism, from the centricity of persons in the scheme of things. The equal motive was to regain access to "reality" in implicit rivalry with science, and defend the poetic or normative imagination against the "pressure of reality" rather as Stevens used those terms and felt the same obsession. It should be observed that although Eliot mentioned the enthronement of reason in the eighteenth century as example of the dissociated sensibility, what he saw in his own time was the rule of random impulse and chaotic naturalist forces. The threat to poetry (and to life) was not from desiccated reason but forces apparently beyond grasp, and certainly beyond the field of sensibility occupied by the poetry of sentiment that Eliot rejected in his youth. On the other hand the "objective correlative" gave safety from Hamlet-like emotions one "cannot understand."

The gist of his thinking insofar as it had connection with a latent theory of poetry was the insistence on depersonalization and the resistance to subjectivity. Dissociation was resolved as in science with a perfect fusion of factual reality with an externalized consciousness which Eliot imagined as "a mechanism of sensibility which could devour any experience" (ESE, 247). The language is curiously significant in its stress on "mechanism" and "devour" as if a neutral process not a sensibility were involved. Thus in his first important essay Eliot made a point of taking science as his metaphor for the poetic process itself. In "Tradition and the Individual Talent" his purpose was to find that emotions and feelings were not the personal property of the poet but data in a field of experience broad enough to include the whole literary and cultural tradition. This could be one anchorage for the emotions but actually the poet went further, for since his mind was the actual field of events, it was as if the poet scientist had entered nature as the intelligent part of it; he could supply himself as chemical agent and become embodied in the truth as well as reporting it.

Almost at the same time, however, Eliot would evoke the classic "framework of accepted and traditional ideas" in the possession of the greatest writers like Dante. Thus he could appeal to a matchless power and authority, gained from nature *and* history. These were both external forces, the artist was simply their instrument, a "mechanism." To go that far in technologizing the imagination may seem a shock today, but the implications are broad for what would later support his political thinking, and even more that of Pound. The themes in Eliot's mind from the beginning were disorder and dissociation on all the levels he considered, personal, cultural, esthetic, and moral. The inner imperative was to avoid the chaos of the solipsist, insufficiently honest in a private futility and despair, like his own Prufrock. The public instruction seemed to be for consciousness to assume either a disinterested detachment or the manner of a submissive and receptive sensibility. Meanwhile the poet-creator was driven to have perfect authority over both.

In the same essay in which he would have the poet emulate a chemical process, Eliot wrote that the emotion of art is impersonal, and "It is in this depersonalization that art may be said to approach the condition of science." (ESE,7) That impersonal power could be a transcendent power, really, because in reporting on experience the observer assumed for a moment the role of omniscience. Experience entered into the presence of the transforming catalyst and the catalyst itself "remained inert, neutral, and unchanged." Science apart, Eliot is quite clear in saying that he is attacking a traditional humanist ideal of personality, "...for my meaning is, that the poet has, not a "personality" to express, but a particular medium, which is only a medium and not a personality..." (ESE, 9).

We might call this a metapoetics. To become a medium and not a person the poet and his art pass from the traditional anthropocentric consciousness and its modern enfeeblement to be identified with the power of nature, or tradition, or society and culture; he may be rewarded by a transcendent omniscience (because depersonalized), and perhaps more important, by a purification (because dehumanized) of the artistic process itself. "How completely," Eliot says, "any semi-ethical criterion of 'sublimity' misses the mark. For it is not the 'greatness,' the intensity of the emotions, the components, but the intensity of the artistic process, the pressure, so to speak, under which the fusion takes place, that counts"(ESE,8). To pass from person to process, from emotion to force, or pressure, is authority transferred from personality to something else, a power that is abstract. In effect, Eliot's critique of personality is not the expression of a humility of spirit but something closer to its opposite, whether belonging to history, or natural force, or to the given institutions of authority.

In the complex dialectic of Eliot's mind all this was in a campaign against romantic subjectivity, whether in his poetics or his politics. He might also seem to have occupied the role of a positivist, even an addict of science, in his early criticism. But this only placed him closer to a religious resolution, a conversion from the stalemate of choice between "naturalist or supernaturalist" strongly supported by new or renewed faith in the traditional church and social order.

Notes

1. "Baudelaire," (ESE,379).
2. *To Criticize the Critic* (Farrar, Straus & Giroux, 1965), p.126.
3. "What Dante Means To Me," op.cit., p.134.
4. From *Syllabus of a Course of Six Lectures on Modern French Literature* (Oxford University Press, 1916).
5. T.E.. Hulme, *Speculations,* p.116.
6. *The Sacred Wood* (London, Methuen & Co., 1950), p.14. (Hereafter noted as SW).

3

"The Silhouette of Man"

Sweeney and the Reductive Imagination

Eliot could produce shock with the succinct image of "Apeneck Sweeney...letting his arms hang down to laugh," and so illustrate his own vision of "that extraordinarily limited animal," man. The Sweeney poems press alternatives to a level that might be called spiritual threat. In a tavern or nightclub, the "silent vertebrate in brown/ Contracts and concentrates, withdraws," while at a short distance, no doubt, the nightingales sing near "The Convent of the Sacred Heart." The effect would make the strictest either/or case for religious belief, and as he wrote in "Second Thoughts About Humanism," "There is no avoiding that dilemma: you must either be a naturalist or a supernaturalist."

"Apeneck" Sweeney is a major symbol in the modernist canon and so is the dialectical pairing of the "vertebrate in brown" and the nightingale's song. The mythic and religious imagination sings above Agamemnon's grave and all higher supernatural things thus confront a dual image of mortal reduction, the slain hero and the sinister animal man. In essence, Sweeney figured as a protagonist in Eliot's severe attack on humanism. Eliot gives more allegorical substance to his character in "Sweeney Erect" to say that Emerson, who called history the lengthened shadow of a man, had not seen "the silhouette of Sweeney straddled in the sun." That would illustrate the intellectual and spiritual distance between two ages, and there were those to influence Eliot deeply who had seen that shape, including Sir James Frazer among early literary anthropologists. Frazer could be called simplistic by modern anthropologists in assuming "that civilization has always and everywhere been evolved out of savagery."[1] Essentially he meant only what was expressed by Darwin when he cast his own longer shadow upon history: "with all [his] exalted powers••Man still bears in his bodily frame the indelible stamp of his lowly origin."[2] Darwin cautioned every expression of "god-like intellect" that ignored its origin, and thus made the reductive consciousness a modern universal of thought.

Wallace Stevens had his own way for dealing with naturalistic reduction, and it also entered into his views of poetry. In the following passage from "The Noble Rider and the Sound of Words" he puts it in such a way as to link the imagination inseparably with the threat of cultural apocalypse, in his case as powerful a stimulus as the First World War was for Eliot and Pound:

> About nobility I cannot be sure that the decline, not to say the disappearance of nobility is anything more than a maladjustment between the imagination and reality. We have been a little insane about the truth. We have had an obsession. In its ultimate extension, the truth about which we have been insane will lead us to look beyond the truth to something in which the imagination will be the dominant complement. It is not only that the imagination adheres to reality, but, also, that reality adheres to the imagination and that the interdependence is essential. We may emerge from our *bassesse* and, if we do, how would it happen if not by the intervention of some fortune of the mind? (NA, 33)

Stevens was describing a sense of crisis in his determination to bring universal poetry, that is, the idealizing imagination, out from the misfortune of *bassesse*, a chronic reductivism of thought and ignobility of judgment. This was a cultural affliction described as if a metaphoric system that once could serve the expansive imagination was now fixed in the condition of what Robert Frost called "comparisons downward."

But where did the metaphors of belief come from? For Eliot it was a strict dilemma - "you must either be a naturalist or a supernaturalist." There is an equally clear rebuttal from Stevens. As he observed modern art, following an insight of Simone Weil, he would say, "Modern reality is a reality of decreation, in which our revelations are not the revelations of belief, but the precious portents of our own powers" (NA, 175). That was an answer to the dilemma between naturalist and supernaturalist; one might choose to be a humanist.

It is clarifying to see Eliot's attack on the humanism of Matthew Arnold or Emerson from this perspective. Without the intellectual candor of either religion or science, humanism could seem a moral complacency betrayed in a thousand ways by the biological animal, whatever the expression of optimistic faith in economic and social existence, ethical culture, or the secular languages of value. As Eliot understood it, humanism meant to salvage a structure of values without confronting the commands from either nature or the divine, or the commitments engaged on either side. His rebuttal would insist that if the human imagination had any creative autonomy it was forced to take instruction from either naturalist or transcendental revelation.

The choices he posed were at the crux of reactive modern thought in the age of naturalist dominance. In this respect Eliot, like Pound, was touching closely to one dominant political dialectic of his time. One could adapt to the laws of animal motivation, find the motor of history, and so control events according to a basic measure. In a naturalistic ideology, like that of Marx, for instance, one should not find the images of Bleistein and Sweeney, Prufrock and Burbank unacceptable. They could represent stages in historical evolution, whether primitive or degenerate, and therefore necessary visions on the road to truth and power. In naturalistic Fascism, that is to say, Nazism, those "images" of Sweeney and Bleistein could be lessons of a species (racial) conflict with conceivably welcome results in the evolutionary cycle of destruction and survival.

These are not gratuitous political analogies. In wider reaction, Bleistein, emerging from protozoic slime, Sweeney, with zebra stripes along his jaws, could be scare images that haunt modern intellectual and political culture. Respectively they reflect the apocalyptic conflicts of race and class. There may be revenge in their creation, as if, subtly compelled, the imagination punishes itself with the real figures of the fallen world. At the same time, these reductive images could provide a stimulus for redemptive visions, either in politics, with drastic modes of revolutionary apocalypse, or in religion, expressed in Eliot's plays, for example, in dramas of martyrdom and salvationary violence.

Discreet but sharp irony reflects Eliot's early style of attack, a better weapon than moralistic or even religious fervor. The young poet from St. Louis and Boston, as quintessentially American in origin as Pound, lived in a limbo of belief systems, or as he could imagine, neither up nor down, neither blessed nor damned. The Sunday faith of Aunt Helen and Cousin Nancy must have greatly heightened the "darkness," in the Conradian sense, wherever the poet had found it, St. Louis, Boston, or London. It was for those "who had not seen the silhouette/ of Sweeney straddled in the sun" that the early poems were written. "Cousin Nancy," whose last name was Ellicott, could keep Emerson and Arnold as "guardians of the faith." Prufrock might be another "cousin" who did not need directly to meet Sweeney or Doris or Bleistein to sense the invasion of alien creatures from "the protozoic slime." These characters inhabit a novelistic universe, a large history best read as narrative without asking whose mind and sensibility is suffering the shock that guides us to a place where "twelve o'clock" on a windy night and its "lunar incantations"

> Dissolve the floors of memory
> And all its clear relations.

But though the world is destroyed many times in Eliot's verse, the aim is to bear witness to the mind or memory,

> As if the world gave up
> The secret of its skeleton,
> Stiff and white.

—leading finally to a city among ruins where there is the strongest threat of violence.

> A broken spring in a factory yard...
> Hard and curled and ready to snap.

But given its "rhapsody," this is a city *after* its agony of struggle, as after a holocaust. A woman appears in the light of a door, with the border of her dress "torn and stained with sand."

> And you see the corner of her eye
> Twists like a crooked pin.

If the eye is spirit, spirit tells us nothing, reduced to a pang of twisted steel, materialized that way, or as the vestigial animal.

> I could see nothing behind that child's eye.
> I have seen eyes in the street
> Trying to peer through lighted shutters,
> And a crab one afternoon in a pool,
> An old crab with barnacles on its back,
> Gripped the end of a stick which I held him.

This is a moment where the reductive imagination, as I use the term, reaches its wholly expressive nadir. As eye meets eye like crab meeting crab, or even as in "Prufrock," descending beyond crab to a "pair of claws / scuttling across silent seas," the effect is toward a cosmic terror, Dantesque, with a world destroyed in its own images. A nausea penetrates existence, rising from "all the old nocturnal smells...and female smells in shuttered rooms." For the crab to meet the woman in her bodily smell is to make a universal judgment. The poem ends with the typical finality of mounting (or descending) purgatorial stairs.

> "Mount.
> The bed is open; the toothbrush hangs on the wall
> Put your shoes at the door, sleep, prepare for life."

But what is immediately offered is the equivalence of suicide in the final line, "The last twist of the knife."

With that murderous closure, what can be the "Whispers of Immortality" in the poem of that title? We know that it is Eliot, in the persona of Webster, who "was much possessed by death/ And saw the skull beneath the skin." In remarkably compact verse "the anguish of the marrow" and "the ague of the skeleton" express frustration for "any contact possible to flesh." Nature is unredeemed but a double horror springs from the peculiar descent into nature which takes place in the unredeemed human city. At the meeting of drawing room and jungle which excites Eliot's imagination Aunt Helen is translated next to the full-breasted Grishkin, who might once have nodded to her across the room at some Cambridge party.

> The sleek Brazilian jaguar
> Does not in its arboreal gloom
> Distil so rank a feline smell
> As Grishkin in a drawing-room.

For Grishkin, to one noticing her breasts and smell, the right accent is death, come to appreciate her with the lipless grin of "breastless creatures under ground."

"Grishkin in a drawing-room," or graveyard, exists on the grandly informal level of Eliot's mind and vision. Grishkin and the "pneumatic bliss" she offers suggest a manufactured gadget, like an erotic device, though it is also a fine pun on the spiritual. Her name emphasizes the ethnic stranger and she is cousin to Bleistein and Sweeney on the same metaphysical level of threat. We take fright at the quick coupling of her "bliss" with the images of death. She suffers in any case the dismissal of any "contact possible to flesh."

In this effect and elsewhere, Eliot points a direction for the reductive xenophobic imagination; a shock is intended, and insofar as Eliot's verse can be accused of expressing ethnic or gender prejudice it puts the familiar emphasis on sexual revulsion and sex linked with death. Bleistein emerges from the prehistoric slime and Grishkin finds her essence in "a feline smell"; the reductive prejudice is against them both. But who is writing the brutal words of disgust for the "protozoic slime" from which Bleistein emerges? It may be out of simple esthetic need that we think of Eliot's personae, Prufrock or Gerontion. The latter particularly is an illustration of neurotic xenophobia even as he invokes "Christ the Tiger," where the redeemer, if he comes, comes from the pit of nature. The parallel question may be why the foreigner is made to represent a lower or "subhuman" species. It is a covert premise of humanism, perhaps as Eliot understood in his attack on it, that the human universal transcends its sub-specie manifestations. But humanism was highly vulnerable so long as its premise could not be disassociated from the reductive denominator suggested by naturalist thought. "Apeneck" Sweeney tells a long story in the epithet.[3]

The usual way to resolve the issue in Eliot's favor or excuse is to pass the responsibility to his personae, chiefly Gerontion, who might be presented as passing through the stages of purgatory toward a possible religious conversion. The dilemma of reductive naturalism without recourse to a higher vision is being presented. Grishkin poses the problem to a refined intellectual imagination, though to put it that way is to suggest an almost grotesque innocence of sensibility in Eliot. Whether in drawing room or jungle, the cat smell, "a subtle effluence" of the senses, quells and drowns the intellect and its "Abstract Entities." The fact that the flesh is warm and "our metaphysics" dry is a starting point, and it can lead in several directions, one of them being a vitalism strangely adapted to the expressive strategies of Eliot's religious conversion. But in every case, the shock of opposition between animal humanity and idealist 'metaphysics' is in the foreground. In "Gerontion," just at the turning point of Eliot's development, the natural life is a betrayal and martyrdom, its symbol the "flowering judas" appearing in "depraved May." That these images are owed to Henry Adams should cause no surprise. "April is the cruelest month" because it reflects the reductive metaphysics of nature.

The prejudice against nature joined with its highest dread is also the basis of two other problematic themes that give tension and size to Eliot's achievement, particularly, of course, in his prose essays. Of pronounced expression is the problem of culture when culture is viewed against the background of cosmic naturalistic thought. Another is the problematic of unmediated reality, that is, the threat to its place in the vocabulary of poets as well as scientists. In Eliot's style of thought, culture and tradition form metamorphic terms to replace the "real," and if the "real" is naturalistically pursued, culture is a weighted essence to defend against nature.[4]

These are major terms of dissociation. Sweeney and Bleistein on one side divide humanity between those who exist debased in the "protozoic slime," and those with sophisticated consciousness (Prufrock, Gerontion) who occupy the purgatory of faith and cannot "turn again" to hope, or pray, or act, or judge, or even finally speak their loss ("the hollow men"). Yet a surrogate consciousness can give figure to these apparitions. Unconditioned humanity (that is, the foreigner) is dangerous and appears at the scene of the historical apocalypse, where Gerontion meets the crowd of them, Mr. Silvero, Hagakawa, Fraulein von Kulp. These figures with Sweeney at their center, gather together the notes of a misanthropy never more keenly rendered in literature. Under its heading Eliot exhibits the terror clothed in irony in his view of decadence and cultural disintegration.

Presumably Eliot was to be a poet whose mind was "the mind of Europe," furnished with what he said was the requirement of poetic creation, a sense of history. That was the epic stage of his small and powerful body of verse and it engaged with renewed large claims for literature as central in the dynamic of human culture. What he called the sensibility (undissociated) had almost a salvationary purpose in his mind, much like what Stevens called the imagination. The intellectual environment in the late nineteenth century was concentrated on historicist themes that paralleled Darwinian curves of descent and ascent. Such ideas were reinforced by ideas from physics, the sensationalized concept of entropy, for instance, which seemed to envision the long or short run decay of all systems of energy. Henry Adams had proposed this for the intellectual self-consciousness of a decadent species, confirmed in its pessimism by both the rivalry of younger or cruder races and by the dismal day of judgment implied by entropy.

The parallels in the writing and thought of Adams and Eliot are important to note, one of them being the attraction of Europe and its monuments of civilization for its audience of the "modern." Such is the effect of reductive tourism in "Burbank with a Baedeker: Bleistein with a Cigar." In that poem Venice represents the modern stereotype of a decayed civilization that had attained both worldly power and utmost refinement. Venice was also the natural habitat for out of mode aristocrats accompanied by images of devitalization or implicit corruption. Thus Burbank (who might have been derived from the life of Adams) is holding a Baedeker travel guide to the heroic ages and is as much like Prufrock as the short poem can suggest. It is he who falls under the spell of Princess Volupine and loses her to Sir Ferdinand Klein, representing "money in furs." Princess Volupine may be highly valued by the merchant, he obviously pays for her, but with "meagre blue-nailed phthisic hand," she is touched by physical and cultural decay. Her name, not incidentally, is a punning synthesis of reactive obsessions, voluptuous, vulpine, vulturous, and perhaps covertly, vulgar. In a compounding of reductive themes wealth in furs is associated with the predatory violence of disease. The Jew is on the scene and attracts the xenophobia that marks the temper of self-conscious decadence. Sir Ferdinand has invaded rank, an impostor, but Bleistein, "Chicago Semite Viennese," is specifically a creature from the source.

Behind the naturalistic nightmare there is the penetrating fear of cultural collapse. There is therefore much more than prejudice here. We "are at the smoky candle end of time" where Bleistein stares at Canaletto, and both are examined in their peculiar opposition. The reference to Canaletto and the allusion to Antony, whose god Hercules left him in the crisis of defeat, are necessary accents to an apocalyptic view of history. The conclusion is appropriately violent; rats, Jews, the fleas on the rump of St. Mark's lion (though it might be the British lion if we take in the meaning of *Sir* Ferdinand), all blend to express the incitement in the question, "Who clipped the lion's wings/ And flea'd his rump and pared his claws?"

In the decadent sensibility, that question, a paranoid whisper among the ruins, becomes passionate. Defeat opens an abyss of resentment, though it is concealed in apathy and self-defacement. The obsession with decadence needs the parallel with animal violence to be understood. Of course, as Burbank recalls Prufrock, so Bleistein is kin to Sweeney. It is fundamental in the spirit of decadence to see Sweeney straddle the world while Prufrock haunts the evening staircase and the twilight hours of fog and depression. His "love song" is the most evocative possible for a legend of passivity and withdrawal.

Prufrock, Burbank, and Gerontion have fallen from a cultural height insofar as Eliot's work is a narrative of the distinction between culture and nature. It is not so much a story of animal or savage uprising, but a fall into limbo of defeat existing alongside the lower depths of avarice, instinct, biological necessity. Prufrock directs attention to an insidious principle of anti-climax where each impulse races with futility in the next thought. The anti-climax is implanted in time; Prufrock is haunted by "decisions and revisions which a minute will reverse." He is not afraid of anything that seems specifically a threat, nor is he diffident for himself in a world of the stronger. Rather his perspective is cosmic, and his mind is penetrated by a sense of universal cross•purposes, an Olympian futility. "Do I dare" and "How should I presume" alternate with disillusioned knowledge, but first in his mind is the problem of valuation. "And would it have been worth it, after all,/....Would it have been worth while,..."   It is the question asked by Stevens, really, in "The Noble Rider" What in our *bassesse* could be worth saying, or imagining? With Eliot's dramatic genius at work a major questioning expresses itself in the mundane social context, with "the smell of steaks in passageways." The successful irony depends on giving as much poetry as could be given to a depression which would in its ultimate development cut off any form of communication, including poetry. No one came as close to articulating the marginal sensibility that floats everywhere richly but attaches itself nowhere. Eliot was here and in all his work the master of an effect that can make the anti-climaxes of reduction seem like cosmic loss without losing the style and setting of "the Eternal Footman's" comedy.

Prufrock is the one who has wept and fasted, really, but the poem does not end with fasting and praying, but a return to the disparity between vital images of being and a loss of affective and intellectual capacity. The allusion to Hamlet is quickly surrendered; he cannot be Hamlet even in the curiously compromised fashion of that tragic hero (as Eliot judged him), whose passion wavers, ascends, and reduces itself in the face of one or more "overwhelming questions." Hamlet is the exception among Shakespeare's tragic figures, where he questions his own tragic seriousness, and Hamlet seems to know the ghost of Polonius better than that of his own father. The failure of tragedy, which the ruminations of Prufrock and later Gerontion acknowledge, is a theme that invites the apocalypse. It is not surprising to recall that Eliot's famous criticism of the play applies itself better to the character of Prufrock than to Hamlet himself.

If Prufrock can only play the fool, or like the sybil at Cumae, pose exhausted in aged and refined insight and wish to die, still it is his sensibility that guards the higher dream and his imagination that descends to the "floors of silent seas" where the crab crawls. In that conjunction of high and low, caught in great contradictions, Prufrock is the purgatorial consciousness to be traced ultimately with Gerontion in a convulsion of spirit that invites the apocalypse. It is Prufrock who might have attended Professor Channing-Cheetah's party where the highly articulate Mr. Apollinax "laughs like an irresponsible foetus." This is the apocalyptic whimper, not its bang, as it is again in the question asked in Pipit's song, "Where are the eagles and the trumpets?" Indeed where are they except in "fractured atoms," blown apart in the imagined violence, past and future, which hides behind Prufrockian futilities.

Notes

1. Sir James Frazer, "The Scope of Social Anthropology," *Psyche's Task* (London: Macmillan & Co., 1920), p.170.
2. *The Descent of Man* (New York and London, 1897), II,387
3. As noted by Calvin Bedient in his perceptive study of "The Waste Land" (*He Do the Police in Different Voices* [Chicago: The University of Chicago Press, 1986]) physical reduction in Eliot is chiefly bodily degradation and linked to the figure of cosmic human self-disesteem which Julia Kristeva gave elaboration under the name of the "abject." Her definition that illuminates the centrality in Eliot's thought and imagination is this: "The corpse, seen without God and outside science, is the utmost of abjection. It is death infecting life"(*Powers of Horror: An Essay on Abjection*, trans. Leon S. Roudiez [New York: Columbia University Press, 1982], pp.4-50), Bedient gives a parallel sense of the abject calling it "unredeemed degradation," with stress on decaying flesh, body odors. "To be abject is to be born of a woman, born to die, incestuously hungering to return to the mother's body yet dreading the death that her body is, even its powers of reproduction, which would give still more life over to nothingness" (p. 22). If this view corresponds with Eliot's own, the abject is the state of human self-judgment appealing for redemption. Michael Andre Bernstein gives strong development to the modern literary parentage of "The Abject Hero" in *Bitter Carnival* (Princeton, NJ: Princeton University Press, 1992).
4. The greater recourse from reductive reality (the "unreal") was the divine "Real." Eliot was bred on the philosophic issue with his Harvard dissertation on F. H. Bradley. There is much useful discussion of Bradley and Eliot in Michael Levenson's work, *A Genealogy of Modernism* (Cambridge: Cambridge University Press, 1984) and that of Calvin Bedient. Bedient discusses the garden experience in "The Waste Land" as follows: "It establishes Reality as the One, and so renders unreal everything palpable, everything multiple." He quotes Eliot's paraphrase of Bradley: "Reality is one. It must be single, because plurality, taken as real, contradicts itself" (Bedient, p.33). See my chapters 11 and 12 below on the access to reality as an important bridging topic with Stevens.

4

Purgatory and Apocalypse

Postmodern literary theory was enforced by the influence of Michel Foucault when he proclaimed the death of Man to parallel the "death of God" which had become the intrinsic byword of modernist thought. Actually the disappearance of the hero or the radical reduction or destruction of his size, character, and possibilities was a distinct feature of modern verse and fiction long before. As good a model for this can be found in the work of Eliot as in Samuel Beckett or any exemplar in postmodern fiction or verse. In Foucault's meaning it was man the protagonist, the focus of interest and value, who had disappeared and along with him any basis for traditional humanism.

The arrival of the anti-hero is most visible in Prufrock or Gerontion, but Prufrock's case is more typically the extreme of passivity, frozen between thought and decision, decision and action. The Prufrockian protagonist who speaks and listens in Eliot's verse, (he has his quotidian youth in "The Love Song..." and his adult despair in "Gerontion" and "The Waste Land,"), and can be traced even to his approximate redemption in the last movement of "The Waste Land" and "Ash Wednesday." It hardly matters that this sequence looks like Eliot's own life for it is clear that in this writing there is no author-person. There are only personae listening to their own and to other voices, the author truly having become something like the strip of sensitive metal called a catalyst. Is the unnamed protagonist the "mind of Europe" which the poet as critic evoked in his essays? It is a serious possibility, but even that is a more concrete identity than the "protagonist" can hold. It is important to note how the passing and disappearance of persons is followed by that highly abstract persona of Tiresias, who represents both the past and the future, both male and female, both blind and seeing, a universal detached from every particular. Tiresias, if he is as Eliot says the narrating consciousness, represents the depersonalization of poetry and myth. His voice is a consciousness set free from agents of action or will, it is the sensibility in extremis, capable only of presenting images while suffering the intense spirit of alienation before offering itself in half-aborted prayer.

But there was soon to appear in Eliot's writing a service to spiritual gain in denial and reduction. In "Ash Wednesday" where "time is always time," and "place is always and only place," the poet-protagonist says he can rejoice, "having to construct something / Upon which to rejoice." The human will being renounced is only as small and dry as the natural air it breathes. In this context it is appropriate to surrender to prayer and patience. "To care and not to care" is one way to deal with suffering. With "Do I dare to eat a peach?" Prufrock asks a question directed perhaps at someone else etherized against the sky. He is answered later by the image of Rachel Rabinovitch tearing at the grapes with murderous paws. The alienation from the will to live can do nothing to express itself further. The next step is perhaps martyrdom.

In Eliot's time it was understandably difficult to write poetry directed toward or about saints and martyrs (though that was the direction in his plays), but poetry could find its values where the defeated sensibility has its own strong appeal, and the highest spiritual heroism hovers directly above a crisis of the will. It is not far-fetched to say that an aroused Prufrock speaks in the cultivated remorse of Harry Monchesney in *The Family Reunion*, and finally and ultimately through the martyr's fervor of Thomas à Becket. There can be no belittling Eliot's determined passage toward the account where immolation transfers from physical void to spiritual victory. However, it is not my essential subject here. The path of the sensibility toward reduction of the will is the intermediate fate of the protagonist I have described; Prufrock-Gerontion in essence, his alienations in the world and the flesh, his "decisions and revisions" amount to an abdication of motive so great that it must demand complete destruction from "Christ the tiger." All these passages translate into a voiding of the material world and the person in that world. In Eliot's achieved imagination the holistic negative can lead to a purgatorial waiting, an outlet from the impasse of the normative imagination, blocked between desire and denial. Transcendence is escape; unable to choose, one escapes choice, unable to pass in time from the state of wanting to the state of acting, one escapes time. But the consciousness of each condition is necessarily more vividly present in Eliot's verse than any goal in spiritual grace and ecstasy. In essence purgatory is a pause between two eternities, and so it is marked by the highly sensitized awareness of the timeless in time, or time in and out of its perceived dimensions. The partner to the dread of the apocalypse is the demonstration of natural entropy.

> . . .what will the spider do,
> Suspend its operations, will the weevil
> Delay?

Gerontion has made judgment of the world's slow death before he beckons for its destruction, "whirled/ Beyond the circuit of the shuddering Bear." The mazes of history do more than the boredom of the senses to defeat the will to live and arouse the apocalypse.

> History has many cunning passages, contrived corridors
> And issues, deceives with whispering ambitions,
> Guides us by vanities. . .

The stalemates of history are essentially those of will, memory, and passion. They are a forced depersonalization, or as Eliot said in prose when ready to welcome it, an "escape from personality" which is thoroughly an escape from self. That these stalemates are worse than the climaxes of destruction is the evident logic of the poem, and it prepares the ground for translating the scene of the predatory leopard into images of redemptive immolation, as in "Ash Wednesday." The point is that there are no proximate justifications in history, moral confusion is absolute and only a divine intervention can save us.

> ....Unnatural vices
> Are gathered by our heroism. Virtues
> Are forced upon us by our impudent crimes.

Reversibility and paradox, anti-climax and betrayal, are the features of time in history, though they make for considerable assets in dramatic verse, and they become poetic principles. Prufrock speaks for the theme where time is baffling and opaque for everyone, "Time for you and time for me." The routine of everyday is no different from that of the universe, which he dares not disturb, a chronological determinism that one might know as history but whose measure is boredom in coffee spoon and clock, the specific and extreme "malady of the quotidian." In "The Waste Land," the bell of Mary Woolnoth keeps the hours, "With a dead sound at the final stroke of nine." In contrast with that dead sound heard in all of Eliot's verse, time's winged chariot in Marvell's image has a Gothic excitement.

> But at my back in a cold blast I hear
> The rattle of the bones, and chuckle spread from ear to ear

And the graveyard rat "crept softly through the vegetation." Time's chariot also brings "Sweeney to Mrs. Porter in the spring," and that measures graveyard time with the humiliation of spirit Sweeney always carries with him.

HURRY UP PLEASE ITS TIME. The capitals are for a loud voice to say that we are in time and out of it throughout the poem, aware of it in its mightiest crescendo and feeblest whisper, fusing several layers of past and present, and ready in some sense to stand at the actual ending of time. The actual footnote of the historic European apocalypse, quoted from Herman Hesse' *Blick ins Chaos*, is only one theme among several, the collapse is universal.

> What is the city over the mountains
> Cracks and reforms and bursts in the violet air
> Falling towers
> Jerusalem Athens Alexandria
> Vienna London
> Unreal

The Baudelarian epithet "unreal" is important as the conclusion to the serial shocks of the imagery. They are "unreal" to characterize temporal mortality and "unreal" is the experiential quality of secular existence. It is the fall of time itself which is emphasized in the climax, and so through sheer stalemate the ground is prepared for the accents of the thunder which are redemptive. As the word "unreal," alone here in its line, echoes throughout Eliot's verse, the concept of true "being" becomes the provocative and paradoxical issue. In its first appearance "unreal" forms the basis of questioning ordinary reality on its naturalistic terms. On that level death and life are both unreal, though death may be the more logical step toward the only "real," The destruction of reality is the mood of those condemned at the netherside of purgatory, as one might say. Appropriately "The Waste Land" breaks up in fragments and dissolving silence, while, and this has emphasis, the last words, sounding like thunder, are borrowed from a foreign language and religious culture as if only a strange language could breach and overcome silence.

I doubt if one can exaggerate what Eliot did for the theme of the world apocalypse that has haunted modern thinking on all levels reaching beyond literature and folk tale to new politics and religions. The refrain, "This is the way the world ends," is the warning sounded by Marx and Lenin in the political wars, with Hitler, too, in calling to his threatened "race" in a deadly competition. It was heard in every rumor or prophecy of cultural decline and death. But Eliot almost immediately chose spiritual and cultural recovery and survival for his theme. What does the apocalyptic reduction of life reality, human cultural reality, invite if not transcendence in its most extreme form of martyrdom in the order of Thomas Becket and Celia Coplestone ?

It is true that Eliot in *The Cocktail Party* emphasizes the coming to terms with commonplace existence for those ineligible for martyrdom. In the context of Celia's fate in that play, however, the unheroic comfort offered the Chamberlaynes is accented to seem hardly worth notice. In such cases the transcendental poet has extended what Stevens called "a malady of the quotidian," a poet's malady, to an unfavorable contrast with extreme suffering in its martyred climax.

These are important distinctions if we look forward to Williams' engagement with quotidian reality and Stevens' major concern with its call for imaginative redemption. The larger point is that the disesteem for mortal humanity and the passive determinism expressed in these brief examples from Eliot's later work penetrate the poetry, early and late, and fix the tone and meaning of Eliot's politics, his "anti-humanism," and his missionary view of culture. As for poetic and dramatic effect in a naturalistic age one must plausibly exceed both naturalist and humanist dimensions; meanwhile the transcendental urge tends to direct all pains to the site of the Fall and postpone human affinities and sympathies to the Last Judgment.

The Nightingale's Song

In every expressed or formal choice in religion, politics, and literary criticism Eliot seemed to turn his back on modernity. But doing so was actually an avant-garde gesture, and that was hidden from no one. For one example, he presented a drama of religious redemption that was linked in character with the apocalyptic politics of his time. In the political dialectic of Marx, for instance, redemption began in the conflict of classes, and with the competition of economic needs and appetites, the low terms are transformed into the highest to achieve a classless society that would be deemed utopian in any other account. Real or naturalistic motivations were to be the instrument of ideal conclusions, and eventual happiness might be measured according to the depth of the misery from which it sprang. The ostensible religious model could be the Miltonian "fortunate fall," or Christ's role of the "suffering servant" repeated in the martyred lives of saints.

Such tensions are the great resource of Eliot's imagination; in a time of confusion the impasse of faith invites extremes and opposite extremes serve to authenticate each other. It can be a shock to renew reading of Eliot and observe how he exaggerates natural cruelty. The motif of total violence, to be murdered and devoured to the bone, recurs with unmistakable implication in the poems and lasts to the end in the plays. To be eaten is nature's rule, the ground for all transitions and metamorphoses; therefore the three white leopards in "Ash Wednesday" attack so that the dry bones may emerge to sing and live. The drowned Phoenician sailor "whose bones the sea had picked in whispers," recalls Sweeney's savage anecdote in "Fragment of an Agon."

> I knew a man once did a girl in
> Any man might do a girl in
> Any man has to, needs to, wants to
> Once in a lifetime, do a girl in. (CPP, 83)

Sweeney then sings to his love, "I'll carry you off/ To a cannibal isle." Musical comedy though that is, it previews Celia Coplestone's very serious fate in another "cannibal" land.

Whatever the perversities of violence, whether the flesh dissolves in acid, in time, in the teeth of the leopard, or on Sweeney's cannibal isle as a "missionary stew," the obsession is meaningful. Dramatic logic, again, forces a choice like that offered by a "Grand Inquisitor" between animal fate and God's redemption. In "Ash Wednesday," in a world pressed to the margin of vacancy, the protagonist imagines his dissolution, proffering his deeds to oblivion and his love to "the posterity of the desert." In suffering dissolution one learns to pray, as in "The Dry Salvages" where "the prayer of the bone on the beach" recalls the earlier poem's prayer of the bone in the desert. It is for the world to give up "the secret of its skeleton." Here as elsewhere Eliot associates both prayer and song with physical martyrdom. Poetry is itself a transcendence of animal consciousness, and playing on that theme with major Hellenic myths, the bones sing to the "Lady of silences" for their resurrection in song.

> It is this which recovers
> My guts the strings of my eyes and the indigestible
>   portions
> Which the leopards reject.

 The reduced indigestible substance becomes compacted with moral, spiritual, even esthetic value, and the theme seems to be that the sacrificial meal found everywhere in nature is the ground for merciful intervention.[1]

  It was in this context that Eliot made his own choices from the archeological museum of myths, among them, dominantly, the savage metamorphic myths of resurrected life. The most complete example for his use was the myth of Philomela, a story of rape, murder, and cannibalism whose gist was converted into the song of the nightingale. This is the justificatory myth of the reductive imagination and it required extreme physical punishment. Philomela is recalled as if to bear witness with the devitalized sexual activity of the "waste land," the carbuncular clerk and bored typist, the Smyrna merchant, Lil and Lil's husband, and finally, Tiresias himself, "old man with wrinkled female breasts." Such images heighten the resplendent sexuality of Cleopatra, Isolde, and the Rhine Maidens, but these latter are death bringers as well, representing death in its existential climax as the love/death, and the love/death itself as the most powerful transvaluation of physical existence. Nothing better illustrates Eliot's dialectic of extremes and the powerful rendering of a chromatic sensibility in "The Waste Land." Vital deficiency is balanced by an over•sufficiency, a splendor of the senses and an almost spiritualized passion that falls into tragedy. The desire for new life in the midst of vacancy is contradicted by images of rape, adultery and murder. But the extremity of violence is followed in turn by an ecstatic metamorphosis of the sensibility. The nightingale's song hovers over the world of violence as well as apathy, and sends the clear signal of its role. It sings within the "bloody wood" where the god dies to be reborn, it sings near the Convent of the Sacred Heart, and that song is Sweeney's epitaph. In the historic view, Eliot's encompassing interest in apocalyptic martyrdom reveals its disturbing aspects. To link vitalist myth and religion, secular and spiritual drama, has its dangers, obviously, and the tendency to reduce (or raise, depending on the perspective) consciousness to a cruel if redemptive determinism has more implications than concern art. In the *Quartets* and in the plays the moment of time's witness to its transcendent dimension is most often a moment of agony. The crisis gathers together the longest history and bears the weight of a divine determinism in all events, illustrated in *The Family Reunion* by way of a summary judgment of the Chorus.

> In an old house .....
> The agony in the curtained bedroom, whether of birth or of
>   dying,
> Gathers in to itself all the voices of the past, and projects
>   them into the future. (CPP, 270-71)

The martyrdom implicit in history, required for its redemptive ends, is emphasized on the stage of great men and affairs in *Murder in the Cathedral*, where the Chorus summons the theme as if giving sanction to Becket's death.

> And war among men defiles this world, but death in the Lord
>   renews it,
> And the world must be cleaned in the winter, or we shall have
> only
> A sour spring, a parched summer, an empty harvest. (CPP, 201)

The superior spiritual dimension pervades nature and resolves its necessary antinomies. The entangled judgment must be that all life is a sacrifice and martyred testament. At the lower mundane level of humanity, in "The Family Reunion," Harry and Mary ruminate over vital existence and its expiation. As Harry speaks,

> Spring is an issue of blood
> A season of sacrifice

Mary responds,

> Pain is the opposite of joy
> But joy is a kind of pain
> .....
> I believe the season of birth
> Is the season of sacrifice
> For the tree and the beast, and the fish
> Thrashing itself upstream:
> And what of the terrified spirit
> Compelled to be reborn.... (CPP, 251)

As darkly fatalist as this is, it defines the apocalyptic theme exactly; where birth has equality with death at the moment of agony, as if all living were pain, judgment is concentrated for meaning at the greatest extreme of pain. In "The Family Reunion," guilt, punishment, and expiation, all center on one act of violence, a murder in fact, which serves to project the past into the future and gives order to the old house and all its experiences. The reader has notice here how a radical teleology, in secular terms a straight historicism, has absorbed Eliot's religious and poetic thought and makes a bridge to his political writing. [2]

Perhaps the best example of this pattern appears in "East Coker," where the threat that the world might end with a whimper is faced with dramatic lucidity. But the certainty that the world *will* end by the logic of natural law, or entropy, drives spiritual fate forward to its own conclusion. To advance from this world there must be further reduction. The Heracleitan way down *can* be the way up, and "darkness" or vacancy, can "purify the soul."

> Emptying the sensual with deprivation
> Cleansing affection from the temporal. (CPP, 120)

In any case the dark is where all go, "the vacant into the vacant" as in "East Coker," "into the silent funeral,/ Nobody's funeral" (CPP, 126).

So many negatives, accumulating, can be a poetic as well as a religious discipline. This is a waiting for the end, and only the apocalypse can come with the force to answer fear and empty nothing of its nothing. The void suggests its own cancellation,

> Whirled in a vortex that shall bring
> The world to that destructive fire
> Which burns before the ice-cap reigns.

Destructive fire, destructive ice, burning above and below the void, make no alternatives, unless one is prepared, as in the poem's fourth movement, to welcome the surgeon who brings pain as the cure of pain.

> The wounded surgeon plies the steel
> That questions the distempered part;
> . . . .
> Our only health is the disease
> If we obey the dying nurse
> Whose constant care is not to please
> But to remind of our, and Adam's curse,
> And that, to be restored, our sickness must grow worse.

This is transcendental paradox, extreme enough to resolve all contradictions; meanwhile men have the companionship of God ("the wounded surgeon") in pain.

If we think that Eliot may have been following the austere discipline of mystics, we may be sure that this pattern of analogy had another resonance for himself as well as his audience. The metaphor of surgery was familiar in the crisis politics of several generations, as were the metaphors of disease and decadent age applied to nations, races, and civilizations. "The whole earth is our hospital" was in fact the self-reassuring imagery of revolutionary leaders, as well as their opponents in therapeutic battle.[3] Whether in the redemptive acceleration of history, or as the means of penetrating routine existence, the apocalyptic temperament gambles on destruction just as purgatory is a progress from hell. "Little Gidding," as the last of the Quartets and most historical in reference, introduces a modern political apocalypse to support the spiritual dialectic. The sequence turns to London at war in the worst days of the air raids. "The dark dove with flickering tongue" evokes the German dive-bombers, observed by Eliot as a fire-warden.

> The dove descending breaks the air
> With flame of incandescent terror
> Of which the tongues declare
> The one discharge from sin and error.
> The only hope, or else despair
> Lies in the choice of pyre or pyre—
> To be redeemed from fire by fire. (CPP, 143)

The German dive-bomber as a metaphor for the Holy Ghost descending would only seem grotesque to those less attuned to the paradox of redemption. To be redeemed from fire by fire is explicit enough, envisioning the ultimate violence that is the release from violent existence. The question again arises whether Eliot was speaking for the secular consciousness of his time in ways he could not anticipate. Was the right metaphor for spiritual experience to be found in a war? Was this eschatology of violence, religious and secular, endemic in the first decades of the century and partly the ground for war itself? Much of the political literature tells us that the ideologues and leaders most responsible for the two great wars thought they were learning to deal with nature on its own terms, and believed in teleologies of crisis that gathered past and future together. They drew their values from natural conflict, and would follow that rule to whatever ends of redemptive destruction their ideologies declared.

As an overtly mild man, a deeply sincere poet, moralist, and man of religion, Eliot himself might be shocked by this juxtaposition. But his imagination was not mild but radical in its violence. The question remains open and it goes deeper than his early affinity with *L'Action Française* and the life-long influence of Ezra Pound. The relationship between the culture of modernism and the era of apocalyptic wars and revolutions is what is at issue, as several students, Donald Davie and Frank Kermode among them, have proposed.

There is some natural credit of course for a major poet to speak in his own voice for large fatal currents of disposition in his time. It is perhaps useless to imagine whether an obsession with the historic apocalypse and its purgative violence was symptom, cause, or effect in the overt political violence of this century. Eliot himself was especially conscious of the sensibility of his age. That he had a share in creating it seems obvious. There was in sum a moral impatience and cruelty of spirit in Eliot's reductive vision of quotidian life and animal being. Obviously there are deeper eschatologies in Eliot's apocalyptic poetry than the oncoming of Fascism and the Great Wars. But the powerful imagination is a mirror. A large sequence of moral and political martyrdom, invited and imposed, haunts this century and is echoed in its poetry and fiction. Is this to give credit or blame? That question has no answer, but the expression of an acute consciousness can become conscience; the important form of moral responsibility becomes that of those who inherit the consciousness of past times.

Notes

1. Eliot wrote "...only Christianity helps to reconcile me to life, which is otherwise disgusting" (Letter to Paul Elmer More, 1928, quoted in John D.Margolis, T.S. Eliot's Intellectual Development, 1922-1939). In the same letter he said that with the religious void not filled he is one driven "towards asceticism or sensuality."
2. I would add in preview of later discussion that the contrast here lies with liberal and democratic humanism which in its meliorism avoids the apocalyptic extreme in all things human.
3. It was in fact the rhetoric of war and extermination used by both sides in the wars of the twentieth century. Close at home see Pound's polemic of political conflict broadcast from Rome, traces of which to be found in the Cantos and elsewhere. Such hospital attributes as "gangrene," "fungus," and "anemia" appear in early verse to describe his enemies. With absolute explicitness Pound could write. "USURY is the cancer of the world, which only the surgeon's knife of Fascism can cut out of the life of nations"("What is Money For," 1939. PSP, 270).

5

A Problem of Order

Eliot's Cultural Poetics

In a retrospective view of his intellectual life as artist, Eliot himself proposed how much he, with greater stress than Pound, was dominated by what he called "a problem of order." This led him to seek the most inclusive sense of human continuity and community; order meant, in effect, culture:

> I was dealing then with the artist, (in "Tradition and the Individual Talent") and the sense of tradition which, it seemed to me, the artist should have; but it was generally a problem of order; and the function of criticism seems to be essentially a problem of order too. I thought of literature then, as I think of it now, of the literature of the world, of the literature of Europe, of the literature of a single country, not as a collection of the writings of individuals, but as "organic wholes," as systems in relation to which, and only in relation to which, individual works of literary art, and the works of individual artists, have their significance. There is accordingly something outside of the artist to which he owes allegiance, a devotion to which he must surrender and sacrifice himself in order to earn and obtain his unique position. A common inheritance and a common cause unite artists consciously or unconsciously: it must be admitted that the union is mostly unconscious. Between the true artists of any time there is, I believe, an unconscious community. (ESE,12)

I doubt if a more ambitious and inclusive statement on the relation between culture and the literary imagination has ever been made, not by Matthew Arnold nor by Wallace Stevens. The search for "something outside of the artist" was in fact a general search for grounding beyond art, beyond personal knowledge or the imaginative will. If we call it metaphysical grounding in the language of post-structuralism today, Eliot would assent under the sanctions of both nature and religious super-nature. The "organic wholes" of common inheritance were natural growths, and for the most part they acted unconsciously, but at the same time they commanded allegiance from the artist, "a devotion to which he must surrender and sacrifice himself." Demanding obedience to an unconscious and inevitable force, culture thus removed itself from the realm of arbitrary human invention and approximated biological fate. In effect Eliot brought forward and insisted upon a cultural determinism.[1]

Certainly for Eliot poetry was the expressive medium for the sensibility of a culture, even if not, as it was for Stevens, the rich ultimate source of the "sanctions" that maintain our lives. I note again that Stevens' wide view of the poetic imagination equates well with Eliot's view of culture. Accordingly Eliot's specific interest in culture can be read from his verse and from his categories of preference in verse, whether classic, romantic, or modern— categories that in his essays represented phases of culture that were more or less desirable. For example, writing about romanticism Eliot gave it one major expression of his seminal principle of dissociation. Where a radical solipsism was its key reality disappeared into literary "strangeness." "Romanticism is a short cut to the strangeness without the reality, and it leads its disciples only back upon themselves." The strangeness became estrangement in personal isolation, the chief symptom of cultural dysfunction. We live in the house of language, his philosophic contemporary, Heidegger, would write, and for the early Eliot the grand echoes of language and culture find contrast with a cosmic silence. This drama of largest dissociation was emphasized by what he once said of Stendhal and Flaubert in a review in *Athenaeum*; they knew "the awful separation between potential passion and any actualization possible in life," and they also understood "the indestructible barriers between one human being and another."[2] The crucial effect of dissociation was in the background of all his essays on culture and community. To cite those barriers is only to stress that the obsessive urge toward human communion in Eliot's mind became cosmic and even mystical.

Under this pressure Eliot led in the large modernist theme that explored the abyss of subjectivity. To escape solipsist experience it would be necessary to escape personal emotion. The poet himself would have to conceal his own person, enveloping a smaller *persona* in a much larger one, a figure like Tiresias in "The Waste Land" who, if his voice is the voice of the poem as Eliot would propose in his notes, it contains all other voices in range, containing history as well as myth (as Pound said of the *Cantos*). In contrast the poet could also become Prufrock, who is cornered and isolated, his voice dropping to a whisper interrupted by silence. Eliot's characters, even when observed in a larger consciousness are creatures of solipsism, like Gerontion feeling the alienation from time and place, or like the "jew" on the windowsill of a rented house, lacking time and place by definition, supremely dissociated and culturally dispossessed.

Calvin Bedient, in studying Eliot's Harvard dissertation on the idealist philosopher F.A. Bradley, focuses with good effect on a central premise in the monograph. "We do not know reality in substance, we know it in relation," and what the waste land represents "is a cancellation of relationship."[3] So Eliot's fleeting protagonists, with names more vivid than their bearer, illustrate a blank at both ends of a relationship, a fragmentized personal consciousness speaking from and to a collective memory frozen in time, "Unreal" until the supra-real appears in the failure of relation just as "the Word within a word" recovers in the failure of language. Bedient does well to emphasize Eliot's familiar linguistic ironies, bringing the most noble and articulate quotations to a level subsisting with pub speech, mock rhetoric, incoherent fragments, and in the background always converging on silence.

The dramatized linguistic failure contrasts and blends with Pound's lessons for Imagist verse, which he celebrated for its effort to achieve the unity of "inward" and "outward" being. This Eliot accepted in his poetics where, as in his essay on Swinburne he wrote in stern admonition, "Language in a healthy state presents the object, is so close to the object that the two are identified."[4] The thought behind this too is Pound's: "When...the application of word to thing goes rotten...the whole machinery of social and individual thought goes to pot. This is a lesson of history...." (PLE, 21). It was a theme of major influence, the dependency of culture on language and the consequent vocation of the poets as language makers and healers.[5]

The ill health of language was found in its barrier to natural and cultural reality. For poets language represents the authority of the imagination and so Stevens and Williams, as they figure in my subsequent discussion, as well as Eliot and Pound responded to a larger crisis than that of art. Meaning, truth, order and communication, all were at stake, and Eliot's profoundly sensitive reactions are at the center of explication. It helps account for his move to transcendent divinity for it was as if the "Real" were only distinguishable on that level from the "Unreal." The apocalyptic divine could appear at the last reduced margin because it was absolute, transcending nature, history and culture.[6] What else could escape the "abyss of subjectivity," the stalemate of language, and the deconstruction of societies, cultures, and persons? The role of divinity for Eliot can be partially understood by seeing the parallel role of art in the thinking of Pound who indeed could conceive essences in his poetry. For Pound art was knowledge and power, it closed all breaches and divisions and it could replace or amend metaphysical, moral, political, and economic truth. This was, we might say in Stevens' terminology, Pound's effort to achieve a "supreme fiction."

But it was only "fictionizing" for Eliot unless art, or poetry, led the way like prayer to supreme insight. Prayer in poetry, poetry in prayer were exercises in mystical vision while divinity still gave access. The only secular or worldly reality (a not quite "supreme fiction") that could unify existence was culture, behind it tradition and the social hierarchies, and above it the orthodox Church to marshal behavior as well as belief. Since in the true spiritual sense as well as secular (as in *The Cocktail Party*) some are able and most are not, some sort of class society must serve culture, preferably a born aristocracy trained in both the religious and esthetic sensibility to impose order. That was the middle or purgatorial way, destined to remain apart from ultimate salvation.

There was that remarkable breadth and simplicity in Eliot's view of culture, even while most of the complex concerns of his religious, moral, and political life were focused on its definition. Specifically, culture was the focus of resistance to modern naturalist myths of power, in all their aspects, nihilist, anarchic, amoral, or simply and sordidly utilitarian. In these respects if culture became the allegiance which Eliot could oppose to the reductive universals of naturalist thought, he followed the preoccupation of a previous generation, notably represented by Matthew Arnold. Actually he took more from the natural supernaturalism of Henry Adams who was curiously ambivalent between the power of physics in the Dynamo and the power of love and worship in the Virgin, who was in turn the sublimated figure of, the classic Venus. Both were fundamental in naturalistic and divine systems of order. Yet Adams could speak of nature as actual chaos and of culture as "the dream of man." Eliot's concern in discussing culture was to certify a reality. Ordinary reality was in his mind always, as when he wrote in *Notes Toward the Definition of Culture* that "one symptom of the decline of culture in Britain is indifference to the art of preparing food." He meant this seriously, as if culture could be described most simply as that which makes life worth living, which generously included for him, or perhaps any Englishman, "Derby Day.... boiled cabbage cut into sections.... and the music of Elgar."[7]

One senses a therapeutic value found in the quotidian as he lingers over his list. The point illustrates how redemptively active the term culture was for Eliot, in the organic sense precisely as something badly needed when Prufrock walks down the city street viewed by "lonely men in shirtsleeves." Sweeney exposes his "apeneck," Bleistein emerges from protozoic slime, and when Prufrock recites, "I should have been a pair of ragged claws scuttling across the floors of silent seas," the whole history of culture is brought into question.

On that base of response, a classic conservative of religious mind daringly pre-empted naturalist and historicist themes (the "protozoic slime" and "time's ruins") to argue for cultural authority. Pre-empt is the right word. What else is behind the respect for "the mind of Europe," that historic mind with its accumulation of treasures and coherent wisdom? The "mind of Europe" is a mind deeper than that of the poet, which he cannot leave behind, which never leaves his under-consciousness as he works, nor that of the reader. In striking contrast with an earlier urgent wish to separate the uses of poetry and the values of religion, Eliot refers to the poet almost as if he were the priestly figure of a primitive society, and in that role expressing "the mind of a whole people."[8] In "The Music of Poetry," a relatively late essay, he wrote that poetry was an advance into the area "beyond which words fail," with meaning extended to "something larger than (the) author's conscious purpose."[9]

> What I call the "auditory imagination" is the feeling for syllable and rhythm, penetrating far below the conscious levels of thought and feeling, invigorating every word;

sinking to the most primitive and forgotten, returning to the origin and bringing something back, seeking the beginning and the end....[it] fuses....the most ancient and the most civilized mentality. (*The Use of Poetry*, p. 118)

One appreciates in passages of this kind the organizing impulse of Eliot's way of thinking. The maturity of a literature is equated with the maturity of a civilization, its vitality with its youth, its depth with its primitive origin and with levels below consciousness; there is no separating its life from its expressions. If a poem reflects the beauty of the culture and the strength and harmony of the culture determines the excellence of the poem, it is because what is brought into exercise is the ability to make an order out of experience. In a mature civilization, "men have a critical sense of the past, a confidence in the present, and no conscious doubt of the future." Decay was the rich opposition to maturity, as he noted, and decay pointed toward apocalypse, leading either to extinction, or to reborn energy in the mysterious metamorphoses of apocalyptic events.

Cultural Politics

Eliot knew that reductive naturalism made a challenge to the traditional distinction between nature and culture. Is culture repression, sublimation, or commonplace philistine safety, and is nature the savage threat or godlike master? The background was set clearly in nineteenth century debates, and today it continues in every discipline and activity, from anthropology to politics and particularly the latter. The passions of modern cultural politics trace their source from premises that somehow equate cultural identity with race or ethnicity or gender and thus give a neo-metaphysical urgency to political conflict. In the lifetime of Eliot and Pound, a time of more savage political wars, the ratios of relation between culture and nature were sensitive and disturbed exactly because of the weakening of a traditional religious metaphysics that closed the gap, or so it would seem surely to the younger Eliot before he "reconsidered" Gerontion's "lost passion." On this ground it may be understood that the apocalyptic political cults of creation and destruction would generate considerable anxiety for the survival of culture itself. The conservative reaction was bound to be heard strongly, whether motivated by truly conservative instincts, as with Eliot, or by the spirit of esthetic order that could take the confidence of the artist craftsman into authoritarian politics, as in Pound's case.

Meanwhile the modern generations might have been able to read Nietzsche's insight into the obsession and ideal of "culture" and see it as a reflection upon their own deficiency.

Knowledge...now no longer acts as an agent for transforming the outside world but remains concealed within a chaotic inner world which modern man describes with a curious pride as his uniquely characteristic "subjectivity."....Our modern culture is not a living thing: it is.... not a real culture at all but only a kind of knowledge of culture....[The Greeks] during the period of their greatest strength kept a tenacious hold on their unhistorical sense, [whereas] we moderns have nothing whatever of our own; only by replenishing and cramming ourselves with the ages, customs, arts, philosophies, religions, discoveries of others do we become anything worthy of notice, that is to say, walking encyclopedias, which is what an ancient Greek transported into our own time would perhaps take us for.[10]

As in so many ways Nietzsche here defines modernism with particular relevance as it applies to the problems faced by Eliot. It is also an outline for the subtle treatment of the same issues in the work of Stevens. What could distinguish "real culture" from a "kind of knowledge of culture?" What could make the imagination that creates and supports culture "a real and living thing"?

It was Arnold who had said that culture shares with religion "the idea of conquering the obvious faults in our animality."[11] That was the accent for Eliot's earliest work; as he said quite specifically, religion alone assured distinction from the animal. Yet the reader notices in his essays on culture that the appeal is not often made to theology or divinity. Eliot defined the peculiar amalgam of his thought as cultural critic when he proposed in *Notes Toward the Definition of Culture* that he was both a Christian and a student of social biology. This was much more than a rhetorical strategy in modern social debate. When he wrote of social unity, he said characteristically that the problem was a spiritual problem "because its solution involves not merely planning, but *growing* a pattern of values..."[12] Yet as a "social biologist" of neo-Darwinian persuasion, Eliot could apply a narrow, again quite determinist standard for judging societies and cultures. It is a political style of conservative stress that asks for fatalist submission as well as strong conviction, and an underlying note is that of the dangerous Fascist politics of his time. In Eliot's treatment particularly it must be called the apocalyptic style, as in his final argument, where one is asked to choose Christianity in the name of the actual survival of a culture and the subspecies or race of people linked with it.

The belief in crisis was certainly genuine for a conservative Christian at the time he wrote his two long essays on culture.

I see no reason why the decay of culture should not proceed much further, and why we may not even anticipate a period, of some duration, of which it will be possible to say that it will have *no* culture. The culture will have to grow again from the soil; and when I say it must be grown again from the soil, I do not mean that it will be brought into existence by any activity of political demagogues. The question... is whether there are any permanent conditions, in the absence of which no higher culture can be expected.[13]

This is essentially the species language of post-Darwinian thought, applied to culture much in the style of Brooks Adams and Pound's teacher, Frobenius. The passage breathes with the warning of evolutionary apocalypse, but its primary emphasis is the bridge it makes between "social biology" and the superior standard of religion. Elsewhere he writes that the conditions of culture are "natural" to human beings, as natural as the family, which in Eliot's thought supplied the rationalization for the necessary existence of social classes. If cultures are primarily natural then there must be a root from which they grow. To Eliot it was no contradiction to propose religion:

> We may say that religion as distinguished from modern paganism, implies a life in conformity with nature. It may be observed that the natural life and the supernatural life have a conformity with each other which neither has with the mechanistic life.[14]

Culture could not have greater metaphysical unity than this. The phrases in his usage were "Europe as a whole" which was an "organism," and in fuller sentence, "European literature is a whole, the several members of which cannot flourish, if the same bloodstream does not circulate through the whole body."[15]

It seemed that the organic metaphor alone enabled culture to compete with plant and animal for legitimacy. In consistency, Eliot could claim the use of words like race and "blood kinship" to emphasize the urgencies he felt. Tradition, for instance, quite simply followed evolution, benefiting from mutation but adhering to the source, that is, as "a mind which changes," abandoning "nothing en route." As he expressed it in *After Strange Gods,* we are aware of some things only when we are losing them, as when we are aware of leaves only "when the autumn wind begins to blow them off/when they have separately ceased to be vital... but the sound tree will put forth new leaves, and the dry tree should be put to the axe."[16] This example of organicism made much possible in reconciling problematic judgments of decadence and decay, stability, continuity, and ultimately adaptive survival in life. In being consistently and subtly "organic," his critical mind became the more authoritative. Maturity, for instance, was a standard for evaluating poets. Criticizing Shelley, he objected to his ideas as those of an intelligent schoolboy, and an enthusiasm for Shelley was "an affair of adolescence." He made the same evaluation for Poe, another arch-Romantic.[17] But growth requires the right environment, and to compound the metaphor he remarked that Poe was not only immature but rootless. On the other hand this rootlessness was itself dictated by history and Poe's culture by "the conditions of the age in which he (found) himself."

Eliot finally brought all his literary weight to bear on the measure of maturity by equating it with the "classic," a remarkable fusion of traditional cultural credentials with those of naturalist growth.

> If there is one word on which we can fix, which will suggest the maximum of what I mean by the term "a classic," it is the word *maturity.*... A classic can only occur when a civilization is mature;... and it must be the work of a mature mind.[18]

The tautology in this definition is the more impressive for its determination to include a whole civilization in its scope, though it was his concern for the growth and decline of civilizations that led Eliot to his organicist vocabulary in the first place. It was almost inevitable that Eliot would deal with the most imperial of classics, Virgil, as the example of what he meant in the concrete if not ideal sense of culture. The Roman empire had historic roots and a vivid destiny, as Virgil expressed it, and culture in such hands, carried by the sense of empire in spatial reach and destiny, became what it essentially was intended to be, an organism to embody the living world. Eliot did not need Frobenius' vocabulary to make his own point on the *paideuma.*

In effect Eliot was very much a voice of his own time when he committed himself not only to apocalyptic prophecy but to imperial "destiny."

> Virgil....is at the centre of European civilization, in a position which no other poet can share or usurp. The Roman Empire and the Latin language were not any empire and any language, but an empire and a language with a unique destiny in relation to ourselves; and the poet in whom that Empire and that language came to consciousness and expression is a poet of unique destiny.[19]

It is noteworthy in this brief passage that he has moved swiftly from "language" to "classic" to "empire." The evolutionary growth is linked to a linguistic and literary determinism and its supreme culmination is with an empire. At that point we are in the hands of the practical imagination whose first loyalty is to order and authority; behind those emblems of safety must lie the realities of power, and the compulsions of "destiny." There is a familiar political intoxication in this language, with ominous echoes directed to the past and future by an appeal to a "higher power behind the gods," the invocation of "destiny," and the political claim on culture for ordinary power and rule. Linked with empire, culture could represent the collective heroism of the race, tested in natural struggle, and directed to a victory of art, intelligence and power. Most impressively Eliot gave culture the force to rival those aggressive fatalists of his time who drew conviction from the rhetoric of class and race. Actually in the political context culture could be the title for racial, national, or ethnic identity, as it is in many quarters today. The equations of cultural contrast in such thinking can be traced in Eliot's early verse, with Hakagawa "bowing among the Titians," and Bleistein contemplating Canaletto.

It is important to remember that Eliot wrote his major essays on culture during and just after the Second World War and under threat from the totalitarian systems. He was himself still insisting on the relative anarchy and cultural enfeeblement of the liberal democracies. He had seen that the Fascists and Communists were basing themselves on such natural forces as the vitality of race and the economic class struggle, and particularly the ethical-esthetic imperative of "order." For this he need only have read the thinking of his old friend in Italy, Pound. Much earlier in his own career he had recognized the quality of that threat, writing in the *Criterion* in 1931: "The Bolsheviks at any rate believe in something which has what is equivalent for them to a super-natural sanction; and it is only with a genuine supernatural sanction that we can oppose it." He never gave up on the call for a superior sanction, but the temptation to rival naturalist politics on its own ground was very strong. It became a combination in his hands, addressing himself to tradition and cul-ture on the terms of social biology, as if he could not quite trust the belief in supernatural sanctions.

Thus in his effective thinking culture and tradition became species con-cepts, where the species transcends the individual and where individual changes or mutations, real novelties that survive, alter the nature of the species. The ideal value of organic culture is clear in the sense that it does not abandon origin, does not abandon the past and the stability of roots, does not abandon the species in favor of the individual, or the individual in favor of the species, but maintains itself as a living entity, encompassing all possible con-tradictions except the death of the species. As this natural force becomes ide-alized as culture, both nature and culture can command sacrifice and submission and seem worthy of it.[20]

As for poetry and the poet, the artist is the emblem of the citizen, the person in the world.

> What happens (in poetry) is a continual surrender of himself (the poet) as he is at the moment to something which is more valuable. The progress of an artist is a continual self-sacrifice, a continual extinction of personality. (ESE, p.6)

In the context of Eliot's writing surrender and sacrifice have more than a vestigial moral and religious accent. Culture was ubiquitous and needed no surrender, except as one might surrender to authentic being. In that interest it approached metaphysical sanction, though for Eliot, as well as Pound, it combined with the more intimate sanction of art, the ideal of culture being the highest expression of the genius of order. The political note comes forward strongly with the "surrender" of the personality or person to the larger whole, even as "sacrifice" suggests the ultimate violent cost, as in the accent on martyrdom in his plays. Precisely at that center of language Eliot's poetics is contemporaneous with the great political struggle of democratic and totalitar-ian ideologies in this century. It is here that essential historic differences lo-cate themselves with Stevens' equally strong cultural enterprise.

Notes

1. Speaking some years ago for contemporary cultural exiles, Milan Kundera observed how "culture" had become a fetish of the modern era to replace religion. At the same time, he declared himself at war in its defense against the alternative threats of marketplace and media democracy and the totalitarian infliction. (*New York Review of Books*, April 26, 1984, p. 36). These latter could be described, with some freedom

of generalization, as forces of nature, expressed as the primary instinct for power and a strong discipline of order. Actually this was more or less the way Eliot described the position of modern culture in his essays "The Idea of a Christian Society" and "Notes Toward the Definition of Culture." The appeal to naturalist destiny may better account for Eliot's cultural "fetish" than the force of super-natural faith. In any case he seemed to need to deal with culture in both the natural and supernatural fields of power, and so he sought guaranty from nature and history.

2. *Athenaeum*, May 30, 1919.
3. *He Do the Police in Different Voices* (Chicago and London: University of Chicago Press, 1986), p.80.
4. "Swinburne as Poet" (SW,149).
5. The ambiguous correspondences between modernism and post-modernism seem likely to rest here. (See my later discussion, chapter 19.)
6. Bedient makes a succinct statement for the metaphysical opposition and reversal in Eliot's work as he moves toward apocalyptic transcendence. "I believe that the poet fiercely nips in the bud....any nostalgia for natural and human values—green growth, fruit, sex, love —in a ferocious dedication to the opposite of all such natural darkness, a devotion to "the heart of light." (pp.6, 23, 33). I refer to Bedient for important intellectual detail in the study of Eliot's mind, making fruitful explanatory use of Eliot's dissertation on Bradley. See also Michael Levenson's discussion of Bradley and Eliot in *A Geneaology of Modernism,* pp. 177-78.
7. *Christianity and Culture* (New York: Harcourt, Brace & Co. 1949), p. 104.
8. *The Use of Poetry and the Use of Criticism, "* pp. 22,26.
9. "The Music of Poetry," On Poetry and Poets, p.22.
10. "On the Use and Disadvantages of History for Life" in Untimely Meditations (London: Cambridge University Press 1983), pp. 78-79.
11. *Culture and Anarchy*, (London: Cambridge University Press, 1960), p. 54.
12. *The Classics and the Man of Letters* (London: Oxford University Press, 1942), p. 24.
13. "Notes Toward the Definition of Culture," p. 91.
14. "The Idea of a Christian Society," p. 48.
15. "What is a Classic?" On Poetry and Poets, (New York: Farrar Straus and Cudahy, 1957) pp. 72
16. It is remarkable how Eliot's cultural criticism and his political views do not seem to age. Religious conservatives today would quote him gladly. Race and gender-oriented multiculturalists today would surely recognize his view of the heritability of cultural values and their importance. That intellectual meeting of right and left is not unique in history. Certainly his organicist vocabulary and his form of cultural determinism could easily be adapted by materialist Marxists.
16. *After Strange Gods* (New York: Harcourt, Brace & Co., 1934), p. 19.
17. *The Use of Poetry and the Use of Criticism* (London: Faber & Faber, 1933), p. 89. His work appeals to readers" at the period of life when they were just emerging from childhood." "From Poe to Valéry," To Criticize the Critic, p. 34.
18. "What is a Classic?" p. 54.
19. Ibid., pp. 70
20. The whole passage is very much worth quoting: "Aeneas is himself, from first to last, a 'man in fate', ...a man fulfilling his destiny.... by surrendering his will *Criterion*, October, 1931, vol.11, no.42, p. 71.

6

The Old Sublime

Despite the well-recorded role that Ezra Pound played as patron, teacher, and editor during Eliot's early career, it is difficult to say now who was master and who was pupil. In nothing were they so alike as in their capacity to dramatize cultural cleavage, to prophesy the apocalypse, or to urge salvation in soft or harsh tones according to their respective temperaments. The germinating concern of Pound's creative life was the threat he felt in the cultural isolation of the artist. For the generation of Paterian lovers of beauty the danger from within was that of the fall from the inane sublime, as if to become major examples of the Dedalian flight which Joyce made his initiating theme. For an American the humiliation threatening artists was even greater, since aspiration so often led to the merely genteel, or to chronic dilettantism. In any case the dread of a meretricious beauty, as vast and vulgar as Jay Gatsby's or Emma Bovary's dreams, dominated the sensibility of artists, and the struggle to avoid its taint characterized the work we associate with vital modernism. Nowhere is that confrontation more transparently instructive than in the work of Pound.

There is clarity of logic to be found in a survey of Pound's developing themes and ideas. He begins, let us say, with a very strong youthful commitment to the esthetic idealism of the late nineteenth century. There is plentiful illustration of that even when he lays the basis of his own esthetic in rich reaction from the vacuity of the "lovers of beauty." He was of course one himself in such early Paterian expressions as the prose poem "Ikon," published in 1913.

> And if—as some say, the soul survives the body;... then more than ever should we put forth the images of beauty, that going out into tenantless space we have with us all that is needful—an abundance of sounds and patterns to entertain us in that long dreaming; to strew our path to Valhalla; to give rich gifts by the way.

The note of pagan worship is magnified in "The Altar"

> Let us build here an exquisite friendship,
> The flame, the autumn, and the green rose of lover
> Fought out their strife here ,'tis a place of wonder:
> Where these have been, meet 'tis, the ground is holy.

55

There seems something desperate in the effort of the imagination to do the work of holiness. But that work for Pound was to enlarge itself toward an omnipotence and scale designed for poetry. The point to be made is that not long after writing in this vein Pound declared himself committed to an effort to "rewrite Sidney's Defence of Poesy." One might add that he would eventually write even more aggressively for Shelley's legislator of the world in poetry. In the first pages of the important essay "The Serious Artist," Pound sets forth his premises for literary art which were to instruct "the nature of man" and "the nature of men when living together in groups"[1]

Was this the modernist hubris half-mocked by Joyce in the character of Stephen Dedalus inviting the powers of God? Pound saw the humor in it himself in adapted lines from Heine,

> I dreamt that I was God Himself
> Whom heavenly joy immerses,
> And all the angels sat about,
> And praised my verses.

But "seriousness" made its call beyond irony. The fact is that he was acutely aware of dissociation in Eliot's broadened sense on higher levels than the adequacy of his verses. The most disruptive forms of dissociation were not matters of individual sensibility but a whole series of divisions and readjustments between the worlds of power and beauty, fact and artifact, or to use Stevens' binary terms, reality and the imagination.

In that respect dissociation was a cultural illness, and in response to it Pound could declare, "I want a new civilization." Eliot, for re-association with the old, brought the artist into perceived relation with his "tradition," a collective sensibility speaking through him. For Pound there was revolutionary redemption in art breaking out of esthetic exile, and thus it could have a triumph embracing politics,(or more daringly, empirical science) passing from an entertainment or luxury by expressing its own essential will to power and order.[2]

Divided between "beauty" and his own dream of imaginative omnipotence Pound felt embattled from the beginning. In the world to which the young Pound summoned his songs transcendent beauty was a dying god. The pathos follows accordingly. In "The Spring" from *Lustra*, "wild desire/ Falls like black lightning/ O bewildered art/" and the lines end, "She, who moved there amid the cyclamen/ Moves only now a clinging tenuous ghost." His inevitable strategy was to escape capture by ghosts while ministering to the high tangible commands of his art. In "The Plunge" he declares "I would bathe myself in strangeness" as if that were to become his long commitment to an expatriate existence in life and in poetry. "New friends, new faces, \ .... among some\ Alien people!" But though the headline is addressed to the "new" it is hard not to see that Pound's actual dedication in most of his poetry is to the old, and that the imagination, perhaps because besieged, turns toward deep nostalgia for its substance. Thus in anecdotal memory,

> So ends that story.
> That age is gone;
> Pieire de Maiensac is gone.
> I have walked over these roads;
> I have thought of them living.

Nostalgia, however, would never do for a poet as strong-minded as Pound, and so he gained his mature style of combat on behalf of the esthetic ideal . "Come, my songs," he writes in *Lustra*,

> .....let us speak of perfection-
> We shall get ourselves rather disliked."

And in "Further Instructions,"

> Come my songs, let us express our baser passions,
> Let us express our envy of the man with a steady job and no
> worry about the future.

Like most of his generation of artists he had selected as his useful enemy the bourgeois philistine. To speak of perfection and thus get himself rather disliked was to be certainly his fate. But in the process he revealed the interesting mental division he suffered, a "dissociation of sensibility" far more revealing and outwardly directed than in Eliot's spare first use. For one thing he had nothing but contempt for the enemies of beauty and for them he could deliver "blasts" of rage that energize the accompanying pages of fine allusions and brilliantly concise imagery. His anger in poetry seems flamboyant today, though it tells of deeper frustrations than those caused by a bad review from "The Times." In "Salutation the Third" published in *Blast*, 1914, "You slut-bellied obstructionist," he writes, "You fungus, you continuous gangrene." In the Roman rage of the poem he writes, I will not die at thirty and let you have the pleasure of defiling my grave. "I will not go mad to please you/ I will not flatter you with an early death."

> Here is the taste of my boot,
> Caress it,
> lick off the blacking.

The coarseness in this had its source in a reaction from his own refined sensibility. Sure of himself as he was, he knew the risks when in "Ite" he asks his songs "to move among the lovers of perfection alone." But "Les Millwin" were also lovers of perfection as they attended the Russian Ballet. There they beheld the "splendours of Cleopatra" "with their large and anaemic eyes." Then why this wicked excess of contempt for the lovers of "beauty" that somehow correlates with his hatred of the philistine? The answer must be that beauty for Pound was to be the inclusive term, close in dignity to Stevens' view of poetry as the intimate source of "the concepts and sanctions that are the order of our lives." As he wrote in "The Serious Artist," "Beauty in art reminds one what is worth while." That was a definition to open his esthetic sense as wide as it might wish to reach.

But first some work of destruction had to be done. London was the right place to observe something like class decadence in the world imputedly devoted to "splendour" and "perfection." In "The Garden" Pound describes a lady from Kensington as if she were a political symbol of irrelevant refinement.

> Like a skein of loose silk blown against a wall
> She walks by the railing of a path in Kensington Gardens,
>
> And she is dying piece-meal
>   of a sort of emotional anaemia.

The contrast for her is harsh proletarian reality.

> And round about there is a rabble
> Of the filthy, sturdy, unkillable infants of the very poor.
> They shall inherit the earth.

It was typical that Pound should sense the class dread behind the threat of decadence, ("In her is the end of breeding"). Two themes of Pound's style of thought flow together with lucid effect in these lines. "Anaemia" was a blunt metaphor from the medical dictionary to characterize the "lovers of perfection," and in turn it suggested a pattern of resistance that is expressed in "Sestina: Altaforte" by the poet-warrior, Bertrans de Born, who sings of scenes of fighting as if they were the sure proof of a sufficiency of vital blood. The sight of blood on the battlefield can bring the singer to howl "nigh mad with rejoicing," and for him wine, music, the violent real weather, lightning or sun, all flash "blood-crimson."

Such contrasts mark the impact of Pound's early verse, as for instance in "Portrait d'Une Femme," which portrays a devitalized sensibility lapsing into fragmented memory.

> Ideas, old gossip, oddments of all things,
> Strange spars of knowledge and dimmed wares of price,
> ....
> Trophies fished up; some curious suggestion;
> Fact that leads nowhere; and a tale or two,

Described so vividly the lady could represent Pound himself in a form of self-criticism. He was already master of pastiche and perhaps he felt threatened to become curator of rare trophies in an historical museum ranging from the Greek and Chinese to Provencal and Italian Renaissance displays. Like the lady in the "Portrait," "...In the whole and all,/ Nothing that's quite your own." But how else could it be for "lovers of perfection"?

In the effort to turn from that vacuity Pound could project Mauberley with a double-edged satire that at once does justice to the things Mauberley loved and yet defends against "beauty" dispossessed by the lovers of "perfection." With notes of violent reality or the sordid quotidian, this was mental therapy against the dense splendors of the imagination. As with Eliot the great buffer of sensitive taste was irony.

The Mauberley poems remain Pound's characteristic success in verse, where he was able to bring the two extremes of his poetic temperament into a blend of tough satire and lyric sentiment. They are poems of discords and ellipses, consciously manipulated by a poet "out of key with his time." The fragmentary references, the abrupt starts and stops, suggest a song forced out against bitter allusions to an older generation which had lost in the struggle for the classic sublime. In rendering Provencal troubadours in pastiche, Pound too might be said to have been "wrong from the start," but in "Mauberley" he can make more convincing reference to "alabaster and the sculpture of rhyme," the ancient "Attic grace" as well as "faun's flesh and saint's vision." The deeper one allusion descends into commonplace or reductive animal existence, the higher another can reach toward myth and the literary sublime. By using the phrase, "the sublime in the old sense," Pound removed himself from strict accountability to it. On the other hand he was in a position to accomplish his other important task, which was to register contemporary lyric protest against what was decreed in the marketplace. Here Pound's theme seized major enlargement with the early strong signs in his poetry of his private cultural war with his time.

Greek beauty was more than the signature of esthetic complaint against a vulgar social order. *"To kalon"* is the sign of the imagination's value, the normative energy itself, here brought down in the marketplace. Similarly, to have "press for wafer" and "franchise for circumcision" is to register insults to the imagination on the level of the religious sublime, though the reference to circumcision, for Pound, poses a double insult, the Hebraic tribal ritual being equated with the basic democratic totem. The reductive contrasts dominate the poem, as with Lady Valentine standing as model in a drawing room.

"Daphne with her thighs in bark
"Stretches toward me her leafy hands,"—
Subjectively. In the stuffed-satin drawing room
I await The Lady Valentine's commands,

The Lady herself then is a caricature of glamor, but her image is needed to trace, in negative, the lost outline of awe in beauty. The quote for Daphne, from Gautier, would never have so much authority without Lady Valentine's presence among "stuffed-satin." For the same reason the poem needs such buffoon artists and esthetes as Lionel Johnson, who fell from his stool in a bar and died, his brain later to be pickled in alcohol.

Those indignities support a deeper imaginative discontent, directed at the apocalyptic crisis for "beauty." The Great War of 1914 threatened mass destruction not only for all contained in Lady Valentine's drawing room, but also in the greater museum that surrounds it in the poem, Athens with its statues of Apollo and memories of Pisistratus, the sage Heracleitus, and the fragmentary relics of Sappho. We know that Pound's friends, Gaudier-Brzeska and Hulme, went to war and so achieved a more dignified pathos in death than Lionel Johnson. As the victims of a great waste they are transfigured in rage to speak for the many who

> walked eye-deep in hell
> believing in old men's lies, then unbelieving
> came home, home to a lie,
> home to many deceits,
> home to old lies and new infamy;
> usury age-old and age-thick
> and liars in public places.

This was a moment in Pound's imaginative career when the disillusioned sense of "beauty" turned to ethical protest. The important point is that the esthetic sublime, expressed by Apollo, Daphne and Sappho, had been absorbed into the view of a disorder in history and even, by direct implication, a great political and moral crime. The sins against taste represented by the "prose kinema," or "the pianola," have been featured (some might say strangely) with "trench confessions," the "laughter out of dead bellies." It was a view of philistinism brought to epic scale. The criminal agents have been identified with the marketplace, the press, the franchise, and ultimately with usury. Those who died "for an old bitch gone in the teeth" endorse the fate of that civilization with their own. The destruction is total, the arraignment is total, and as a concise polemic against an identifiable culture and its signals of self-destruction, "Mauberley," in its two parts, may be the best political poem written in several generations, understanding that the issue is cultural politics and the threat is the apocalypse of culture.

It adds something to the cultural history of modernism to see that the keystone in this structure of thought was exactly the loss of the "old sublime" and the defeat of the ruling imagination. The ultimate victim is Mauberley himself, a man of sensibility, now transformed to become "a consciousness disjunct." With the artist's urge destroyed, he is confined to a grotesque subjectivity, "washed in the cobalt of oblivions." The artist victim had replaced the artist-hero of the Provencal poems; the latter survived only to serve pathos and rage alongside the Chinese glory and that of the Italian Renaissance.

For Pound to think of artists so reduced was enough to activate the poet militant and revolutionary. Pound passionately believed that at one time, in certain eras and places, there was harmony between imagined perfection and actual custom and rule. The need was imaginatively holistic; usury, for example, was the best of targets, for it claimed the imagery of parasitic waste. The "greenish souls of the little Millwins" were among its products, because usury represented the breach between imaginative desire and its locus in action. Thus the god Pan is invoked in order to find the vitalist power of natural reality. Pound's "usury" is most simply defined in the Hell Canto, XIV as the practice of "the perverts who have set money-lust\ Before the pleasures of the senses." Usury was the emptying out of measure and meaning in the life force itself, and their replacement by an abstraction that was pure counterfeit. Therefore for Pound usury might be called the exact enemy of "poetry" in Stevens' large sense, or his own of "beauty." Specifically usury opposed itself to creative *work*, and so art verified its centrality for Pound and could substitute for deeper but more distant moral and political implications.[3]

However, there are no portraits of the poor and oppressed in Pound's verse; it is the high, creative imagination that suffers most in the regime of usury. Mauberley, who is not Pound but much like Prufrock, is doomed in his passive sensibility, no more able to support full and fluent lines of verse than he is to face out the impasse.

> Nothing, in brief, but maudlin confession,
> Irresponse to human aggression,
> Amid the precipitation, downfloat
> Of insubstantial manna,
> Lifting the faint susurrus
> Of his subjective hosannah.

Pound's career began I think with that contempt for a mere "subjective hosannah." The key is in the "Portait d'une Femme," for the lady who possessed "nothing that was quite her own." The same theme is in "Ortus," an early statement of the poet dealing with a subject that refuses to take form:

> How have I laboured?
> How have I not laboured
> To bring her soul to birth,
> To give these elements a name and a centre!
> She is beautiful as the sunlight, and as fluid.
> She has no name, and no place.
> How have I laboured to bring her soul into separation;
> To give her a name and her being!
> ....
> I beseech you enter your life.
> I beseech you learn to say "I,"
> When I question you;
> For you are no part, but a whole,
> No portion, but a being.

The poem could have been forwarded to himself, or a part of himself. To have "laboured...to bring her soul to birth....To give her a name and a being!" is an honorable dedication of poetry, but here it is as if the poet were questioning not only beauty but the world itself and his own "name and a centre" in it. Was the world a collection of random effects and he a collector of equally random appreciations? The hypothesis suggests that Pound too felt a struggle with the unanchored imagination and unmediated reality, and so approached the theme invoked by Stevens.

There is much later support in an isolated and therefore ambiguous remark from Canto 98, repeated in 102:

> "But the lot of 'em, Yeats, Possum, Wyndham
> had no ground beneath 'em."

The ground that was lacking in Yeats, Eliot, and Lewis would presumably include "name, "place," and "being." Surely the dispossession of ground can apply to Pound as well. But that issue aside, the early lines from "Ortus" and "Portrait d'une Femme," and then from "Mauberley" give more poignance to his verse than is usually received. The "museum" of the lady's mind is in the first place a search for a "name" and a "place," though made more attractive for strangeness than familiarity. To use contemporary theoretical language, it is a search (in an ethical-esthetic void) for "presence" (or "grounding") in what is distant in time and place. So Pound's early subjects and styles from *Lustra* and *Cathay* deal with exotic differences. The range is impressive that includes intimacy with Rome and ancient China, the artists of the Italian Renaissance and the poets of Provencal, and "names" like Sextus Propertius, Quintus Septimus, Cino, En Bertrans de Born, Perigord, Maent, Richard Coeur de Lion, Arnaut, Dante, and Rihaku. We may understand Pound's taste for translation, quotation, and pastiche, and for languages in general as if the foreign tongues could find a new path to the ground of being.

More directly there is a lesson in the title he used in publishing *Personae*. Did he himself have the need to take on such adequate surrogate powers? If we say it was for the writing of strong verse there is no need to investigate a psychological problem. "Personae" was well named for the adoption of masks and armor; to live within the styles and languages of older poets was both weapon and defense. The poet is in fact multiple, not one, not immediately and directly a person, just as "personae" are not persons. It might be argued today that Pound in his early work is a "post-modernist" poet and critic of poetry, though standing in the advance guard of modernism. The parallel is with Eliot's catalyst theory of poetic creation, a view of a neutral instrument between the inherited language, its conventions and its "personae," and between the completed poem and eventually the reader.

I call the issue at hand dissociation in its deepest sense, that is, the separation of primary identity from the ground of name and place in a narrative of being. Such awareness of loss or division leads directly to satire, as we see evidenced in what Pound called his "Moeurs Contemporaines" where his poems shifted from exotic distance to the plain present. This could lead to his writing essays in depersonalization, with people evacuated of substance, made abstract and classified, and then reduced to the neuter pronoun as in "Sketch 48 b. II"

> At the age of 27
> Its home mail is still opened by its maternal parent
> And its office mail may be opened by
> its parent of the opposite gender.
> It is an officer,
> and a gentleman.

The officer has become the formula of the conventional abstract to contrast those others who seek to occupy the absurdly solipsist realm of fine surrogate experiences.

Notes

1. *Literary Essays* (New York: New Directions, 1935), p. 41 (hereafter noted as PLE).
2. The wider issue reflects the seminal work of Henry Adams, as I have viewed it in an earlier work. In his world at the turn of the century the religious, esthetic and moral agents of sensibility wander the universe without sanction from truth or from nature. Adams' effort was to find and redeem the naturalist sanction, (in blend with the religious), as if to give everything to the vital force in the icon of the Virgin-Venus in order to match or in fact overcome the modern power god, the Dynamo (Power and Order [University of Chicago Press, 1981]). I strongly recommend that students read my chapter on Henry Adams for its relevance to the lives and work of both Eliot and Pound.
3. Pound's adulation of Henry Adams and Henry James was particularly warranted for the three were Americans of enormous sensibility who transferred what might be the ordinary esthetic sense in others to the highest level level of ethical-esthetic perception and judgment.

7

The Vortex of Art

"A Scientific Definition of Poetry"

It was said of Pound, as of Ford Madox Ford, that he was the last of the pre-Raphaelites. Both, however, were in a personal position to repudiate the older generation of taste, and in the revolution conducted by Pound and Ford, Hulme and Eliot, deeper cultural changes were necessarily involved. At the start both Pound and Ford criticized the hypertrophy of the poetic dialect, its increasing isolation from serious as well as practical expressions of language. They wanted for esthetic language the kind of authority now offered to science, which seemed then, progressively, the only language that could gain and keep intellectual attention. In his poetic "Credo," printed in Harold Monro's *Poetry Review* in December 1911, Pound bluntly takes more than personal authority as his esthetic standard.

> I believe in an 'absolute rhythm,' a rhythm, that is, in poetry which corresponds exactly to the emotion or shade of emotion to be expressed. (PLE, 9)

But absolute only meant exactitude in expressing a truth. Emotions were not subjectively locked responses released in art; they were its materials or "facts" to be accurately recorded. No more than for Eliot was this phrased as an aspiration to do justice to profound emotional experience, but rather as an effort to get rid of "rhetorical din" and "emotional dither"; it was, more than anything, an effort to touch the "hard and sane" surface of reality.[1] Modern poetry, he wrote, "will be as much like granite as it can be." As Ford himself noted in a review of Pound's *Cathay*, there was nothing new in these strictures, and by that he didn't necessarily mean to refer to his own role in teaching the young Pound, but to the teachers of both, Flaubert, Remy de Gourmont, and the Goncourt brothers. For Pound the emulation of science was explicit and went far. He wanted a poetry freed from the emotions that had no link to the "perceptual faculties," and an experience in poetry moved by the "inevitable laws of nature," rather than what he called "the stupidity of the experiencer."[2]

In that context "stupidity" is the harshest pejorative to describe romantic and subjective dissociation from the "perceptual faculties" or the laws of nature, and so Pound made his own effort to formulate a "scientific definition of poetry."

> The Art of Poetry consists in combining these 'essentials to thought,' these dynamic particles, *si licet*, this radium, with that melody of words which shall most draw the emotions of the hearer toward accord with their import, and with that 'form' which shall most delight the intellect. (PSP, 330)

But "delight" or esthetic pleasure was not, for Pound, distinct from more ambitious aims.

> Now that mechanical science has realized his ancient dreams of flight and sejunct communication, he (the poet) is the advance guard of the psychologist on the watch for new emotions, new vibrations sensible to faculties as yet ill understood. (PSP, 331)

In writing this he embraced rivalry with science, believing that art, as much as science, advanced the boundary of known experience. Pound's own faith installed poetry on the highest level next to mathematics where " the poet's true and lasting relation to literature and life is that of the abstract mathematician to science and life." It was hyperbole for him to say that a new cadence or rhythm might rank with the intellectual adventure of a new mathematical theorem, but it suggests how impassioned Pound was on behalf of art's authority. Pound thus transferred the intellectual hubris of late nineteenth-century science (raised to half-mocking idolatry by Henry Adams) to the hubris of art and eventually to the true tragedy of hubristic politics.

Within intellectual presumption the artist-scientist illustrated Pound's need to bring poetry to the level of the philosopher king whose highest aspiration only genius might understand. Such a genius (in surprising juxtaposition for many) was Henry James, as Pound wrote about him in 1920, when the language of scientific naturalism most attracted him. James, he says, set titanic masses, volumes, weights into position. These were of course social volumes and weights.

> His art was great art as opposed to over-elaborate or over-refined art by virtue of the major conflicts he portrays. In his books he showed race against race, immutable; the essential Americanness, or Englishness, or Frenchness... "why" there is always misunderstanding, why men of different race are not the same. (PLE, 298)

Examined on James' microscopic slides, the forces in race and character were as absolute as any in nature, "permanent and fundamental hostilities and incompatibles." Difficult as this may be to grasp in its emphasis for James, the master of nuance and subtle modulation, it is possible that Pound in his enthusiasm was over-arching toward a less attractive persona than the artist or scientist, a leader of men and a leader of races in their "major conflicts."[3] Perhaps it was a necessary culmination for the religion of art to become "science" and the politics of art, seeking the sort of holism where art and science, nature and culture, combine forces in the search for ultimate order and authority. The essence, however, was a rivalry for power, one pressure of the imagination meeting another that would master nature, both facing "the pressure of reality" with the instruments they had at hand.

The Esthetics of Energy

When it came to emulating science, Eliot's view of the imagination as catalyst was much too passive for Pound. He was more interested in basic energy, the power that might be engaged in "making a new civilization," such being the higher function of poets. In the excitement of change one could believe that the stripping of old forms, whether in art or culture, would purge the imagination in order to renew its vital energy. That energy, and its purity of impulse, was the prize sought by modern poets in many devices and strategies. It became a truism eventually that modernist art tended to value its own deconstructive force as much or more than its finished forms. One of the most notable effects was the use made by Pound and Eliot of an explosive contact between words, images, ideas that offered violent impact as well as a very important gain in detachment. The effect was homeopathic; if the sensibility was brought sharply above complacent illusion, it was also given distance from ugly or violent contrasts. For Pound further, the command to redeem the imagination made him propound his earliest slogan for artists, "make it new." Any newness would be a test of creativity, and any genuine new work would be a message from a world about to exist, indeed it would be the making of that world.

The authority for this intellectual ambition began with a respect for "facts" and closed with a greater respect for the energy that took mastery over all phenomena. Thus Pound discovered and delivered Fenollosa's words, "All truth has to be expressed in sentences because all truth is the *transference of power*."[4] To bring language into equivalence with natural truth and to make it a "transference of power," was to give the poet an immense confidence, close to that of a metaphysician-priest, or to mention the obvious, the best of orators at the newest Roman forum. As energy was released in the universe, transcending its ostensible structures, so art was energy, always transcending its own forms or pre-established systems. In this Pound was touching one of the clearest principles of a modernist esthetic. As in so many other respects Pound conveyed the meaning of art movements such as Cubism, Abstract Expressionism, and particularly what was later called "action painting," which featured the energy of the creative act as its own subject. He also was engaging, through Fenollosa, with the simplified Nietzschean formula of the "will to power" in its most problematic implications for discourse and action.

The equation of language and rhetoric with power (like the equivalence of knowledge and power) has usually the effect of reducing if not dismissing the civil and ethical uses of language. Traditionally that use of language tended to resist power or give it a moral dimension in terms such as persuasion, invitation, empathy, identification, self-offering, and love. Of course all these could be dismissed as sublimating rhetoric serving power, But the argument itself has reality, and here, as I shall try to illustrate, is where a poet like Williams changes path with his original master. The clearest parallel for Pound's impersonal vortex is with Eliot's rejection of poetic personality which would seem to eliminate the dialogue of subjects and mutuality of response. Speech and writing in that context would be closer to rhetoric than poetry, subordinate to the swirling force in history and politics rather than persons and things. Here what was once voiced as truth or love or praise speaks realistically in the language of power.[5]

That language of power dominates in the effect of Eliot's poems and plays where images of impotence and fatalistic passivity alternate with the expiatory violence endured by martyrs and the more prosaic but quite brutal violence hinted in the life of Sweeney. It is in the same context that the spiritual resemblance between Prufrock and Hugh Selwyn Mauberley can be recognized. Both speak in ironic de-creation, and both find the most succinct images of impotence projected from themselves onto a world in a moral and esthetic impasse. But while Prufrock dramatizes a solipsistic break between person and person and the psychic distortion of the environment in which he lives, "Mauberley" blames a degenerate powerful world for the breaking of his spirit.

> The age demanded an image
> Of its accelerated grimace,

If Apollo and Pisistratus are invoked for the missing "god, man, or hero," it is to stress the need for a classic strength of imagination and will.

It was after the first issue of *Blast* and the launching of *Vortex* that Pound met the crucial defining words from Fenollosa, "all truth is the transference of power," without knowing perhaps that the source of this inspiration and much else from Fenollosa was Emerson. Emerson thought of truth and beauty and right as manifestations from a source of sacral energy, but his naturalist idealism was never misunderstood by his contemporaries. Pound, in his own earlier work, published his thought of poetry as the controlled transformation of energy, the good work feeding response with its energy, and presumably in a fruitful chain of cultural reaction, the bad work drawing it away.[6]

That was Pound's emphasis in the year that the Curies isolated radium (1910), a few years before he read Fenollosa's manuscript and before the advent of *Vortex*. He wrote then on Cavalcanti in praising *virtu*, or the integrity of force in the poet, that this was like radium in expressing "a noble virtue of energy."It was also axiomatic that energy entailed order, a principle he might have gotten from Henry Adams. The ideogram, as eventually instructed by Fenollosa, was in effect a logic of opposed energies in which images, words, ideas discharge against each other in opposition and attraction, in essence a species of natural form. The method had Pound's own training ground in the "Mauberley" poems.

> The tea-rose tea-gown, etc.
> Supplants the mousseline of Cos,
> The pianola "replaces"
> Sappho's barbitos.

> Christ follows Dionysus,
> Phallic and ambrosial
> Made way for macerations;
> Caliban casts out Ariel.

In these important stanzas one notices first the density of abstract metaphors. Christ follows Dionysus as one image of force follows another, in fact, "supplants," "makes way," and "casts out," so that whole civilizations appear as immense abstractions of power. These sharp transitions and steep drops, demonstrating the large reach of metaphor, were basic in Pound's delighted recognition of Eliot's early verse. The theme became clear; if energy moved into patterns of order, than order moving from disorder was structured in conflict. Temperamentally the theme of conflict was most congenial. He was a poet of intensities after all, and as he could maintain the short lyric intensity of poems like "The Return" or "Virginal" or the blissful harmonies of his imitation of Waller in "Hugh Selwyn Mauberley," he also seemed to spur himself with anger, as if combativeness were inseparable from his poetic inspiration. Thus, in "Salvationists," inviting his songs to take arms and sing of perfection, he reads little distinction between being at war and aiming for perfection because perfection of any sort, whether in art or life, raises targets for attack. Poetry itself is a kind of war, and poets are warriors, since they battle with the world's stupidities and ugliness.

In that setting Pound was to be consistently fascinated by artist-rogues and roisterers like Bertrans de Born and François Villon, and such greater, more authentic rogue rulers like Sigismundo Malatesta. By affirming that poetry was the interest of warriors and princes, he might hope to bring it abruptly out of the "esthetic twilight" of the late nineteenth century. It was invitingly simple to repeat that beauty itself was the expression of a superior energy, authenticated by its force within the shapes of order. The contrast with decadence was brilliantly ready when he explored the old poetry of the Chinese, as in this example of Rihaku:

> The lords go forth from the court, and into far borders.
> They ride upon dragon-like horses,
> Upon horses with head-trappings of yellow metal,
> And the streets make way for their passage.
>   Haughty their passing,
> Haughty their steps as they go in to great banquets,
> To high halls and curious food,
> To the perfumed air and girls dancing,
> To clear flutes and clear singing;
> ("Poem By the Bridge at Ten-Shin")

Pleasure, power and beauty are certified here, sanitizing "the perfumed air" and purifying "the dance" by linking it with the adventurous hardships of lords who ride dragon-like horses. "Haughty their passing," for this was the dignity of living.

If there is a tradition here for this thought of the literary sensibility it turns again toward Henry Adams, who felt the same need to give vitalist explanation to a surpassing achievement in beauty such as Mont St. Michel, with its source in the virile empire of the Normans. Wallace Stevens understood that imaginative hunger when he chose Verrocchio's statue of the condottiere, Colleoni, for his image of the "noble rider," a symbol diminished in modern art and life. Colleoni and Malatesta—there are final differences in the usage made of these figures by Stevens and Pound, but the parallel points to a shared imaginative need at the source. For one image of the hero he wanted, Pound followed Joyce to the *Odyssey*, because, like Joyce, he saw Ulysses and myth in large concession to the most sober modern realism. In fact he flaunted realism in using the Greek term *polumetis* which suggested the survivor who kept a primitive force intact.

> The things that the *polumetis* knew were the things a man then *needed* for living. The bow, the strong stroke in swimming, the how-to-provide *and* the high hat, the carriage of the man who knew how to rule, who had been everywhere, Weltmensch, with "ruling caste" stamped all over him, so that a red, cracked skin and towseled hair as he came out of the underbrush left him " never at a loss."[7]

He came out of the underbrush and he knew how to rule, these were the true naturalist virtues; vitality and the shrewdness for survival earn the right to rule. The pagan gods recognize Odysseus for this, "And as Zeus said, 'A chap with a mind like THAT! the fellow is one of us. One of US.'" Perhaps there is something characteristically American about that colloquial fellowship with the gods; Pound may have thought of himself, poet from Idaho, as coming out of the frontier underbrush. In the same essay which attends to red-skinned Odysseus, he directs invective at his enemies as gorillas, amoebas, "primitive congeries of protoplasmic cells." The ultimate reduction tells us something of his demand on the hero to reabsorb his primitive substance, as if that could achieve so far unimagined evolutionary excellence.

Even more than Ulysses, Malatesta suited Pound's imagination as an example of successful metamorphosis. Sigismundo carried himself close to the underbrush, part gorilla himself, though he was also the condottiere patron of poets and painters. His figure is seen in focus with Canto 9 recording the year he fought in snows and hail, trapped in the marsh, standing in water up to his neck. As he fights there and in the street fight at Fano, he remembers Basinio, the poet who won a debate in the courtyard of Malatesta on the value of Greek for the Latin•writing poet. In another reference, Malatesta fights and is swindled in an involved series of manipulative relations with the Sforzas; from a whirl of deceit, hatred, and violence, including a reference to his second wife, Ollizen, whom Sigismundo was believed to have poisoned, the sequence of thought turns to his stealing the marble in Classe in order to build his own "*Tempio*" at Ravenna. That devotion to the *Tempio,* grand monument to art and culture, underlies these accounts of criminal rowdiness, which include a "row about that German-Burgundian female." "Row" is quite a euphemism for what actually took place. The German-Burgundian "female" was a noble woman assaulted and killed on the way to Rome, supposedly by Sigismundo, condottiere and "taker of cities" (PC, 36).

The narrative is a good illustration of the transgressive style in modernism. The recognizable theme is to make the hero a gifted breaker of conventions who proves himself first in his defiance of rule and second in exceptional acts of creative imagination. Thus Pound described François Villon in *The Spirit of Romance,*

> . . .thief, murderer, pander, bully to a whore, he is honoured for a few score pages of unimaginative sincerity; he sings of things as they are. He dares to show himself.[8]

To sing of "things as they are" reflects the mischief of thieves and murderers. Choosing such heroes was, as Donald Davie notes, itself a matter of Pound's conforming to the convention of the avant garde in its offensive against the establishment, bourgeois genteel or bourgeois philistine. But all this is produced on behalf of "things as they are." Li Po, another of Pound's rogue-poets, was called by contemporary anecdote a drunkard, an idler, undependable, without self•respect. "His intellectual outlook was low and sordid," observes Davie, quoting directly from the contemporary record of Chinese criticism.[9] In these respects the principle of metamorphosis itself guided Pound to his choices. The careers of Villon and Li Po certified the miracle of imaginative redemption from what was "low and sordid."

Charles Olson writes that Pound's chief reaction in his themes and subjects was from the quotidian existence of America at the turn of the century. He was right to call Pound "terribly American" in this war against boredom.[10] Eliot produced "the boredom and the horror" to give his view of these cultural pains. With much less fear and revulsion Tocqueville knew what was American in predicting the future of poetry in the real world of democracy. "Nothing conceivable is so petty, so insipid, so crowded with paltry interests—in one word, so anti-poetic, as the life of a man in the United States."[11] The range and eclecticism of Pound's imagination receives explanation at once on that basis, as does that of Eliot. Probably no writers in the American tradition, even Poe, were as far-reaching in the search for distant allusions, esoteric knowledge, epic personalities, and apocalyptic themes, all in the most acute view of the lowering "anti-poetry" in everyday existence, which brings Stevens and Williams into the same purview, though with greatly different effect. Pound's voyage of the imagination in search of heroes is a very American voyage, even in its conclusion, as he moves from the Greek and Roman, to the Provencal and Renaissance stores of legend, and then to the Chinese as if to reach the height of the exotic, and finally, as it were, back to early America in the persons of Jefferson, Adams, and then, of all people, Martin Van Buren. It is both an irony and earned progress that Pound's mind should be so thoroughly invaded by the quotidian after all. Van Buren was home-folks as presidents go, and the problems of taxation and fiscal policy for which Pound gave him credit in the *Cantos*, are at first very mundane items of interest. But that challenge to the imagination was central to Pound's theme; money, through usury, could assume a malevolent role equivalent to all of the enemies of romance.

In any case it was not a journey of exotic discovery that led Pound to his heroes. The intention was certainly deeper than the impulse to shock bourgeois pieties or even, more largely, to invade "tedium," which Edward Dahlberg, speaking for a slightly younger generation, called "the grand malaise of the Western World," "at the nether-most core of history, and at the underside of war and poverty."[12] Baudelaire, and then Eliot, could confirm that "malady of the quotidian" (to borrow Stevens' enormously evocative title) in the now traditional view of the modernist psyche. But Pound in his search for colorfully outcast and creative energies was committed to affirming values that were at home in a world defined in vitalist terms. As Davie observes of his version of "The Seafarer," Pound not only eliminates Christian values but "replaces them by something positive, not just pagan but barbaric."[13]

The bombast of such heroes and the shock of their violence gave relief from the oppression of the everyday world. Life at its high points of pressure in fighting, seduction, and rape are small apocalyptic notes, climaxes of destruction which reveal a transvaluation of values. Once Malatesta, for example, a scoundrel if ever there was one by conventional definition, has manifested his *deep* nature he can rightly be seen as patron of the arts as well as ruler of the city. This was one contemporary political theme, certainly accepted in the totalitarian society to which Pound eventually gave allegiance. Like art, a secular order expressed itself in the manifestation of intense energy. It was a vitalist energy capable of breaking through all sublimations. What might be creative would follow what was destructive and order itself be renewed in the state. This was not, of course, the apocalyptic sacrifice figured in Eliot's late poems and plays, but there is a clear parallel. Pound was as demanding in sacrifice for his politics as Eliot was in religion, and in that respect closer to the temper of his times.

The Vortex of Culture and Race

To summarize, the theme was simple enough, nature provided systems of force that verge regularly on chaos and destruction. It was probable that nature was not inhabited at all by an intelligible genius of order, or that its order, if present, was antithetical to the temperament and needs of mankind. Entropy was one major example, and even more destructive to human teleologies, there was soon to arrive the Heisenberg principle of uncertainty. This was part of the intellectual atmosphere that Pound's generation breathed, and it hardly needed reinforcement from the Nietzschean talismanic phrase, the "will to power," to place the artist in heroic focus. Pound may have had a disordered mind but it was one peculiarly susceptible to the magnetic particles of thought, or as he would put it, his generation's vortex. If authentication had to come from nature it came helpfully, for as he said, "energy creates pattern." The artist not only records but creates, and in creating he moves as a force producing "order-giving vibrations," by which, Pound says, "one may mean merely he can departmentalize such part of the life-force as flows through him" (PSP, 346).

Energy, then, was something like an abstract deity endowing form and substance. In equating energy with form, Vorticism in Pound's formula could establish a respect for pure form unmatched by any previous art theory, since form was endowed by nature to exceed arbitrary invention. Here Pound could anticipate the modernist disdain for traditional form-content dualities as he writes of "energy, whose primary manifestation is in pure form..." The word "pure" has its meaning now entirely divorced from sentimental or idealistic implications. The fruitful implication is that form achieved itself best insofar as it deviated from conventional or traditional patterns, and indeed, as in abstract art, from the restraints of its material content. What this meant for Pound was that energy, a vitalist power in the artist and the work, is the value attached to the work beyond other values. The supreme effect, given and received, is the energy *in* the form. Accompanying the fetish of form, a fetish of the "new" arises, which clings to the redeeming principle that energy manifests itself in change.[14] At that point the attribution of genius has the old metaphysical magic, a semi-divine principle like that which once endowed the magus and seer, or a semi-divine ruler. In the face of this power, abstractly generalized, what is ordinarily called subject matter—things, persons, ideas, values, the matter for debate in usual discourse—may simply fade before the superior energy in order-making. Whether it was the abstraction of esthetic form or the abstraction of physical force that led to this point is not easy to measure, but the result was a fiercely authoritarian abstraction of power which could lend itself as easily to politics as to art in suit of Pound's need.

The ambition to rival physical nature meant that art could have the immediacy of a physical event and make the same demand for attention. This was implicit in the original definition of the Vortex as Pound proposed it in 1914, writing that a poetic image is "a radiant node or cluster...a VORTEX from which, and through which, and into which, ideas are constantly rushing.[15] In that vocabulary of description, art entered the direct world of action. If it was energy, it was reality, and no longer the mere instrument of ideologies at a second or third level of response. The meaning in the Vortex and Futurist movements was that art could find the "node" of reality, the gifted energy that moved the world, and as the future developed, the artist would be the natural ally for the great order-makers of life in society.

The Vortex was indeed the "node" itself for ideas of culture, cultural rivalries and energies, and cultural fate that obsessed the minds of Pound's and Eliot's intellectual generation. In Pound's ninth Osiris essay he wrote that words, made analogous with electrified cones in fields of force, are filled with "the power of tradition, of centuries of race consciousness, of agreement, of association."[16] In that view, the "vortex" was a pattern that drew on everything, so that there could be a national vortex, presumably a racial vortex (since it grew from "centuries of race consciousness"), as well as the personal vortex which Pound called *virtu*.

The impressive effect in this development of thought from vitalist premises was the way in which art was used as the bridge between the laws of life and a highly tribalistic view of culture. Cultures, or civilizations, were complex concatenations of forms and forces, they existed in the life cycle, they have their birth, youth, and death, they triumph with energy and fail with its absence. Pound took this vocabulary from Leo Frobenius, an anthropologist viewing culture in terms of energy cycles—a sort of pre-structuralist, we might say from this distance. The *paideuma* added point to the teaching of Fenollosa by addressing itself to the appearance of a culture and people as a unified pattern of force in history. This was what Pound needed to validate *The Cantos*, as Hugh Kenner suggests, and they should be read on that basis to bring them a coherence not otherwise understood. They were "the tale of the tribe"; everything else was refinement and superstructure, narrative values that were quite illusory unless supported by the source in the "vortex" and its latent form in the *paideuma*.

Such terms were neither fanciful nor esoteric in Pound's usage. His acute sensitivity to the vitality of language had earlier carried him to the distinctive cultures of Provence, Renaissance Italy, and the Chinese. His art was anthropology in its need to find large patterns in the link between language and action, or between language and the imagined personae of his poet-rogues and poet-emperors. Vortex, and later the *paideuma*, made it possible to draw together the heroics of personality, the vivid particles of immediate experience, the evident design of whole cultures, and an underlying deep respect for a metaphysics of force which in its naturalist expression would be manifest in race. A metaphysics of force prescribed an ethos of order. It is on this ground that Pound's work could become the testament of a modern discipline of value, with its far-reaching effects in politics, cultural politics, and war.

We live or shall live in a poeticized culture, Richard Rorty recently wrote, where metaphors will take the place of revealed or dictated truth. That may be so, though in Pound's case one might argue that he and his poetry lived in a culture conditioned by the lordship of fact and by vitalism and evolutionary science. Pound's personal political influence did not extend very far, but it is remarkable how well he expressed a modern political myth that is both activist and determinist at the same time, both fatalist and aggressive. For this he allied the dynamics of personality and will with the compulsory rule of the group and its history, that is, its pattern of energies. A "vortex" might be found anywhere but most convincingly it might characterize the imperial force and *virtu* (culture) of nation or race. To say this is to do nothing to detract from the value and importance of a "poeticized culture" (in Rorty's meaning), but the opposite, particularly as we reflect upon the sharply contrasting poetic thought of Stevens and Williams.

Notes

1. *Selected Letters of Ezra Pound*, 1907-1941, ed. D. D. Paige (London: Faber & Faber, 1950), p. 49.
2. "The Wisdom of Poetry" (*Forum*, New York, April 1912), *Selected Prose, 1909•1965*, ed. William Cookson (London: Faber & Faber, 1973), p. 330 (hereafter noted as PSP).
3. *Instigations*, (New York: Boni & Liveright, 1920), p.114.
4. "The type of sentence in nature is a flash of lightning. It passes between two terms, a cloud and the earth. No unit of natural process can be less than this. All natural processes are, in their units, as much as this. Light, heat, gravity, chemical affinity, human ill have this in common, that they redistribute force." Text from Fenollosa, "The Chinese Written Character as a Medium for Poetry" (*Instigations* 1920, pp. 366, 363).
5. One can see here how current trends in language theory and literary criticism share focus with classic modernism. Much of the controversy in postmodern theory deals with its use of Foucauldian theories of power and knowledge, power and language, treated in general effects in later. chapters.
6. "I Gather the Limbs of Osiris" (PSP,30).
7. *Guide to Kulchur*, p.146.
8. *The Spirit of Romance* (London: J. M. Dent & Sons, Ltd.), p. 181.
9. Davie, op. cit., p. 25.
10. *Charles Olson and Ezra Pound*, ed. Catherine Seelye (New York: Grossman Publishers, 1975), p. 90.
11. Democracy in America, vol.2 (New York: Vintage-Alfred A. Knopf, 1945), p. 78.
12. Edward Dahlberg, *Can These Bones Live?* (Norfolk, CT: 1960), p. 21.
13. Davie, op. cit., p. 26.
14. Such insights for modern art are what make the title of Hugh Kenner's influential book, *The Pound Era*, most relevant.

15. *Gaudier-Brzeska*, p. 106.
16. Hugh Kenner, in commenting on this, suggests that the Vorticists rejected Futurism because it denied tradition, and were distant toward Cubism because "it seemed indifferent to personality" (*The Pound Era,* p. 238).

8

Esthetic Politics

The Scourge of Beauty

Believing that for artists the issue was returning to active battle in the world, and that art was in fact a form of higher politics Pound proclaimed his manifesto. He had first thought of defending the arts in the ordinary way of persuasion, but trying to influence "an unbearably stupid" humanity, at last the artist had to be "aroused by the fact that the war between him and the world was a war without truce."[1] In this call to arms Pound was headlong in expressing the extreme attitudes of avant-garde modernism. It wasn't a case of winning a decent respect but that of winning power. The "aristocracy of the arts" could save aristocracy itself against democracy, "that folly." As for the philistine, he was the direct enemy who carried oppression into his indifference or contempt for the arts. The clerks of politics and religion had failed; in the view of Pound's direct aggressive spirit, the field was open for art, even if one were an artist only by analogy, as in the case of Mussolini. *Il Duce*, Pound announced, had told his people that poetry was a necessity of the state, and one of his followers had urged that poets preoccupy themselves with the matters of money and credit. "These two facts indicate a higher state of civilization in Rome than in London or Washington."[2]

The warlike accent in his work was familiar long before the adventure with Mussolini and its aftermath. Writers and artists were an oppressed race or class in his earliest manifestoes — "artists mistrusted," "lovers of beauty, starved." From a very early point he thought of art and poetry as administering its own form of violence, and in a rather bizarre invitation to Whitman to join him in this task, he wrote,

> It seems to me I should like to drive Whitman into the old world. I sledge, he drill—and to scourge America with all the old beauty (for Beauty *is* an accusation)...[3]

Was the scourge a metaphor or did it propose actual violence? The distinction did not carry strongly, one supposes, if Mussolini had become the champion. Earlier, the Futurists of Italy shared in the inspiration of the first Vorticist manifesto which proclaimed that "We will convert the King if possible. "A VORTICIST KING! WHY NOT?"[4] But that round assertion was followed by one more threatening. "And we will sweep out the past century as surely as Attila swept across Europe." Discounting a bit of Dadaist comedy, this was the artist as tyrant as well as scourge, and to know how invigorating this could be, one need only recall the portrait of *fin de siècle* estheticism drawn in "Hugh Selwyn Mauberley."

Historic hindsight is useful in this most important phenomenon. There is now a rich literature on the links with Fascism and Nazism in modernist thought. A recent book by Philippe Lacoue-Labarthe discusses the work of modern thinkers under the heading of the "estheticization of politics," and he speaks to the experience of Pound when he refers to the age of totalitarianism. Around 1935 or 1936

> ...Brecht and Benjamin coined their classic slogan: to the "estheticization of politics" one must respond with the "politicization of art."[5]

After concluding that the estheticization of politics was exactly the program of Nazism, Lacoue-Labarthe points to its philosophic roots — "what Hegel calls 'the political work of art' ..in effect 'the formation (Bildung) of man himself....'" And on Nietzsche and Hegel he writes,

> ...when dealing with the Greeks, both men identified politics with esthetics and such an identification is at the heart of the mimetic *agon* in which they both (and many others with them in fact, almost everyone, including Heidegger) saw Germany's only chance of finding its identity and acceding to existence.

Whatever the philosophic antecedents, the emphasis on the "esthetic" politics of Nazism (to the surprise of some who do not pay sufficient attention to Hitler's strong fantasy of himself as artist-statesman) suggests the basis for Pound's own political choices. When Pound writes in Mauberley "We have the press for wafer;/ Franchise for circumcision," he makes his most succinct attack on democracy. The coupling of the Jewish and Christian rituals with the franchise and press was more than aimless malice. Religious rivalry, however, was certainly not Pound's concern; his concatenations are post-Darwinian symptoms of an antihumanist and antidemocratic age. Was circumcision a defacement of the natural body, or was it a certification of the reductive base of religion? Was the franchise the sign of the equally reductive base of democracy? The questions point the way to an esthetic-aristocratic standard of judgment.[6]

To summarize how closely Pound was in touch with his political era, we have him choose the man of strength at the seat of power and judgment. Values depend on his force, and the substance of value is provided by the creators, artists and poets, statesman-philosophers for whom he acts as patron.

The object is to create the ordered society and state; clarity of standards, lucidity of values are ideals of order, order is power expressing itself successfully. Furthering such hypotheses, an aestheticized politics could discriminate between the ugly and the beautiful, between the weak and the strong, the brave and the cowardly. As a universal basis of discriminations aesthetic judgment would deny equality at every turn, and even elevate prejudice to a working principle of the state. Given metaphysical ground judgment had license to be ruthless in the name of beauty which begins as an "accusation." The natural power of the imagination was responsible to nothing except that contained within its own order. As judge, beauty was in fact a scourge, willing to destroy without mercy, for what was mercy in aesthetic judgment? Art did not yield to consensus, did not survive in compromise, the artist destroys what he rejects.

Armed with aesthetic and cultural confidence Pound focused on the case of usury where its judgment was summed up as "CONTRA NATURAM." But how then did usury become an instrument in the struggle for survival and power and still be against nature, and how did art serve in that struggle? This may have been a problem for other naturalist politicians but not for Pound. Allied with the vocabulary of health and disease, art more than matched any other authority from nature. It offered the exercise of valuation at its source, in its purest motive, while usury, as a large pervasive economic parasitism, was the opposite of any authentic labor, or skill, or created beauty. In its uncreative essence usury was the negative principle, and Pound's fixation upon it must be understood from that point. With it Pound could generalize broadly.

> You can probably date any Western work of art by reference to the ethical estimate of usury prevalent at the time of that work's composition....The kind of thought which distinguishes good from evil, down into the details of commerce, rises into the quality of line in paintings and into the clear definition of the word written.[7]

Reversing the order of the last sentence, one observes that the quick and confident esthetic judgment expands to distinguish "details of commerce" and from there moves to the higher categories of good and evil. Art gave assurance that judgment was possible. It thereby anchored a world of uncertainties and inconclusive facts. Aesthetic judgment could hardly leave the great moral categories alone and serve a lesser sphere. As for finance and usurious interest, the esthete under his leaking roof could gladly make welcome the powerful forces of industry and commerce cleansed of usury. Joined with nature and under the rule of art the result would be perfect unity and control. The master imagination could not aspire to more.

The Total Order of Beauty

It has been argued germanely by Lawrence Rainey that Pound's "symbol of his own poetic and cultural enterprise" in the *Cantos* is Malatesta's *Tempio*, his architectural monument at Ravenna.[7] The monument was a cultural memorial where for Pound the esthetic and the public values, practical or ethical, combined without argument. Certainly Pound's *Cantos*, like Sigismundo's *Tempio*, have a lesson of order toward which everything points, both as a natural principle and a supreme virtue, extending from life to art, or with more emphasis, from art to life. This is true despite the *Cantos'* ostensible effect of literary disorder. In Pound's case one might question whether it was a personal incoherence or that of history, or observe a conscious break from the traditional narrative intelligence, but disorder functions in the *Cantos* finally as a claim on order which was compiled, as with Eliot, from epiphanies of allusion and example. The largest support was drawn from distant sources, compact entities in the historic imagination like classical China where the Confucian creed gave priority to order in personal life and in the state.

Linking nature and art, the Chinese emperors patronized the arts and were great builders like Malatesta. Their laws and works and their pictured ideals are always in tandem with the seasonal changes and the phases of fertility and drought. The intelligence of order had analogy with science, and the Confucians were the best of scientists. "You can no more fake in this company than you can fake in a science laboratory." Pound goes on to say,

> ...at no point does that Confucio-Mencian ethic or philosophy splinter or split away from organic nature.... The nature of things is good. The *way* is the process of nature, *one*, in the sense that the chemist and biologist so find it. Any attempt to deal with it as split, is due to ignorance and a failure in the directing of the will.[8]

Here Pound returns with simple clarity to Eliot's organic view of culture. The difference is Pound's stress on the "directing of the will," a political difference of major importance. Though the words give confidence to an esthetic discipline not to be distinguished from ethical rule, we can say that like nature in its highest power these were humanities of an unforgiving character. As much or more than wisdom, it was a question of honesty, a brutal candor could be redemptive, violence too was a form of honesty, supported and made sovereign by "the directing of the will." If power was truth, it needed only to be conveyed exactly to form a universally legitimate standard.

> It is of the permanence of nature that honest men, even if endowed with no special brilliance, with no talents above those of straightness and honesty, come repeatedly to the same answers in ethics, without need of borrowing each other's ideas. (PSP, 103)

With faith in nature and with the command of honesty Pound located the terms that answered his needs, first with the Chinese sign for "sincerity," which meant "naming the emotion or condition," and then for "the action of fixing and perfecting" words. From these come the Confucian answer when asked about the first act of governing, "call things by their right names" (PSP, 99). Equally important in the system was the Chinese concept of virtue, which

Pound translated from its ideogram: "It is, in Chinese, the whole man and the whole man's contents." This brief dictionary of signs was sufficient to bring art (a right naming), science, and politics together, never to be separated.

Between science and politics, however, there was an intervening study, namely history. If it were read properly, history could speak with the same authority as nature. That was an ambitious form of the typical historicism that absorbed Henry and Brooks Adams and which affected their generation and a succeeding literary generation to include Pound and Eliot. It was Brooks Adams, more than Henry, who was in the background of Pound's mind, particularly in a neo-Darwinian, holistic reading of history. He called Brooks the first to formulate the idea of *Kulturmorphologie* in America, creating a "cyclic vision" of serial conflict, " a consecutive struggle against four great rackets, namely the exploitation of the fear of the unknown (black magic, etc.), the exploitation of violence, the exploitation of the monopolization of cultivable land, and the exploitation of money."[9] The passage from Pound's writing is expressive for it locates the naturalistic ground of this vision of history; it is placed in time cycles which are life cycles and structured as systems of energy, manifested in struggle and through monopolies of force.

In Pound's assertive temperament history could be made to read what his political themes dictated. During World War II he simplified most aggressively. "We find two forces in history; one that divides, shatters, and kills, and one that contemplates the unity of the mystery."[10] The grand symbol and mystery appeared in the sign of the *Fascio*, a thousand candles, he writes, burning with intense brightness without injuring each other. To invite mystery was not really characteristic of Pound's mind, though with his usual bluntness he wished to idealize unity and sanction the magic paraphernalia of Mussolini's system. Reducing fateful conflict to "two forces" gave support to Pound's own abstract form of political demonism. The Semitic force in history was the "one that divides," being against any scale of values. But even the Greeks, and he preferred the Romans, were lesser in contrast to the Confucian East.

The search for a cosmic order of values associates significantly with Pound's use of the word "totalitarian." For him it meant first of all a holism founded on absolute good faith in conforming with the rule of nature. It was secondly hierarchical and anti-egalitarian, being an order of valuations. "A totalitarian state uses the best of its human components."[11] Located in "the nature of things," the totalitarian state acknowledged the pattern of history and regarded itself either as a culmination or a falling off in one of history's cycles. Kung himself, according to Pound, was both naturalist and historicist, for as a supporter of the Chinese imperial order he "recognized an historic process, including the alternating periods of order and confusion."[12] All orders followed that cycle, as in thinking of the successful Christian empire in the Middle Ages, Pound says it came in a transition from being "a merely seditious sect to a bulwark of order," in part by releasing itself from what he called the "self-centered lust for salvation." [13]

The examples of holistic thinking proceeded with their own logic from Pound's theory of art, or what might be called his poetics of cultural creation. For art he says,

> ...the aim of technique is that it establish the totality of the whole....The total subject IS the painting.

This was the basis of important political analogies.

> When the usurer climbs into the saddle you have attention absorbed by the detail, colour, lighting, etc. to DETRIMENT of the total reason for the work's coming to be.[14]

The dominant metaphors for such thinking draw support immediately from biology, with all systems complete in their dependence on disease or health.

> ...the one thing you shd not do is to suppose that when some-thing is wrong with the arts, it is wrong with the arts ONLY. When a given hormone defects, it will defect throughout the whole system.[15]

When the whole "system" is diseased the whole must suffer purge, or per-haps destruction. Here, beyond metaphor, totalitarian politics could find its sanction of greatest violence. In full paradox the naturalist mentality is more drastic in its moralizing than any other. The "whole" becomes a new god, mysteriously abstract as it may be, and the virtue of order is as much a state of grace as that offered in any religion.

> If a man have not order within him
> He cannot spread order about him;
> His family will not act with due order;
> And if the prince have not order within him
> He can not put order in his dominions.
> And Kung gave the words "order"
> And "brotherly deference"
> And said nothing of the "life after death."
> (Canto 13, PC, 59)

This is the straightforward ethical logic of naturalist reasoning. If nature defines a system of forces as its primary rule, than civilization must define order as its primary virtue. There is immense implication here for a modern pathology of politics in its link to art and literature. Insist on a cosmic force (that finds pattern) in nature, insist on a hierarchy of values, find security or intelligible enclosure in the group's collective sense of itself as the whole, and subordinate all values to a dread of dissolution, all this was a formula for his time, "Pound's era" in a sense that confirms his importance. Pound's poetics is at once a politics and both are committed to the "rage for order," the term suggested by Stevens to describe the esthetic will. It is remarkable how little Pound had to say in his later years about the imagination as such. The dictating force in literary and political invention was to be called power and its components were determinist and impersonal on two counts, the first in favor of nature in its *virtu*, a vitalist factor and therefore the neo-metaphysical source of power and order. The second as history simply borrowed the *virtu* of great antecedents like the large sized emperors of China. Behind all this there was the ideogram illustrating the unity of language and thought, thought and action, that which absorbed history and nature and therefore was already beyond the dialectical engagements of the imagination. But regardless of how it is reasoned the doctrine of an all-absorbing physical-cultural force in history and nature, whether called Vortex or Jehovah's thunder, will surely meet the classic contradiction and conflict between imaginative freedom and established power. Here again the relation between poetry and politics receives emphasis, but in a sense that reverses direction in the work of the poets who are the subjects of the next portion of this study.

Notes

1. *The Egoist*, "The New Sculpture," February 16, 1914, p.67.
2. *Guide to Kulchur*, p.249. Few would now disagree with the minimal judgment offered by Donald Davie: "*Guide to Kulchur* is an overtly Fascist book. Pound even compliments Wyndham Lewis on having discovered Hitler before he, Pound, discovered Mussolini. Though one dislikes admitting it, nothing has happened since to invalidate this logical and chronological connection between modernism in the arts and Fascism in politics" (op. cit.,146).

    The unpleasantness pertains to a specific manifestation, reactionary and Fascist, but the point in large applies to the apocalyptic politics favored in the modernism of both right and left.
3. "What I Feel About Walt Whitman," 1909 (PSP, 116).
4. *Blast*, No. 1, June 20, 1914.
5. *Heidegger, Art and Politics* (London: Basil Blackwell, 1990), p. 69.
6. Lacoue-Labarthe writes that "racism-and anti-semitism in particular- is primarily, fundamentally, an aestheticism." (p. 69).
7. *Aryan Path*, August, 1937 (PSP, 90).
8. *Ezra Pound and the Monument of Culture*, op.cit., p.2.
9. "The Ethics of Mencius," *Criterion*, July, 1938 (PSP, 100).
10. "A Visiting Card" Rome, 1942 (PSP, 277).
11. Ibid.,p. 276.
12. "The Jefferson-Adams Letters." 1937-38 (PSP, 128).
13. "The Ethics of Mencius," *Criterion*, July, 1938 (PSP, 104).
14. *Guide to Kulchur*, p. 43.
15. Ibid., p.60.

9

Prejudice and Abstraction

"Go In Fear of Abstractions"

This chapter forms a bridge in my study between the work of Eliot and Pound and that of Stevens and Williams on a subject that is central to the important contrasts that interest me. The bridge of contrast is the struggle between the immediacy of poetic detail, things, persons, facts, and the abstractions inevitably summoned by the images and meanings they suggest. Pound himself led in that effort in modern art to shake off the burden of abstractions, whether conventional or foreign to the experience of most minds and sensibilities. The point is clarified in the work of Williams if one takes seriously his own slogan, "no ideas but in things." That was of course his effort to translate Imagism, and it was Pound's own strong early instruction to writers to "go in fear of abstractions," particularly in stripping from poetry the opaque shape of generalized ideas and the stereotyped rhetoric of emotions.

The fact has first importance, Pound writes, a fact is the "luminous detail" to oppose mountains of scholarly documentation as well as expressions of sentiment and judgment. In sharpest example, physics gave "luminous details" their cosmic values. Such details of "fact" were really forces, the energy that controlled and moved ostensible facts and circumstances in the actual world. This authority is what he wanted for poetry, and if it was absolute, in his word, it could make poets the actual legislators in the world. But a "stupid" subjectivity had nothing to do with that role; the poet spoke for "the inevitable laws of nature."

Here in his prose declarations Pound immediately expresses a seeming contradiction. Forces, energies are abstract words that lead to a major abstraction "the inevitable laws of nature." The point is that Pound had a talent for abstract thought and rhetoric possibly stronger than his love for the "luminous details" of poetry. (Gertrude Stein's made her succinct description of him as the "village philosopher" making his appearance in sophisticated Paris.) The question is how Pound led himself from that point to what he told himself very early in writing the Cantos, "We no longer think or need to think in terms of monolinear logic, the sentence structure..."[1] The late Cantos, numbers 101-109, for instance, can have the effect of delirium; with cohering passages left out and the breakdown of syntax, the phrases become fragments of mind and audibles of sound. But this assemblage aimed to reflect the largest experience, "The Cantos are a poem containing history," Pound asserted. They were aimed originally at the simultaneity of times past and present, a correlation of languages and cultures, a multiplicity of persons and an anthology of ideas, something resembling Joyce's ambition in *Finnegans Wake*. Pound himself called it his "grab-bag," perhaps reflecting a moment of dejection. But the abundance emphasized an implicit need to fill a void.

In the best understanding of this aspect of Pound's work Hugh Kenner examined an effort to forge a ground between modern empiricism, drowning in facts, and the method of "sentiment and generalization" that functioned for past eras.[2] In effect Pound would try to compact the presentation of facts with the set of meanings that he could find to cling to them. Factual statements then became images, or even headlined ideas without passing through a process in causal logic or imaginative exposition. Exceeding the license of poetry and deserting the privilege of fiction, images and ideas were now equal to facts, had become facts. As I understand it, Pound was doing more than raise poetry to the level of science. He was bypassing the progress from evidence to interpretation, hypothesis to law, subjective impression to objective truth. It was closer to an older mode of truth by revelation. In his essay on Cavalcanti, Pound announced the basis for radical fusion, "all truth is the *transference of power*" and effects in poetry were "magnetisms that take form" in a "world of moving energies."[3]

As Hugh Kenner observed, where for others the process would be that of metaphor or simile, the figure for Pound passed beyond figuration; the image was commanded to be both 'real' and metaphoric, and in the effect achieved abstraction without, one might say, paying the price in credibility. Thus the symbolic abstract in persons and character could be presented as *"La virtu,"* "the potency, the efficient property of a substance or person." The parallel with "modern science shows us radium with a noble virtue of energy."[4] It is obvious that this is both magnifying and reductive in the approach to persons; the "patterned energy" in people is made a normative term and people as such become abstract instruments in a vitalist world. Thus, as I see it, Pound opened his thinking to the most powerful abstraction, a possibly prejudiced view of persons and things where ideas and valuations became compacted with their presented substance.

What seemed hidden for Pound in his commitment to the model of science was the understanding that facts in science are always the servants of abstract hypotheses. He liked "the inevitable laws of nature" but all laws are classifications and ultimately abstract. The truth was that his intellectual temperament was holistic and deeply dependent on terms like "inevitable laws." His respect for "absolute forces" was matched by an equally strong obsession with determinist causality. In his own venture into historiography he expressed a simple faith, remarking that the history written yesterday had fatal *lacunae*, telling us next to nothing of causes.

> We know that these causes were economic and moral; we know that at whichever end we begin we will, if clear headed and thorough, work out to the other.[5]

This was scientific authority and the effect was intoxicating. He knew how to account for literary and art history with equal completeness.

> Greek poetry as we know it flows into decadence. Anyone with Gaudier-Brzeska's eye will see Greek art as a decadence. The economist will look at their usury. He will find the idea of it mixed up with marine insurance.[6]

To explain Greek art and its development in relation to marine insurance seems eccentric, but it is an expression of the factualist mind that seizes a distant circumstance to explain large results. The broader term, usury, suggested analogy with unifying principles like gravitation, moving Pound as naturally as Marx himself toward economics as the field of real force in human affairs. Moreover, usury was an ethically weighted term from the past, and so in Pound's monomania it helped the sobriety of the scientific economist with the moral fervor of religious proscription and thus became a giant abstraction.

The process has its very strong irony. In the move away from abstraction in poems Pound found himself mixing the elements of holistic abstraction in his deeply involved normative thought. Dissociation in his case was that between facts and valuations—the ancient quarrel between science and poetry, or political and moral philosophy and poetry. The subsidiary issue was between theory and action, which led Pound's mind to activist totalitarian politics. This of course was the longest distance from images of faces in the rain at the Metro.

His thought grew that way because it was difficult to remain within the language of mechanics in a world of moving energies and still maintain the moral pressure that a politics (and poetics) required. For that purpose the better language was biology and medicine, and in Pound's sustained invective usury was less a physical force and more a disease infecting society.[7] The large result of this vein of thought was to bring politics to the rank of therapeutic surgery as the decade of the thirties went on to its explosive end. It was then Pound wrote, "USURY is the cancer of the world, which only the surgeon's knife of Fascism can cut out of the life of nations."[8] Thinking of this sort had its own momentum, with its blend of esthetic, ethical, and "scientific" judgment, and leads finally to a naturalist metaphysics of evil. The point where science, art, and politics converged was in power, and the fact that it was automatic and unconscious, on an animal or bacterial level, certified the dehumanization in this view of historic conflict.

The mode of abstraction in Pound's *Cantos* could be described as a stream of essences interacting with a formed ideological sensibility and expressed by metaphoric snapshots, fragments of history, headlines and letters, fragments of mind and items of a journal as it might have been kept by a corresponding secretary of the world. There is an approximate analogy with the novelistic technique of John Dos Passos in using capsule biographies, newspaper events and familiar stereotypes of character, all a form of naturalistic reportage that conveyed a political perspective, as if the fragmentation that aims for realistic immediacy must at once call for support in abstract conceptual treatment.

Pound's ultimate device in this respect, and his urgently considered asset for all poetry, was the ideogram. Early in his magisterial work on Pound Hugh Kenner describes him in St. Elizabeth's hospital, trying to absorb the conflict of fact and interpretation between Maoists and the U.S. State Department during the Chinese Revolution. Kenner comments on his behalf,

> Like the I Ching's divining sticks, the ideogram, being part of a system of archetypes, should govern such bewildering facts had we but the wit to apply it. For 30 years it had been Pound's Sisyphean lot to read and misread newspaper facts in the light of archetypes with which his mind vibrated, never willing to concede a shift of dimension between crystalline myth and the polymorphous immediate.[9]

This is a major perception, important for any consideration of Pound's working thought. The ideogram was in practice a kind of absolute governance of "reality," facts ruled by archetype, or stereotype and myth, and these in turn expressed under the sign of fact or image of value. In political reference the effect of the ideogram gives authority to prejudice; it comes close to the totalitarian spirit that enforces the ideological unity of theory and practice, idea and person and idea and thing.[10]

One can, I think, hypothesize a political as well as literary turn taken from early Imagism toward the ideogram and then the *paideuma*, both with their irresistible pull toward the authoritarian Vortex, "from which, and through which, and into which, ideas are constantly rushing." But that paradoxical result came from the initial impulse of Imagism against the abstract sign or symbol, in the process breaking down the burden of convention, traditional language, and standard ideas and meanings. Certainly that was the work that Williams took for himself and thought he had learned from Pound when the latter wrote in his code for young writers "go in the fear of abstractions."

With the authority of the ideogram the esthetic imagination took exclusive possession. This could happen presumably when the imagination lost its traditional mythopoetic base. There is a natural linkage between esthetics and politics, both being concerned with ordering and synthesizing facts and ideas. But licensed in the power of the ideogram, the imagination may turn in service to a fiercely and narrowly abstract ideological politics of money and usury.

Monuments of Prejudice and Abstraction

Pound's early practice of the ideogram appears when he mourns the death of close friends and companions in "Hugh Selwyn Mauberley." They become, like Gaudier-Brzeska, monuments of ideas or values. Are there no actual *persons* in Pound's verse? Yes, but allegorical persons rather like Jefferson and Sigismundo in leading the *Cantos* toward epic treatment of the decline and crisis of modern civilization. Many of his readers find the poem most accessible as a moral drama occupied by the figures of Confucian emperors, artist warriors, troubadours, bankers, Jews, Jefferson, Van Buren, and Mussolini, all types and figures of abstraction even if we include more intimate figures like "Possum" Eliot and "Uncle William" Yeats.

On the whole, for example, one judges that the "Jew" and usury are different names for the same essence, basically metaphors pressed to become ideograms or normative signs. To understand such reductive essences one must envision transcendent values of health, or social harmony, or the absolute good. Similarly when Eliot signs an effusion about Bleistein with "Chicago Semite Viennese"— he is indulging essences that classify and are stereotypes. Of course such massive metaphors serve needs beyond poetry. As Christopher Ricks wrote in his discussion of this theme, "Once you think about prejudice you are taken into a great deal of and about Eliot—into the nature and boundaries of his imagination."[11]

The creator of Prufrock and Gerontion turned out to be a thinker almost compulsively interested in communal order and predisposed to cultural politics. He disliked personal intervention in either his poetry or criticism and even his most fervent religious and moral beliefs were expressed institutionally, as if speaking as a dean or bishop. Pound's was a personality too strong and explosive to be contained by the ideas of a collective order, but he early found his masks in the variant personae of his poems. We know quite well for example that his Jefferson belongs entirely to him, as do his Homer and his Chinese. He was not so much a translator as a transmigrating genie taking possession of his subjects. As such the impersonal abstract is greatly potent and can even support a megalomania in control of the precepts of art, history, race, and economics.

Readers and critics of Eliot recognize that for him the attraction of the impersonal rests on the fragmentation of the individual self. In his most influential essay Eliot was at war with the romantic (or humanist) poetics which exactly wished to focus on personality and the emotions. It was really a strike against individualism; and the impersonal rule blends easily with *ex cathedra* authoritarian judgment, as if God or Church or History were speaking. Even in his poetry, passionate in its resonance as it was, he drew on literature as an institution—Dante, Shakespeare, Sophocles. Eliot's great achievement in "The Waste Land" was to give a voice, or voices rather, to a configuration of culture that included fragments of Dante, the speech of the Buddha and of London Cockneys, a voice from the bedroom of a neurotically matched couple, and vibrant echoes from the work of dead poets. All these were perhaps ideograms that presented what he called "the mind of Europe," and all were matched against the naturalist chaos and urban void. Expressions of that sort in the *Cantos* are the more problematic because what is so highly personal and idiosyncratic in delivery presumes to be the voice of history.

In his study of Eliot, Louis Menand points further to a related issue of interest. He describes in Eliot's Harvard dissertation his view of "the extreme ontological relativism" in modern thought.[12] If Eliot saw this as a ground issue of his intellectual life, his reaction would plausibly be to lean on the collective tradition through allusion and quotation, or as Pound does, through translation, so that the individual voice had ballast, or was, as Eliot said of Tiresias, not individual at all but the voice of culture and the race. The opposite reaction to the threat of solipsism is almost automatic in Williams' resort to pure immediacy in his verse. We should imagine Williams listening as Menand describes Eliot's intellectual commitment that began with his Harvard dissertation.

> Individuality—the set of qualities that "belong" to the object- is by the lights of the dissertation, a phantom; it is an accident of the shape ordinary knowledge happens to take, the inexplicable residue that remains after everything else about a thing has been explained.... How can we then speak of "an object's distinctive character?[13]

Many degrees of difference were enough to convince Williams that Eliot was seriously his poetic antagonist, but his own concentration on "an object's distinctive character," or "the inexplicable residue that remains" after definitions and explanations have been rejected, would be foremost in opposition.

In any case what criticism might observe in Eliot's verse is the strength of abstract prejudgment in a style that seems to summon an appeal to actual experience. "Chicago Semite Viennese" can call up little but prejudice in this sense, compounded in abstraction by three terms presented as a list of attributes but consisting of conventional images of decadence or corruption. Prejudices fixate on cities or people or whatever it is that is surrendered to abstraction. In Pound's case obviously there is nothing wrong with being opposed to usury, as it may be defined. But to bring groups or individuals to represent it under the sign of a medieval sin is at once prejudicial and eliminates their immanent being. Eliot's Bleistein or Sir Ferdinand Klein, with "money in furs," are caricatures in a cartoon; violent as the revulsion Bleistein arouses may be, he has no real existence. As a figure of prejudice, he arms an abstract hatred against an abstract target. He is most real in his death, as in "Dirge," Bleistein in sharp detail is beneath the seas being eaten by crabs.

Persons, we sometimes say "real people," arrive in Williams' verse as a kind of surprised discovery, their concrete existence is what forms the poem, as illustrated by the young housewife (in the poem of that title) who comes to the curb in her negligee in the morning, "tucking in/ stray ends of hair..." while the poet in his car passes over in the sound of crackling leaves. The brevity and the syntax are a tribute to immediacy. Immediacy, for Williams certainly, was a principle that tests the imagination, and if abstract prejudice is in the writing it would arguably be a fault of the imagination. Prejudices strain to become myths or are borrowed from myths, but myths require distance and narrative conviction. The effect of prejudice is to encourage disbelief not its suspension. The effect on those who already share the prejudice is not important for poetry.

The sensible context of Eliot's "prejudices" can lead to lightening if not forgiving them according to measures of literary justice. They are the prejudices of a despair that is *total* and reflects back upon the prejudicer. The persona who speaks of the "jew" squatting on the window sill [the lower case is a perfect illustration of an abstraction moving into an image] is himself squatting in some limbo, not a window but perhaps worse. If Prufrock and Sweeney illustrate a prejudice among humans, they also share the affectless sensibility that has lost the human in itself, and so Prufrock descends to meet Sweeney in the modern Inferno Eliot's early verse so powerfully rendered.

Nevertheless, in his recent book Christopher Ricks opened up a discussion with large pertinence to the evaluation of Eliot's sensibility and mind. On that level of interest the topic broadens and the contrast with prejudice is not humaneness or impartial judgment but a quality of the poetic mind and imagination. In fact the literary instincts of both Eliot and Pound were most active when the emphatic effects of prejudice gave basis to the use of surrogates and personae, i.e., Gerontion, Mauberley, Prufrock. The observation points to the way that even incidental names of unique beings, Hakagawa, Mme Sosostris, Fraulein von Kulp, do in fact still emphasize the prejudice of ethnic or racial generalization. The poetry of allusion gave momentum to the move that Pound and Eliot made from the poetic scene into cultural criticism. They had become categorical with great force.

The question comes forward, are not all poetic metaphors led by the impulse of classification and abstraction and thus add prejudice to a view of reality? They may indeed but supply the antidote as well. It is clear that Stevens loved to play mockingly with big concepts and figures as when he addressed himself to the "emperor of ice cream." A favorite for me among his poems is the early "Metaphors of a Magnifico" where he riddles with the distinction between "Twenty men crossing a bridge,\ Into a village" and "Twenty men crossing twenty bridges,\ Into twenty villages," "Or one man\ Crossing a single bridge into a village." He could not summon or refuses to summon the necessary abstraction, and so lets the abstraction of numbers to collapse into "one man crossing a single bridge." This is for sake of the health of metaphors.

Any discussion of abstraction in poetry must attend to the first section of Stevens' major poem, "Notes Toward a Supreme Fiction," where Stevens' declared that the "supreme fiction" must be abstract. Abstract is here a word that explains the relation between fiction and reality. "In this invented world" the mind in its "first idea" begins the process of abstraction, that is inevitable and of the nature of mind; there is no other direct path to meaning. But in the essential movement of Stevens' poetry abstraction is severely supervised and restricted. As a process it can be reversed and that is the theme and dynamic of much of his verse. He adds a necessary dimension to abstraction by following its source, its making, and its ending. "Begin...by perceiving the idea/ Of this invention, the invented world." The poem moves from the beginning (with "the first idea") to the end of abstraction. "You must become an ignorant man again/ And see the sun again with an ignorant eye/ And see it clearly in the idea of it" When "the sun is seen in its idea" it is an abstraction "washed clean," an abstraction that purges itself, to reach "the remotest cleanliness of a heaven/ That has expelled us and our images." We examine abstraction as we abstract and the equal energy of the poem is devoted to the process of de-abstracting, (or de-creation), which for Stevens' was the greater part of poetry. "The sun/ Must bear no name, gold flourisher, but be/ In the difficulty of what it is to be."[14]

When Stevens wrote against abstract "monuments," as in "Mr. Burnshaw and the Statue," he seems to suggest that "supreme fictions" were best created (and destroyed) in poetry rather than politics. The poem begins with a quick answer to his presumptively Marxist critics, who were its provoking source.

> The thing is dead. . . .Everything is dead
> Except the future. Always everything
> That is is dead except what ought to be.
> All things destroy themselves or are destroyed.
>
> These are not even Russian animals.
> They are horses as they were in the sculptor's mind.
> They might be sugar or paste or citron-skin
> Made by a cook that never rode the back
> Of his angel through the skies. They might be mud...

The introduction aimed at its political target continues a few lines later:

> The statue seems a thing from Schwarz's, a thing
> Of the dank imagination, much below
> Our crusted outlines hot and huge with fact,
> Ugly as an idea, ...

The long shadow of Emerson suddenly intrudes in the reader's consciousness, where the "love of the hero corrupts into worship of his statue." Almost as a polemic Stevens writes of "crepuscular images" — "Made to remember a life they never lived....(and) "Made to affect a dream they never had." And he writes further of

> A time in which the poets' politics
> Will rule in a poets' world. Yet that will be
> A world impossible for poets....

That is as if to say that Pound, as poet, could not live in Pound's Fascist world. The impossible world for poets was the world of crude abstraction, an actual antithesis, even a subversive relation existing between poetry and politics. It is a complex but fruitful paradox if we assume that the "supreme fictions" of both worlds have the same source. A major discourse is added to Stevens' poetry from the address to General Jackson's humble statue in Lafayette Park and its inept boast for the hero. It is emphasized by another monument, ruined Ozymandias in the desert, as he is approached by the "spouse" of the heroic imagination who begs to be clothed in "precious ornament" and "the spirit's diamond coronal." Ozymandias of broken stone is in a position to reply

> ...the spouse, the bride
> Is never naked. A fictive covering
> Weaves always glistening from the heart and mind.

Notes

1. Vincent Sherry, *Ezra Pound, Wyndham Lewis, and Radical Modernism* (New York: Oxford University Press, 1993), p.179.
2. Kenner, *The Pound Era*, pp 152-53.
3. "Cavalcanti," *Literary Essays*, p. 154. I find no reference to Nietzsche in Kenner's reading here but the parallels are remarkable with the Nietzschean declaration that there are no facts, only interpretations and with the accent on power that subordinates both fact and interpretation.
4. Kenner, p. 154. I should say here that I am indebted to Kenner for some of these observations and insights but I take full responsibility for my own interpretation of them. The same is true for what I take from Donald Davie on Pound and Calvin Bedient on Eliot.
5. *Guide to Kulchur*, p. 31.
6. Ibid., p. 33.
7. Thus general principles absorbed or were the source of his images and analogies. Example: "The brutal and savage mythology of the Hebrews was revived with the fall of mediaeval civilization and the festering mind of Calvin.... distilled a moral syphilis throughout the whole body of society. The grossening and fattening of European architecture was the contemporary imprint of (this) diseased condition." *New English Weekly,* June 6, 1935 (PSP, 235).
8. "What Is Money For," 1939 (PSP,270).
9. Kenner, *The Pound Era*, p. 15. Kenner very usefully quotes Pound from New Age, Dec 7, 1911, p. 131 on his effort to forge a ground between modern empiricism and the abstract conceptualism of the previous age, between "the prevailing mode of

today, that is, the method of multitudinous detail, and ...the method of yesterday, the method of sentiment and generalization" (p. 152).

10. In a recent critical study of Pound the writer, Vincent Sherry, goes so far as to describe Mussolini's political propaganda as his Poundian manner. He finds this in opposition to the "normal linguistic consciousness" which, he says imaginatively, is in opposition to "extreme political authority." "The absolute identity of meaning and sign," which Sherry finds in the signs of the Vortex as well as the ideogram, "shuts out all processes of linguistic analysis, inquiry, debate" (Sherry, op. cit. pp. 178-9). I do not find this view excessive or unreasonable.

11. Ricks, *T. S. Eliot and Prejudice*, p 78. Ricks advisedly warns criticism against counter-prejudice in the reader, and the conflict of prejudices that breed as they do in war or retrograde politics. But this only certifies, it seems to me, the imputed flaw of prejudice in the writing. Anthony Julius' recent book, noted previously, puts much detail behind Ricks' point that prejudice was integral in Eliot's poetic method.

12. *Discovering Modernism* (New York: Oxford University Press, 1987), pp 139-43. Menand writes perceptively that " the subject of the impersonality of the artist- a model of the mind ...seems both reductive, because such passivity is ascribed to it, and extravagant, because it is required to generate such an exalted kind of truth..."

13. Ibid. p. 77.

14. There is a good review by James Longenbach of Stevens' meaning of the "abstract" to indicate that it was a pluralist concept. "The danger for Stevens is to become content with any single representation." Longenbach writes further, "The job of the ephebe is consequently not simply to dispense with all previous ideas of the sun but to build new ideas, new sets of value, all the while recognizing their contingency, their status as humanly constructed metaphors" (Longenbach, op. cit., p.256). This is sound if we assume that the "abstract" is necessarily the attribute of a fiction or metaphor at the start. In that sense any artistic invention or fiction is abstracted or selected from the uncoordinated details of experience and thought. Stevens certainly meant to preclude the notion that literal realities, photographed things and sensations could suffice for a fiction. But the conceptual abstract was a greater danger, particularly when applied to persons.

Part 2

Stevens and Williams:
The Source of Poetry

10

"A Confidence in the World"

"Modern reality is a reality of decreation," Stevens wrote; the thought was not voiced dispiritedly, as the fuller sentence reveals: "in which our revelations are not the revelations of belief, but the precious portents of our own powers."[1] The distinction, as he derived it from Simone Weil, was between decreation and destruction, the first being a passing from the created to the uncreated and the second from the created to nothingness. At the border of nihilism Weil thus indicated a mode of redemption for modernist thought. Though Weil may have meant something quite different, Stevens makes use of reality's decreation to give praise to the source of creation, that is, the imagination. Despite the paradoxical statement from a religious mind and believer in revelation, Stevens adapted this to his own view of the secularized poetic imagination in an age of disbelief.

The imagination can be redemptive not to reveal higher things in spirit and religion, or the official artifacts of culture and the collective imagination, but to reveal "the precious portents of our own powers," intrinsic in the person, universal in their latency. The imagination itself in its freedom and power is the most "precious portent." In reductive or "destructive" effect the imagination may work against itself to reveal the portents of weakness, or animality, or the void in the world and the person, or more demonstratively, the subordination of things, persons, and the imagination itself to naturalistic fate and historical and cultural determination. This may serve as ground for distinguishing modern perspectives for poetry in their wide normative range.

It is striking on this theme to see Stevens gain an inspiring premise from a very brief poem of Williams.

> It's a strange courage
> you give me ancient star:
>
> Shine alone in the sunrise
> toward which you lend no part!
> ("El Hombre")

Stevens reproduces the poem as a prologue to his own, called "Nuances of a Theme by Williams," and follows with these lines:

I

Shine alone, shine nakedly, shine like bronze,
that reflects neither my face nor any inner part
of my being, shine like fire, that mirrors nothing.

II

Lend no part to any humanity that suffuses
you in its own light.
Be not chimera of morning,
Half-man, half-star.
Be not an intelligence.
Like a widow's bird
Or an old horse.

The collaboration is important for it expresses the strong impulse in both poets directed against the anthropomorphic (pathetic) fallacy as well as the blind impasse of solipsism. We don't know how Williams reacted to the interpretation of his poem but the appeal to the star's external immunity of being should have had his sympathy; as well would the definition of courage, a strange courage indeed, and a new courage in a world only half-inhabited by humanity. It was in fact a commitment for Stevens, as it was for Williams, but that was exactly based on the reality that shines like fire, rejecting a mirror or a reflected intelligence.

They agreed, it seemed, on the imagination's first move. This I propose is the correlating theme of the work of Stevens and Williams, addressed to achieving or maintaining " a confidence in the world" against the stresses of epistemic skepticism and alienated consciousness. It will be also against Eliot's dominant religious belief in a fallen world and his indictment of a secular "wasteland." The latter of course express more than the lack of courage or confidence and much, much more than skepticism, but at low moments it looked like the purest depressive nihilism and at high moments a reactionary politics and religion deeply opposed to the liberal democratic ethos. At that level, with the great impact of his early poems, Eliot stimulated an extraordinary fertility of response in the verse and thought of both Stevens and Williams. In their poetry and thinking about poetry it is clear that they are drawn into dialogue and argument with the dominant ruling authority of Eliot and Pound.

The context for Stevens gave his response the sharpest modern accent. In "The Man with the Blue Guitar" he voiced the premise of the guitarist's new song,

Throw away the lights, the definitions,
And say of what you see in the dark

> That it is this or that it is that,
> But do not use the rotted names.

Here is where courage is needed, acknowledging the decay of forms.

> Throw the lights away. Nothing must stand
>
> Between you and the shapes you take
> When the crust of shape has been destroyed.

The lines are a tribute to Stevens' power of concentration. What shape can one have when the very crust of shape, the *believing* by which it is formed, has been lost? The threat is nightmare.

> How should you walk in that space and know
> Nothing of the madness of space,
>
> Nothing of its jocular procreations?

Eliot knew them, but in Stevens' case the jocularity is not a mocking pathos, close though it may seem to madness. For Williams there was a true joy in creation, as he writes in prologue to *In the American Grain*, "...it has been my wish to draw from every source one thing, the strange phosphorus of life nameless under an old misappellation."[2] But both Stevens and Williams would speak more typically of decreation rather than creation "in the madness of space," that is, for the sanity in seeking a footing in space. Stevens for instance wrote the following in self-examination.

> Someone here wrote me the other day and wanted to know what I meant by a thinker of the first idea. If you take the varnish and dirt of generations off a picture, you see it in its first idea. If you think about the world without its varnish and dirt, you are thinker of the first idea. (SLTR,427)

The awe associated with the phrase" a thinker of the first idea" may seem less esoteric if one considers that by it Stevens meant an analogy with the immediacy of sensibility and perception expressed by poems. Thinking the first idea could be illustrated by the early poem from *Harmonium*, " Metaphors of a Magnifico." The bluntly ironic title is important; there are no metaphors in this poem, and far from expressing a "magnifico," the voice in the poem seems to be of someone falling asleep in the midst of an arid meditation. Is the experience of twenty men crossing a bridge into a village the experience of each separately or the experience of all? Whichever it is, the question asserts the starting point, the perceiver knowing his sensations and the general perceiver hovering nearby with a general concept. It is almost a delight, not a confusion, to acknowledge in the words of the poem that the meaning will not declare itself, and that as it breaks down the experience renews itself—the boots of the men, the boards of the bridge, "the first white wall of the village,/

The fruit trees..." As fragmentary perceptions these have a physical security, though they are struggling to decompose a possible metaphor that encloses the experience of twenty men. The confusion or uncertainty applies most to the abstract identity of twenty men together. How do you make an experience of that collective identity? Isn't it spurious, doesn't it require a breakdown or reduction to elements of a consciousness? Here I think the meaning of "decreation" receives full illumination as Stevens uses the term. The problem of the poet in his metaphors is how to deal with collective abstractions, whether in scientific, political, or ordinary conventional discourse. Obviously the project of the poet is intimately involved.

Another "failed" poem which turns failure around with distinct poetic power is Williams's "Portrait of a Lady." It traces the inverted growth of metaphor by beginning with one of marked exaggeration.

> Your thighs are appletrees
> whose blossoms touch the sky.

The poetic hyperbole is tasked in the next words, "which sky?", a question which is answered by an even more farfetched gesture of the imagination. "The sky/ where Watteau hung a lady's/ slipper." Hyperbole is recognized for what it is, as if the poet were desperate for an uplifting allusion. But this is what gives the poem license to proceed. We are in the workshop of poetry itself, casting about for alternatives, struggling with irrelevance.

> ....Agh! what
> sort of man was Fragonard?
>
> —as if that answered
> anything....

One might say this is a poetry that is more interested in process than effect– as if to gain a stronger impact of authentic feeling than any completed effort of traditional lyric praise such as Eliot's borrowing of Shakespeare's description, of Cleopatra, "the chair she sat in" is after all a throne. From Watteau to Fragonard in a short space reflects an almost sublime distraction, and the "agh" is a suitable expression of disgust, as if frustrated by the pretentious allusions and the full-blown metaphors that begin the poem. But there is no escape from the dilemma of the poem at hand, and it wins its way finally to an image which reaches its actual intention.

> ...Ah, yes—below
> the knees, since the tune
> drops that way, it is
> one of those white summer days,
> the tall grass of your ankles
> flickers upon the shore–

Is it a poem of passion at all, of love struggling with the frustration of words and tunes? That it certainly is, for the fragments turn from the frustration of high metaphor to the deeper frustration of local and personal being. "Which shore?" interrupts a memory of white summer days, impossible to recapture as the question repeats itself four times in the remaining lines and is answered irritably, "How should I know?" But frustration of that sort is set off by an ecstasy obliquely remembered in the interrupting line, "the sand clings to my lips." This fragmented image suggests an overpowering experience as it approaches limitation on all sides, in memory as well as in fact. The abasement is that of the imagination itself before ineffable experience. One is left impressionistically between the ejaculation of disgust, "agh" and a stray phrase, "petals maybe." But this is repeated for the last line, as if impatiently. "I said petals from an appletree." Conviction and sincerity have restored those lyrical apple trees whose blossoms can now still touch the sky. Sincerity in such form can do anything, for it stands for the inexpressible. Williams' "Portrait" can then be called successful. The petals from an "appletree," all that is left from the original inspiration, now float in the poem as if shredded from the structure of language, contracted into an essence. As an "image" it is doubtful that anyone has more successfully defined what was meant in the original credo of Imagism, or the context of imaginative frustration in which it arose. It was the same resistance that led Stevens to one of his fertile summations: poetry is realized in "simply the desire to contain the world wholly within one's own perception of it."

If resistance and interruption became stylistic maneuvers as the work of Stevens and Williams suggest, and if poetry remains the expression of a sensibility striving to be in possession of experience, the modern poet may be seen as confronting two opposite barriers to expression. One is the threatened fall of a structure of belief imposed through cultural forms. The other is the unmasking of a reality perceived as below culture, beyond it, actually at war with it, or perhaps simply a void. The alienation (a better word in this context than dissociation) may begin at either end of this scale, though ultimately, the alienation is either total or not alienation at all in the sense that both culture and "reality" are deemed imaginative and linguistic artifacts. What was a vital drama becomes a subject for linguistic free play, after passing through language pressed to the margin of silence as in the writing of Samuel Beckett. In the case of Williams poetic reduction of that sort can go almost as far but does not anticipate the void, (or rather puts itself into the void in order to make poetry in the struggle to get out), and somehow revitalizes itself as poetry in stripping away old and safe screens of experience.

The unmerciful double threat was defined by Stevens at an acute moment of sensed crisis for general civilization during the Second World War. Probably no one has ever spoken for both poetry and culture with such simultaneity of passionate concern. Modern reality had become violent, physically and spiritually violent, Stevens wrote in 1942, as if aware of the ultimately destructive reductionism of the political ideologies now at war. Given the poet's function, the focus then had to be upon "a maladjustment between the imagination and reality," an infliction in which "we have been a little insane about the truth." The work of the imagination was to be redemptive against that obsessive "truth," voiced in the "spirit of negation." That was the spirit of naturalist realism, and, he wrote, it " provoke(s) us to wonder if our salvation, if the way out, is not the romantic."[3]

Stevens could say in "Adagia" that "Realism is a corruption of reality," but "a maladjustment" is clearly the key when he refers elsewhere to the "taint of the romantic," as if it carried the aura of decay (OP, 166). Babbitt, Hulme, Maurras, Eliot, and Pound had done everything to make anti-romanticism a prejudice of modernist culture. Science and the classics set the standard for intellectual dignity, and "the taint of the romantic" could easily be interpreted as the taint of the human, expressed by the anthropomorphic sensibility. In this context and carried by the force of truth, it was possible, in Stevens' terms, to "become wholly prejudiced against the imagination." On the other hand, the imagination had exercise in unmasking itself. Stevens wrote his essay, "The Noble Rider and the Sound of Words," as if the "noble rider" represented an inaccessible monument of the past. Williams, as though in rebuttal, wrote the following lines of coarse brevity:

> The revolution is accomplished
> Noble has been changed to no bull.
> ("Poem for Norman MacLeod")

This was not mere mockery. The first nobility lay in candor. The pride of authentic experience was achieved largely through what Stevens called "negations," stripping away the old "noble" of the idealizing sensibility. Unclothing it was almost enough to suggest a redeeming truth, nakedness was both a natural virtue and a purification from lies. Alternatively, as Stevens suggested, the operative term could be "force," expressed in violent experience authenticated by the realism of pain, if by nothing else.

For those bent on a cure for the "romantic" this was viable. For Stevens, however, under war and the totalitarian terror, the "real" in its sanction of force was itself the greater source of alienation. It is "reality" that is estranging, Stevens wrote with a sense of crisis in "The Noble Rider," and his statement requires the premise that reality is accommodated or transformed by the imagination, or else it is mere violence or chaos or the "snowman's" blank. There is a language for reality in sharp contrast with the "romantic," but it is a foreign language, estranging the sensibility in a world called real. Williams himself wrote "no bull" as if dismissing every anthropocentric myth of the past, but he was not thereby endorsing either force or chaos, or even the neutral sensibility. One must understand Williams' sphinx-like phrase, "so much depends," in addressing himself to the perception of a red wheelbarrow. What depends? Nothing less than the effort to bring an estranged reality back into poetry. There had been, for Williams' generation, redemption in the attack on the "tainted" imagination, going forth boldly to strip away old styles, old myths, alienated values, and in breaking those screens, to penetrate .... what? That on which "so much depends."

"Our Hold on the Planet"

As usual Robert Frost made simplicity profound when he entitled a short poem "Our Hold on the Planet."

> There is much in nature against us. But we forget:
> Take nature altogether since time began,
> Including human nature, in peace and war,
> And it must be a little more in favor of man,
> Say a fraction of one per cent at the very least,
> Or our number living wouldn't be steadily more,
> Our hold on the planet wouldn't have so increased.

Frost's style is mock-didactic, but he communicates a center of inspiration shared with his two fellow American poets. What saves or increases "our hold on the planet?" Stevens reacted in a letter written in 1948, at a time when he was most concerned with the fundamentals of his own thought, and made the following observation on modern painters.

> These men attach one to real things: closely, actually, without the interventions or excitements of metaphor. One wonders sometimes whether this is not exactly what the whole effort of modern art has been about: the attachment to real things. (SLTR,601)

In verse published a year earlier Stevens would declare in "The Motive for Metaphor" that one shrinks from "The weight of primary noon,/ The ABC of being," but meanwhile finds himself opposing the "interventions" of metaphor. The urgency behind a deeper motive for poetry, as well as the unsimulated relief in it, can be understood from a remark in the same letter.

> And thinking about the nature of our relation to what one sees out of the window for example, without any effort to see to the bottom of things, may some day disclose a force capable of destroying nihilism. My mind is as full of this at the moment as of anything...

Full of this as he was, the statement deals clearly with what is needed to understand Stevens' obsession with problematic reality; it deals with the nature of "our relation with what one sees outside the window" and it is "a force capable of destroying nihilism." Was it a banal and uninteresting world in which men were condemned to live? No, but if it was not seen outside the window, much less at the bottom of things, the formal language of reality was foreign, not reality at all in a painter's or poet's sense of the word. Conventional realism was descriptive, not experiential, and a coded form of description at that, not directly or immediately true, but true only by a formula of method and consensus. These were established by strangely abstract institutions such as the higher science, specialized technologies, or the ideologies of religions and political parties. The latter, in their modern accent, seemed to transform their believers into non-human creatures, difficult to reach except in their own coded reality systems. The mixture flooded the world with competing and exclusive realities, unintelligible in the long run except to native sectarians.

On this account Stevens was much moved by his correspondence with Jean Paulhan, who, it seems, could verify his thought that the "essential value of poetry today" was the *"confiance que le poete fait, et nous invite a faire, au monde"* (SLTR,725). Stevens brought this into his one direct effort to write his poetics, "A Collect of Philosophy." There he said that in a world dominated by the philosophy of science, "nothing, absolutely nothing, constitutes an assurance that the external world resembles the idea that we form of it." But in that "it is an invitation to much poetry" for it is "opposite to the confidence which the poet, by nature, reposes, and invites us to repose, in the world" (OP, 195). He goes on to dwell gratefully on the phrase, *"la confiance au monde."*

> So many words other than confidence might have been used—words of understanding, words of reconciliation, of enchantment, even of forgetfulness. But none of them would have penetrated to our needs more surely than the word confidence. (OP,200)

If for Stevens poetry was "a force capable of destroying nihilism," at stake was nothing less than the deepest need implied by the title of Frost's poem. The effort to regain hold on the planet motivates the modern styles of reduction in both fiction and poetry. One thinks of Hemingway as an example where so many of his effects, the syntax itself, are charged with a concentration on navigating the physical details of existence as if straining for metaphysical security. In significant counterpoint the theme in Eliot goes furthest in its willingness to engage with insecurity. His interest in reduction is absolute, but it is a need to reduce phenomenal existence to essential "nothing" in order finally to throw the mind and spirit more completely into the gamble with God's being. Thus the dry bones of Ezekiel speak or sing, and so the Pentecostal fire is invited in the midst of a war's destruction. To extend the contrast, one could say that Pound, a poet of sharp sensibility and low spiritual force, made his gamble on the side of ultra-aggressive political humanity. If fascism had only one quality it was the motive to gain imperial hold on the planet and reduce the unformed rabble of people and events to ordered submission.

It is precisely at this point of summary, in the frame of these widely opposite forms of spiritual and secular redemption, that Stevens' voice is most evocative and intends a personal and familiar human security to be felt. In "Notes Toward a Supreme Fiction" the reconcilement with the ordinary earth is made explicit without metaphysical bombast or pretense.

> We have not the need of any paradise,
> We have not the need of any seducing hymn.
>
> ....Tonight the lilacs magnify
> The easy passion, the ever-ready love
> Of the lover that lies within us and we breathe
>
> An odor evoking nothing, absolute.
>   ....
> For easy passion and ever-ready love
> Are of our earthy birth and here and now
> And where we live and everywhere we live,

It is there, "where we live," that the issues of reductive thought lead. How much mastery does reality require in order to live in it? Stevens' imaginative life suggests that modern writers must write as if "present at the creation," or alternatively and apocalyptically, at creation's end. The temptations of vitalism are strong, as if the void challenged warriors and athletes.

At that point temperaments diverge and modern poetries suggest large-scale divisions in the styles of personal and public order. Williams' verse seems to inhabit the center of anarchic impulse, and yet, as in writing to Kay Boyle, he would affirm a shareable world in immediately felt experience.

> You know, I think, enough of me to understand that I have no belief in the continuity of history. Everything we know is a local virtue....In other words, art can be made of anything—provided it can be seen, smelt, touched apprehended and understood to be what it is—the flesh of a constantly repeated permanence. (WLTR,130)

He writes in the same letter that poetry in its contact with the actual world has nothing to do with what he called "the social eye," that is, the ideological patterns of a socialized view of reality. "As I have said for me, its virtue lies in relating to the immediacy of my life. I live where I live..."

For Williams there was no substitute for poetic immediacy, for beyond it, it seemed, there were only the oracles of reality who spoke for science, religionists speaking for God, the ideologues of politics, "or anything else (that) tries to swallow" poetry. All these led either to false authority or to the alienation of sensibility. To understand the cult of immediacy, which was Williams' thematic contribution to a modernist poetics, requires appreciation of all the forms of alienation available in the modern world.

Similarly the way to read Williams is to perceive the exile and struggle of the sensibility at the starting point, his own version of the "first idea." Although his personality dominates his verse, it does so in a kind of blissful and painful intercourse with objective existence. His images and language in "The Wind Increases" stress this crossing over from consciousness. There in a wind—stormed harried earth, with tulips and trees sidling and tossing in the force outside, he evokes a response so sharply defined. Without premonition the word love simply erupts out of notations of the external world in storm. Love is a response to gratified assurance, a hold on the planet.[4] Whose love is it that flows and meets the wind? The answer arrives with a deep—rooted image so typical of his work.

> Good Christ what is
> a poet—if any
> exists?
>
> a man
> whose words will
> bite
> their way
> home-being actual
> ....
> new
>
> upon the tortured
> body of thought
> gripping
> the ground.

In its "tortured body" thought must have ground to grip, must become pure body and action and be no longer thought. The all-sufficient image, the only image, one might say, in his poetry, is not descriptive of being but joins being itself "to the last leaftip." Even the words that bite take their imagery from vital process, turned toward a prayer made explicit in the lines from "Drink."

> Where shall I have that solidity
> which trees find
> in the ground....

To accompany these life images there are the words that point to the hard edges of self-defining existence. If in "The Road to the Contagious Hospital" spring is the rooting season, it is also the time when objects, one by one, outline themselves. They "grip down and awaken" and so make culmination of the actual in "the stark dignity of entrance." It is difficult to do more than quote that phrase to express the sympathy for objective existence. "Clarity of outline" is another such phrase, verified and expanded in a remarkably eloquent poem, "The Rose."

> The rose carried weight of love
> but love is at an end-of roses

Even love ends in the geometry of being but that has its comfort, "each petal ends in an edge." It is a reality, "cold, precise, touching," and the word that follows is "What," a word alone on the page, a word alone in space, needing no question mark. It is the all-sufficing edge of being, and at that point the poem begins again.

> From the petal's edge a line starts
> That being of steel
> Infinitely fine, infinitely
> rigid penetrates
> the Milky Way...

and with the poem's ending,

> The fragility of the flower
> unbruised
> penetrates space.

It is an illumination in Williams' work to perceive that "reality" no longer bears a distant metaphysical imperative but is the object of love, a fixed pole of imaginative desire, and so eludes mentalistic and linguistic skepticism. Such a poem as "The Rose" marks an impassioned plea for existence on the ground where perception meets and equals valuation. It is poetry written, as Stevens said, "for the spirit left helpless by the intelligence," with meanings salvaged from the marginal chaos and the fragmented mind. When reduction becomes affirmation, it is to clear the way, to get rid of the wreckage, so to speak, of abstract being and approach its pure state. In this liberated state of the imagination acts of poetry are anchoring acts, truly aimed to gain a hold on the planet.[5]

The anchorage wins a certainty in object and place but there is more. A third agent, the reader, is present in the intercourse between a single consciousness and the world, as if the reader were to be a generalized consciousness inhabiting the world. For that form of the sensibility the act of poetry exists, it is the whole burden of its function. Robert Frost memorialized this in "Mowing," where when he writes "Anything more than the truth would have seemed too weak" he is giving the truth of perception its role of making the bond with others. So more explicitly, "The Tuft of Flowers" presents the insight that a community of the real is based on the search for a world that can be shared. The inspiration joins that of Williams. The rhetoric that fails the test of immediacy has failed to seek valid community, and its words are alienating because they are the words of a consciousness seeking to interpose meaning from within itself, whereas true confidence can only come from without. If such private discourse doesn't tyrannize the consciousness of others, it suggests only individual or factional isolation, or the abyss of solipsism.

The tradition has its American roots marked in the lessons of Emerson and Whitman. Williams was as exuberant as Whitman in believing that no alienating distance separated the writer of the poem, the protagonist of the poem, and the reader. More than most poets he was intent on gathering perception into a participation *in* reality. What is the end of poetry, he asked, and answered thus: " To refine, to clarify, to intensify that eternal moment in which we alone live..." But that single moment of apprehension did not exclude others. On the contrary,

> In the imagination, we are from henceforth (so long as you read), locked in a fraternal embrace, the classic caress of author and reader. We are one....Whenever I say 'I' means also 'you'. And so, together, as one, we shall begin.[6]

This is essential Whitman at the opening of "Song of Myself," and both poets make emphatic statements to combat the impression of eccentric subjectivity or even a ripe tendency to megalomania. For the American poets, Williams, Stevens, and Frost, the imagination was uniquely personal in its immediacy, but at the same time it was profoundly socializing. Such dialectical effort may be basic in an individualist democracy; one has to think of Thoreau, Emerson, and Whitman and their great simultaneity of confidence in both self and world. For the failure of that confidence, or its tragic complications, one may adequately bring to mind the writing of Melville, and in his very different context, Eliot.[7]

Notes

1. "The Relations Between Poetry and Painting" (NA,175).
2. *In the American Grain* (New York: New Directions, 1925), facing page.
3. "The Noble Rider" (NA,17).
4. The parallels in fiction are close; in Hemingway "love" is buried in each detail of overt physical acts, fishing, cooking a meal over the campfire, crawling into a tent, carefully swording the bull. The same naturalized "love" is in the existential nearness of a protagonist, as with Faulkner treating a character like Lena Grove, who never kisses nor embraces but simply walks placidly across the landscape to her goal, hardly doing anything, saying anything but offer her metaphysical "presence."
5. Sister Bernetta Quinn wrote Stevens, requesting specific affirmation of this perception of his work. She said that she understood he sought a center, an anchorage in being. He said yes, but without specifying any goal, spiritual or metaphysical. "Your mind is too much like my own for it to seem to be an evasion on my part to say merely that I do seek a centre and expect to go on seeking it.... It is the great necessity even without specific identification."
6. *Imaginations*, p. 89.
7. Students of the theme in American nineteenth-century writing may wish to consult my extended treatment in *Democratic Humanism and American Literature* (Chicago: The University of Chicago Press, 1972; reprinted, New Brunswick, NJ: Transaction Publishers, 2005).

11

"A Malady of the Quotidian"

"Earthy Anecdotes and Banal Sojourns"

Verrocchio's statue in Venice of the Renaissance warrior, Colleoni, presented Stevens with his protagonist of the high imagination. In choosing him as "the noble rider, "as lost to us as Plato's rider in the *Phaedrus*, he was expressing a theme of key importance to him in application to poetry and to a general crisis of culture. To see it properly one must remember Pound's quite different treatment of Renaissance condottieri, as well as his respect for their modern avatar, Mussolini. What was involved was the loss of the noble or almost any category of the human sublime, reduced to "a tin wreath" for god and man. We hardly need to recall Eliot and the strategy of his early verse, based essentially on quixotic ironies that were touched with the despair of a fallen cultural aristocracy. For many readers the same principle operated in the influence of Joyce over modern image-making as in *Ulysses* he pursued the anti-heroic to mock-epic proportions. The pairing of Sweeney and Agamemnon and that of Bloom and Odysseus must have permanently marked the literary consciousness of several generations. Could a bumbling Jewish businessman, reflecting the bourgeois anti-hero in every petty dimension of his life, have become the protagonist for an epoch of civilization?

The modern anti-hero arrived earlier, perhaps with Flaubert with his piercing expression of class irony in *Madame Bovary*. The revenge of the aristocratic sensibility has a long history, and in recent decades the blending of under-class revolt with aristocratic criticism is a fact of life. We don't really know how much modern revolutionary, radical and reactionary spirits were mixed with a deep, half-conscious revulsion from mediocrity on every level of social leadership. The unrest may thus have been largely a protest of the imagination, rebelling against its poverty in all the public forms of life.

But behind the rage against cultural leveling and imaginative poverty there was a deeper rebellion, only partially understood, against reductive naturalistic thought and the normal progress of science. The anti-hero, a term I believe that cast its first spell in Dostoevsky's *Notes from Underground*, has inhabited modern fiction much as the "anti-poetic" installed itself as an essential theme and style of modern verse.[1] The terms locate a range of existential humiliation on both the petty and grand scale. What was the insult that motivated the Underground Man's profoundly meaningful and self-destructive "spite"? In their animal essence all men are truly equal, but beyond that in what sense equal? No doubt in their flaws and limitations, or in the capacity for self-deception. The democratic creed of equality was in many aspects not a blessing, since the imagination that draws the heroic or sublime was repressed and then usually reversed to search for images of abject mediocrity. To deal with this reduction became the theme of a modern poetics, shielded behind the condescensions of irony, the refinements of estheticism, or the various forms of the revolutionary and apocalyptic spirit. The grand project in art was to concentrate and resolve those responses, as in the work of Flaubert, Eliot, and Joyce. It was here that Stevens also found inspiration, and he consciously accepted the task for himself and other modern writers to deal with the "anti-poetic" given world without sacrificing what Robert Frost called a "hold on the planet."

The American poets who refused exile in Europe, Stevens, Frost, and Williams, possessed the instinct to refuse aristocratic ironies or a standpoint of spiritual detachment. More deeply, they would not be put off by naturalist truths on America's ground of nature. I propose that what moved these Americans at the base was an intrinsic allegiance to democracy. All forms of leveling are at home in the culture of democracy, including metaphysical leveling. If equality is a universal, than reductive effects have somewhere a positive basis. Stevens' "major man" (or his major everyman) was most vividly present where the "first idea" of the imagination arrives and begins its task of construction.[2] In Williams the margin was at an almost mystical place in the perception of other lives. For example he remembered in his *Autobiography* a fulsomely awkward school•teacher and the dingy children in her classroom. Their "thing" was their irreducible being as he apprehended it, and this vision, for him, was no less mysterious and beckoning than that for Eliot of Mary in blue, walking in the garden.

Near the end of his life Stevens described a commitment to "the circumstances in which people actually live..." and to give them "the poetry that they need in those very circumstances" (SLTR, 711). His words reinforce what he expressed in many letters and poems. As if to dedicate a poetic paradigm in "An Ordinary Evening at New Haven" he wrote, "Here my interest is to try to get as close to the ordinary, the commonplace, and the ugly as it is possible for a poet to get" (SLTR, 636). But how was this a dedication to "the poetry that people need?"

To indicate his sustained interest, fifteen years previously he described "Sailing After Lunch" as the abridgement of a theory of poetry, where the subject of the poem, he said, was the false romantic, the romantic in a "pejora-tive sense." He added, "But poetry is essentially romantic" (SLTR, 277). The conflict is fairly constant in Stevens' mind, though the poem makes the effort to distinguish.

> Mon Dieu, hear the poet's prayer.
> The romantic should be here.
> The romantic should be there.
> It ought to be everywhere.
> But the romantic must never remain,

The romantic that remains becomes false,

> ...a heavy historical sail
> Through the mustiest blue of the lake
> In a really vertiginous boat
> Is wholly the vapidest fake. . .

The romantic, giving "slight transcendence to the dirty sail, " is ultimately "the way one feels, " before being translated into its heavy historical portrait.

Obviously Stevens would separate the "romantic" from its "pejorative sense" to be made to adhere to the normal and the commonplace, but how one would do that becomes the problem in Stevens' poetics. Was it only normal security in the world that Stevens wanted? He had something more impersonal in mind, closer, as he said, to a theory of poetry. It was poetry that needed anchorage, but also it seemed a moral obligation to achieve "a reconciliation with everyday reality" (SLTR, 643). As a young man writing to Elsie Moll, who would become his wife, he voiced his theme from the dense commonality of New York.

> The *teeming* streets make Man a nuisance a vulgarity, and it is impossible to see his dignity. I feel, nevertheless, the overwhelming necessity of thinking well, speaking well. 'I am a stranger in the earth.'(SLTR, 141)

The directive to himself could reach to an evangelism of the commonplace, as in these selections from the *Adagia*.

> Poetry is a purging of the world's poverty and change and evil and death. It is a present perfecting, a satisfaction in the irremediable poverty of life.

> Feed my lambs (on the bread of living)....The glory of god is the glory of the world...To find the spiritual in reality...To be concerned with reality. (OP, 167, 178)

One thinks of the antic titles of his poems where the imagination lays its style on the ordinary: "The Emperor of Ice Cream," "The American Sublime," "A Rabbit as King of the Ghosts," "Loneliness in Jersey City," "The Man on the Dump," "The News and the Weather," "No Possum, No Sop, No Taters," and finally a very poetic evening in New Haven presented as most ordinary. In the explicitness of the informal, poems are "anecdotes" or offered in the most ambitious of his poems in the form of "Notes."

He remarked in comment on "The Emperor of Ice Cream" that it "wears a deliberately commonplace costume, and yet contains "the essential gaudiness of poetry" (SLTR, 263). It was in this letter, written in 1933, that he named the poem his favorite. He called it an instance of "letting myself go, " not to a whirlwind of passion, of course, nor even to a drifting hedonism. The "lets" are several: "Let the wenches dawdle; let the boys bring flowers; let the lamp affix its beam; let be be finale of seem." It was really a case of *letting* himself and the world *be*. There is a magnificent surrender to the "not-seeming" in the poem, a philosophic ecstasy. It is a finale of poetic attitude, but with a curious dynamism, not limpness in the approach. This emperor is a muscular being warm with life to pair with the dawdling wenches. Reassurance comes from what is old and used, the dress, the dresser lacking three glass knobs, last month's newspapers. The woman who is dead, does she consent to this order of her rites? Her horny feet protrude from the sheet on which she once embroidered her own fantasies. There is deep harmony here. Let the poet persona whip the erotic ice cream from such stale substance as he can claim. The humble ecstasy is expressed in playful alliteration, "kitchen cups of concupiscent curds." This is the ice cream of language, and the poet, hungry and alive, is the ice cream maker. "...In short, ice cream is an absolute good, " Stevens said in his brief commentary. Again he carefully explained that he meant "being as distinguished from seeming to be," the latter a good enough phrase to define a "false romanticism."

"Cortege for Rosenbloom" is another comedy of the quotidian which may have been written to answer the need of people captured within the quotidian. The anti-hero is the wry Rosenbloom, "the wizened one." He is borne in the cortege by the "infants of misanthropes, and the infants of nothingness." A heavy accent is on them, climbing the sullen hill to bury Rosenbloom, but seen from below they are bearing his body into the sky. This is where poetry, in "the endless tread that they tread, " will carry him, and for this the pallbearers wear turbans and boots of fur, a costume carrying the pathos of the sublime. Nothing else surrounds the funeral but the chitter of cries, the jumble of words, the jangle of doom. These obscure voices are a more definite closure than death. Still we have Rosenbloom in his essence, memorialized in his own "intense poem" and his own "strictest prose." The sky where he is buried is a sky of imagination and truth, and there Rosenbloom may transcend the comedy of his name, the frost, the jangle of doom, borne staunchly by the infants of nothingness.

It is not straining rhyme and resemblance to see Rosenbloom in the order of tropes dominated by Leopold Bloom in *Ulysses*. Texts have been written on the Jew as a highly charged agent of the modern imagination where he can appear both a figure of the quotidian and a carrier of naturalist reduction, as in the pantomime which includes Sweeney and Bleistein. The latter, lying in "protozoic slime," would have enjoyed mercy if given the semi-comic fate of Rosenbloom.[3] Stevens in this case, like Joyce, adds another dimension in seeing the Jew as the protagonist of the quotidian, but on the basis of which we might even discover in Rosenbloom an "Emperor of Ice Cream." He may be the protagonist of humanity in a secular age, redemptive in significance pre- cisely *because* he comically survives naturalist humiliation without super- natural favor, having lost it. Rosenbloom reminds us that Stevens' Comedian, whose name is a letter, is a ubiquitous character in his poems, a man of forty and bald amorist, ward of Cupido again and again, the fop of fancy for certain. But whether he sees "nightgowns with blue rings or yellow rings" he wears his own plain nightshirt in any case. The high gloss of artifice, the dandyism of language in the invocations of Eulalia, Solange, Semiramide, Chieftain Iffucan of Azcan (with the half hidden "if you can" and "ashcan") are appeals to the spirit of the poverty-stricken knight, Don Quixote, and Sancho Panza,

This form of comedy carries imaginative relief as an expression of the ideal and a cure for its torment. Prufrock himself, as a "ward of cupido" in his own fashion, is not far off. The key is a pathos of the imagination and the unex- pressed sensibility. Chaplin is a prototype for poets, as Hart Crane felt along with Stevens, perhaps blended with Cyrano in the latter case. To strut on a stage, to be actor and fantasist, is a primary definition of man.

> From this I shall evolve a man
> This is his essence, the old fantoche
>
> Hanging his shawl upon the wind,
> Like something on the stage, puffed out,
>
> His strutting studied through centuries...

He exists, puffed out, and though reinvented in the song of the guitar, there is assurance in that he exists. Where he lives is Oxidia, "banal suburb, one half of all its installments paid." Was this the conventional attack on the stage prop of middle class existence? No, "Oxidia is the seed/ Dropped out of this amber- ember pod....Oxidia is Olympia."

It may be that the quotidian is redeemed by affection in the unassailable claim of the known. "Fat girl, terrestrial, my summer, my night, "is Stevens' final apostrophe to earth in "Notes Toward a Supreme Fiction." "You are famil- iar, yet an aberration," and Stevens then draws the portrait of earth-life in the figure of a woman "bent over work." But she also becomes the "more than natural figure," "soft-footed phantom," the "irrational distortion," a part of the dear earth but incompletely containable in it. She carries "the fiction that results from feeling," but that is where her more than natural reality begins. He concludes with lines that warm the poised detachment of the poem.

> I call you by name, my green my fluent mundo.
> You will have stopped revolving except in crystal.

The plain fat girl earth in its constancy, once justified by name, has become the pure artifact of crystal. The vast repetitions of earthly existence are expressions of things final in themselves and therefore good, the poem says, and what we enjoy in these repetitions (as in the bird's song, the woods, the spinning of a leaf, and the wine that comes to table) "we enjoy like men." Repetition is a function of the quotidian, its peculiar character, and with that in mind the poem moves to another conclusion.

> Perhaps the man-hero is not the exceptional monster,
> But he that of repetition is most master.

Not the least of the complex affinities between Stevens and Williams was the fact that they both dedicated long careers to poetry, felt themselves champions of poetry, and simultaneously, of their own choice, gave themselves up to mundane time consuming occupations. Neither one seriously complained of the life of insurance lawyer or small-town general practitioner, and both continued their work well after they might have retired, Stevens into his terminal illness in his mid-seventies, and Williams after a disabling stroke. In part at least they acted as if a threat lay in giving themselves up entirely to the life of the imagination and in that sense receive the fate of Mauberley.

Appropriately for this and other reasons Stevens wrote the introduction to Williams' *Collected Poems*. What he said about Williams in that essay reflected his own character as a poet. He meant no insult surely when he called Williams a romantic poet, a writer with a sentimental side. He might have said the same about himself, or about Hemingway, whom he praised on similarly equivocal terms. Sentimentality has an abhorrent name, Stevens wrote, but the reaction from it has its sentimental side. The inversion of sentimentality expressed itself in anti-poetry. As Stevens applied it to Williams,

> The anti-poetic is his spirit's cure. He needs it as a naked man needs shelter or as an animal needs salt. To a man with a sentimental side the anti-poetic is that truth, that reality to which all of us are forever fleeing. (OP, 255)

For Williams, he says, the anti-poetic is not mere rhetoric and not even a scourge for the complacent. The latter is a significant reference, since Stevens knew well how much the reductive spirit in modern writing was precisely intended to be a scourge, a convention to whip the conventional. Rather the anti-poetic for Williams was "a phase of man's spirit, a source of salvation." Stevens was not one to use excessive language, and it is incumbent on readers of his poetry as well as that of Williams to consult what proposes to be the resource for "salvation" in their work. At the least it may lead to the chief energy in the poetry.

Williams as much as said so in "Apology" where he gives himself a motive for writing verse.

> The beauty of
> the terrible faces
> of our nonentities
> stirs me to it;

Like so much in Williams the simple language stirs an unrest. One might remember Yeats' own presentation of a "terrible beauty" in events that aroused his poetry, but the word "nonentity" puts the response into a different world. The terrible truth of nonentity comes in metaphysical terms as well as social, and as Stevens suggested, behind it was a redemptive urge, demanding some basis for nothing less than the "spirit's cure."

The motive that operates may exist on the margin of a blind compulsion. Indeed Stevens carries romantic irony to its ultimate hilltop in the following passage.

> What, then, is a romantic poet now-a-days? He happens to be one who still dwells in an ivory tower, but who insists that life would be intolerable except for the fact that one has, from the top, such an exceptional view of the public dump and the advertising signs of Snider's Catsup, Ivory Soap and Chevrolet Cars; he is the hermit who dwells alone with the sun and moon, but insists on taking a rotten newspaper. (OP, 256)

One might see the application to Fitzgerald's classic novel where the whole cast of characters are forced to a view of the public dump. Similarly in Eliot, who warmly praised *The Great Gatsby*, there is always a view available of the dump. It belongs to the habitat neighboring the ideal, which gives the latter chance to achieve ineffability, as in the distant unheard song of the mermaids, or the recall of some "ineffably suffering, ineffably gentle" thing. Less transcendently, Steven's own poem, "The Man On The Dump, " marks the transition.

> Between that disgust and this, between the things
> That are on the dump (azaleas and so on)
> And those that will be (azaleas and so on),
> One feels the purifying change. One rejects
> The trash.
>   ....
> One sits and beats an old tin can, lard pail.
> One beats and beats for that which one believes.
> That's what one wants to get near.

There is much to accent the true act of the imagination in the phrase, "the purifying change"; one can reject the trash.

In Stevens' introduction to Williams' poems he describes "the realist struggling to escape the serpents of the unreal" and avoid becoming the realist "with a sentimental side." Of this Williams is the undoubted master. Take the example of "This Is Just To Say," about those well-known icebox plums.

> I have eaten
> the plums
> that were in
> the icebox
>
> and which
> you were probably
> saving
> for breakfast
>
> forgive me
> they were delicious
> so sweet
> and so cold

The reader is first disoriented, but then forced to ask where does the aura of plain intensity lead? The last three lines do illustrate poetic logic and structure, they are finalities. "Delicious" is a sensual summing up, generally descriptive, but "so sweet" is the concentration of that pleasure, pressed into the syllabic long ee closed sharply with the t. And then the blunt impact of "cold" on the tongue and teeth, as if before the sweet and with the sweet there must be the physical shock of something actual and external, something happening.

However, in one sense the poem remains unwritten, reflecting luminosities in the mind of the reader that an unwritable poem would attend to if it could. There is nothing here but the taste of those plums. Such experiences are never communicable, but the concentration on *that* fact turns to the benefit of intensity in the experience. This is accented by the dragging syntax and rhythms of the broken lines, "and which/ you were probably/ saving for breakfast." A heavy matter of fact reference, it has only a household meaning and cannot tell us how the plums were delicious. But perhaps it tells how much that is sweet and cold and delicious is concealed unsaid in such household routines. After all, the very short exclamation of the poem lives in the interval of night and morning, the family sleeping, the icebox waiting for the next day's use. So much depends on what is not said. For instance, the line "forgive me,"—how much else in a marriage and household is there to forgive, and doesn't this item of forgiveness connect with all the others? It must, and it also pulls the delicious plums into metaphoric standing, though of the most reserved, understated sort. "Forgive me" slips without interruption into the final assertion which *is* a form of ultimate reconcilement, "they were delicious, so sweet and so cold." It may be a rhetorical pleasantry, "forgive me," even a comic excess, but it comes out of the guilt of pleasure, the pleasure in guilt. Pinned to the icebox the note is an unforgettable voice from immediate experience, and it may not be too far to say that this is the quotidian value for which Stevens searched.

Stevens could understand such a poem celebrating "mere being" though he perhaps had less gift for treating it himself. A poem by Williams, called "Poem" to say how little and how much it presumes, features a cat stepping down over a jam closet into an empty flower pot. Carefully recorded, "first the right foot carefully and then the hind..." the movement is that of a living thing among objects, the familiar alive, as the cat is alive, and the empty flower pot is not. With that connection objects suddenly become luminous, as if the empty pot were actually filled, awkwardly, comically, with tangible life. In a distinct geometry of existence, the first two stanzas climb up and over, the last two stepping down. The jam closet has a function, of course, sheltering sweets, just as the pot, in future or past, contains flowers. But this is background for the cat and his cat-life. In a cat's intense life, climbing and descending, for that matter even sitting and sleeping, are dramatic actions. But then for this cat there is some embarrassment, an almost human ineptitude, which gives him an affinity with the people for whom the poem is written. In such awkwardness the cat gains new consideration of his life. When the pot has been conquered, he is still the graceful cat, the bottoming out of reality in the empty pot of space. It is an epiphanic moment in the poetry of the mundane, as keen in its intensity as any of spiritual implication in Eliot's verse, a mark of contrast that almost suggests intention on Williams' part.

"To A Poor Old Woman" is another example of that experiential absolute to which Williams gives utter respect. The old woman is munching a plum on the street, half of it still in her hand, a paper bag in the other. On one side the paper bag links with the blank external while the plum is being absorbed in a purely private experience. One should say by the way that the street is the home for experience in Williams, the place where it gathers together and is both observable and community bred. A question reasonably asked is why in the second stanza does the poet repeat "They taste good to her" three times?

> They taste good to her
> They taste good
> to her. They taste
> good to her

It might be that this registers only an inarticulate concentration on his subject, again a poem at the margin of what can be written. But we notice that the repetitions vary the line breaks and accents significantly, delivering emphasis in this order, "good," "taste," and "to her," as if each reference had meaning by itself. A sentence is being parsed for poetic value until the final accent on the pleasure, "to her," closes the sequence. And then these words command the observer, "you can see it." What we see is her total surrender to this experience.

You can see it by
the way she gives herself
the one half
sucked out in her hand

Comforted
a solace of ripe plums
seeming to fill the air
They taste good to her

Again a relevant contrast comes to mind of a very different poem featuring Rachel Rabinovitch who "tears at the grapes with murderous paws, " Both poems have absolute relation to physical experience, but Williams' poem makes no large reference, has no theme of life against death, and no great historic or mythic context to call up Agamemnon. The old woman gives herself to the plum, the plum to herself, and the childlike erogenous quality radiates from her body, "a solace of ripe plums fills the air." If plums fill the air like an army of angels, they are the ordinary angels of appetite and pleasure. The remarkable thing is how Williams' strictly objective projections can have this powerful synesthetic reach, as if the reader were to be engaged with experience as in Williams' view of Mark Anthony with Cleopatra, appreciated from her feet to the roots of her hair. As for Rachel Rabinovitch (or Sweeney) who occupy a different phenomenal world, the animal with tearing paws also radiates a synesthetic effect, that of sharp revulsion. It is a difference to marshal whole layers of value and sensibility. In the Eliot poem Agamemnon exists in the safely transcendent pantheon of mythic past, his image is like that of a medallion or piece of sculpture. He is there to represent a god or hero and heighten an existential duality which is one effect of "the malady of the quotidian."

The Malady of the Quotidian

If one asks a question quite simply, what did the four poets I study and the writers and artists of their generation have in common, a fair answer might be that they lived in a world that disappoints the imagination. If we ask in turn why this is called "modernism" it is because what is expressed is the sometimes successful or victorious struggle of the imagination to live in that world. In *Herzog,* Saul Bellow's protagonist was impressed by reading Heidegger on the "second fall of man," a fall into the quotidian, and he responded in ironic complaint: it was necessary to fall far enough, no one yet had fallen deep enough. If that was reconcilement with the earth and life it was a challenge greater than any other. It may be that at this center the whole of modern moral life concentrates its dangers: nihilism, passivity, acedia, megalomanias of power, apocalyptic urges for the sake of ultimate liberations and ultimate harmonies, and behind all the alienation from life often masked in cynicism but expressed on behalf of ideals already defeated.

No one knew or suffered the "malady of the quotidian" more than Eliot, it was the loss that stored his gift. He drew power from recalling the awe of the superhuman with figures from the heroic pantheon, Agamemnon, Hamlet, Dante and Beatrice, Ezekiel and Isaiah, Sir Perceval and the Fisher King, Wagner and Michelangelo. It was Eliot's genius to propose them to the imagination while simultaneously making the descent to Prufrock and Sweeney, cohabitants of the world of "birth and copulation and death." He wrote his Venice poem for Burbank and Bleistein as if he also knew, like Stevens, the neighboring statue of the "noble rider," Verrocchio's Colleoni. The fact is that these lower figures live chiefly by their dominant contrasts; they have the vitality of the almost moribund. Prufrock was called into existence by John the Baptist and Hamlet, as much as they by him.

The way to see the issue most directly is through Pound, who had an inveterate appetite for heroes, paragons of battle, patrons of art, though there was a curiously thin antiquarian quality in his transcription, as if in life they had no more body than a literary allusion.[4] On the other hand his view of democratic reality had specific force in a world "where all men in law are equals/ and we choose a knave or eunuch to rule over us." In the same poem Pound asks the question which must be felt by all students of his poetry who wish to understand its spirit.

> O bright Apollo,
> ....
> What god, man, or hero
> Shall I place a tin wreath upon!

The problem of the hero, as Stevens well knew, was a problem of the reflexive imagination. If the valuer could not be valued, nothing of the world, inanimate or living, could receive value. One looks at heroes as if in a mirror, and whether for envy, emulation or contempt, the secret is the need for human self-esteem. To understand Stevens on this issue we refer to his poems, but also to his quiet thoughts in letters to close intellectual companions like Henry Church, this one written in 1945, in the twilight of the Second World War's political heroes and the passing of Roosevelt and Churchill.

> What is terribly lacking from life today is the well developed individual, the master of life, or the man who by his mere appearance convinces you that a mastery of life is possible. (LTRS 518, Nov., 1945)

He goes on to say that he hoped the new men (Truman and Bevin) would win over Stalin, "but they don't make life a particularly agreeable thing to experience." Much earlier he had expressed an interest in Mussolini in the early wave of Fascist Europe's heroics, while combining it with sympathy for the blacks of Ethiopia, then being conquered by *Il Duce*. That Stevens, like others, was decidedly ambivalent on the subject is reflected in another letter to

Church where he mocked the Nietzschean "*uebermensch*." He was referring to his figure of "major man" in "Notes Toward a Supreme Fiction." "My interest in the hero, major man, the giant, has nothing to do with the Biermensch; in fact, I throw knives at the hero, etc." (STLR, 409).

The point suggests another challenge for Stevens to come to terms with the quotidian, or rid himself of its "malady." If he was tempted by the artist or grand thinker as hero his answer would have been "For myself, the inaccessible jewel is the normal and all of life, in poetry, is the difficult pursuit of just that" (SLTR, 521). The remark is an emblem of his link with Williams, who made the commitment even more openly.[5] The two poets were making their stake in a time dominated by longing for the imperatives of the aristocratic sensibility, applied with accuracy to Pound who once wrote, "The study of literature is hero worship." When Stevens addressed himself to the theme in "Notes Toward a Supreme Fiction," it was as if he recognized the threat of making too much of "major man," seeing the danger of hero cults, potency obsessions, the sinister overcompensation of Nietzschean figures. It is with no surprise then that the reader finally comes to Stevens' definition of his "hero," after proposing that "The major abstraction is the idea of man."

> Though an heroic part, of the commonal.
> The major abstraction is the commonal,
> The inanimate, difficult visage. Who is it?
>
> What rabbi, grown furious with human wish,
> What chieftain, walking by himself, crying
> Most miserable, most victorious,
>
> Does not see these separate figures one by one,
> And yet see only one, in his old coat,
> His slouching pantaloons, beyond the town,
>
> Looking for what was, where it used to be?
> Cloudless the morning. It is he. The man
> In that old coat, those sagging pantaloons,
>
> It is of him, ephebe, to make, to confect
> The final elegance, not to console
> Nor sanctify, but plainly to propound.

The transfer from heroic rabbi ("furious with human wish") and chieftain to Chaplinesque clown suggests a figure made comic for the reach of his imagination more than his limitations, but why is he a subject to propound "the final elegance?" Perhaps the context requires knowledge of what can be provoked by a boring mediocre world—for example, the destructive political malice of Pound, the defacing ironies of early Eliot.

The significance of Stevens' comic figure as "major man" may in part be expressed by something Williams wrote in response to a widely circulated negative review of *Ulysses*. Rebecca West had seen Joyce as a Shakespearean fool in his cloacal japes and antics. Williams answered her from the heart of his own writing. She wants to be somewhere else, he said, in a transcendental dream. "Whereas *here* is the only place where we know the spirit to exist at all, befouled as it is by lies" (WSE, 87). With good literary sophistication Williams understood that the role of the Fool was to cleanse the spirit of lies. But more than that, as he said in his enthusiasm,

> The true significance of the fool, is to consolidate life, to insist on its lowness, to knit it up.... Life is not to run off into dream, but to remain one, from low to high. If you care to go so far, the fool is the premonition of the Russian Revolution, to modern revolutions in thought.[6]

The statement has generous sweep, as usual with Williams, but it has more profound implication than first appears. It is a great claim on behalf of the reductive imagination, the most affirmative that could be made. The fool, in Joyce and Shakespeare, is an articulate spokesman for mankind. His mode of reduction, in his being and from his words, is an approach to the universal, knitting up life from low to high in a web of affinities. The reductive fool is revolutionary as well as healer, or in the optimistic vein, both at once, since he would rid mankind of oppressive hierarchies of value and the manic prejudices that arrive with transcendental authority. Williams revealed himself here as a writer who recognized the dissociation of low terms and high terms, the consequent alienation of the normative spirit, and his insistence on reaching for low terms is to bring reality and value together on the demanded basis of truth, not lies.

It can of course be pointed out that Prufrock, in his simulation of Polonius, is a Shakespearean fool, though Williams would differ heatedly and I believe he would be right. If Prufrock *condemns* himself, he is not the true fool, and if he further invokes a pair of ragged claws on silent seas for his biological past and future, he has surrendered all possibility of comic redemption, for comedy is of the human and defines its borders. Prufrock illustrates the exacerbated sensibility that would choose either to purge itself of existence or purge the world of all traces of both the animal and the quotidian. If Rachel Rabinovitch yawns as she pulls her stocking up, she expresses the banality of existence in her own being. But this image is blended with violence; she tears at the grapes with murderous paws while an assassin waits at the window. Eliot in this verse seems to give that choice, as if violence were the only relief from boredom. One might add parenthetically that there are no fools in Pound, whether Shakespearean or Chaplinesque, though Mauberley is the object and agent of an angry, more than slightly self-pitying satire. Anger was the force of Pound's esthetic spirit, as well as his intellectual style that revealed itself best in polemic. Beauty itself was a polemic in Pound's hands, a reproach, a purge of unseemly being. In the grand debate between the high and low terms there was in Pound the fanatic spirit of the priest of the absolute, eager to bring victims to the sacrifice.

But for the poetics of failure, or poverty, just escaping the "sentimental side," as Stevens wrote, one should look at Williams. "It's the anarchy of poverty/ delights me." This, from "The Poor" was a manifesto of the reductive and it links with his search for affirmation in the dead end of winter, the raw start of spring. What can be the delight in poverty, or could it be a delight in poetry while thinking of its source?

> Chimneys, roofs, fences of
> wood and metal in an unfenced
>
> age and enclosing next to
> nothing at all

This is a sharp move from anarchy to the surface restraint of buildings and streets, chimneys, roofs and fences of wood and metal, abstract lines of enclosure for they enclose "next to nothing at all." The pathos of nothing is forced against the enclosure of form—that is a subject for poetry, reinforced by the allusions to anarchy and custom, the life of the children of necessity.

These terms set, the actual man of poverty appears, "an old man/ in a sweater and soft black/ hat who sweeps the sidewalk." The line following, "his own ten feet of it," is one of those unexpected phrases which appear in Williams' poems, making the casual drift of notation suddenly rise to sharp impact. The old man has taken possession of his space, he is sweeping it, even, as in the last lines,

> in a wind that fitfully
> turning his corner has
> overwhelmed the entire city

That is an effect of being truly present in language and beyond language. Such members of the poor can do nothing but affirm their existence, since they are at the margin of all opportunities and capacities, fenced in by necessity, as well as at the margin of meaningless space. The act of sweeping his place is the best action to gain a poet's respect, a model for the reductive hero, forcing a lesson from poverty.

There is a tradition in American writing, as I've proposed, which consults the democracy of nature and life, a metaphysical democracy enforced by the absence of fixed hierarchies. When Stevens called in the "emperor of ice cream" to replace the more grandiose rulers, he was following the distinct American tradition that began to fulfill itself with the work of Emerson. "The American Sublime" is naked and bare, and must be clothed, the imagination is hungry, though capable, and it is therefore thoroughly at home with the realities of reduction, or decreation. Decreation, or deconstruction in its ambiguous meaning, if they prove nothing else, prove creation, and so prove ultimate equality in the imagination. It is to say naked we create and so prove freedom over and over again in our nakedness. By tradition or necessity we have nothing, pointing to the nothing of death. But between these borders of nothing, between the two abysses of past and future where Tocqueville so memorably placed the hero of the democratic imagination, there is the freedom to exist meaningfully within a re-created world.[7] 'n imagining the hero of a democratic poetry Tocqueville produced one of his most relevant insights.

> Man springs out of nothing, crosses time, and disappears

That faith in the eternal invitation to live accounts for the peculiar exuberance and freshness of the verse of Williams, the calm restorative effects in Stevens, and the simple inevitable moves they both were capable of making toward the very beginning or "source of poetry."

Notes

1. A parallel term in modern art criticism is anti-literary usually applied to painting.
2. See "Notes Toward a Supreme Fiction" for both these important references which I discuss later in this text. But in advance I should add this interpretation: "major man" is the hidden protagonist in much of Stevens' poetry and the "first idea," I believe, stands for the creative root of the ethical and poetic imagination. One of the most recent contributors to a related view of poetry invents the word "poethics" to discuss the philosophic base of literary humanism. (See Michael Eskin, *Ethics and Dialogue* [New York: Oxford University Press]).
3. Readers who contemplate Eliot's specifically anti-Semitic references in his early poems may be puzzled by the extreme insult of animal reduction offered to Bleistein, Rachel whose "paws" tear at the grapes, and "the jew" who crouches like a predatory bird on Gerontion's windowsill. The reference that is appropriate is this one from "Second Thoughts About Humanism": "If you remove from the word "human" all that the belief in the supernatural has given to man, you can view him finally as no more than an extremely clever, adaptable, and mischievous little animal." One must choose between a natural and supernatural identity, and in Eliot's mind the higher choice was Christian. Accordingly the task in his thinking as a poet is modeled upon Dante who used his gift to define "the adjustment of the natural to the spiritual, of the bestial to the human, and the human to the supernatural" (from "What Dante Means to Me", previously quoted in Chapter 3, p. ??). Accordingly the Jew takes an inevitably degraded place in this hierarchy; in what might be called metaphysical anti-Semitism, once chosen to be redeemed the Jew has fallen far into unredeemed nature toward animality, ultimately protozoic or viral in the hands of the obsessively naturalistic and secular Nazis.
4. Charles Olson, writing about Pound from personal knowledge during the St. Elizabeth days, expressed insights that deserve reflection from students of Pound's work "he has little power to compel, that is, by his person. He strikes you as brittle and terribly American, insecure....he does not seem to have inhabited his own experience. It is almost as though he converted too fast (presumably, converted his experience to literature). The impression persists, that the only life he had lived is, in fact,

the literary, and, admitting its necessity to our fathers, especially to him who had such a job of clearing to do, I take it a fault. For the verbal brilliance, delightful as it is, leaves the roots dry. One has a strong feeling, coming away from him, of a lack of the amorous, down there somewhere" (*Charles Olson and Ezra Pound*, p. 99).

5.   In talking about *Paterson* in his letters he once said,

"I don't want to be thought an *artist*.I much prefer to be an ordinary person. I never wanted to be separated from my fellow mortals by acting like an artist...I want to be something rare but not to have it separate me from the crowd" (WLTR, xvii).

6.   " A Point For American Criticism" (WSE, 88).

7.   In imagining the hero of a democratic poetry Tocqueville produced one of his most relevant insights.

Man springs out of nothing, crosses time, and disappears
forever in the bosom of God; he is seen but for a moment,
wandering on the verge of the two abysses, and there he
is lost. (*Democracy in America*, vol. 2, book 2, chap 17, p. 80.)

12

The Necessary Angel of Reality

To understand the framework in presenting what Stevens' called the two necessary angels of verse, the angel of the imagination and the angel of reality, we might confirm the intellectual context by quoting Gottfried Benn who lived through the peak period of modernist activity. "Between 1910 and 1925 the anti-naturalist style reigned supreme in Europe to the exclusion of almost everything else. For the fact is that there was no such thing as reality, at best there were only travesties of reality."[1] Steven's response would have been to declare the "angel of reality" necessary to poetry. If the term was problematic in Stevens' mind and Williams' poetic practice, it was also central and must be understood if we wish to understand their views of poetry. Meanwhile, it might make sense to say that for Stevens reality simply stands for that which lies just beyond the constructs (or deconstructions) of the imagination, never quite reached or confirmed but inextricably related. In sum reality is one pole of a reaction, the stimulus of a response, the raw colors of a palette next to a painting, the materials of the imagination which was first, in Stevens' view, simply an act of the mind upon something external to it.

For the theorizing poet such terms, imagination and reality, (perhaps Stevens meant they were, alternatively, the *guardian* angels or *fallen* angels of poetry) have definitions which are multiple and belong in the context of their use altogether. As in a marriage they have more meaning together than apart.

> The poet finds that as between these two sources: the imagination and reality, the imagination is false, whatever else may be said of it, and reality is true; and being concerned that poetry should be a thing of vital and virile importance, he commits himself to reality, which then becomes his inescapable and ever-present difficulty and inamorata.[2]

However, in the dialectic of the mind, the reality term may be reduced to being empty, the apotheosis of nothing, the "mortal no" in void and death. Is that a matter of "vital and virile importance"? Yes, of course, death being the "mother of beauty." Stevens might say the obscurity left behind is a feature of poetry that copes with such difficulties. Perhaps it will help to define the terms as normative, not illusion versus truth but meaning versus non-meaning. Imagination bestows a value to experience—objects, persons, actions. Reality may be the resistance to that value, or the welcome to it, and if not indifferently negative in its violence. However, in its resistance reality may have a promise like that of a lover. It is without doubt in Stevens' mind the "source of poetry." In one succinct metaphor of definition, Stevens wrote,"A poet looks at the world as a man looks at a woman" ("Adagia," OP, 165). The poetic act is basic, almost libidinal in its readiness to seek reality.

> ...we find the poetic act in lesser and everyday things, as for example, in the mere act of looking at a photograph of someone who is absent or in writing a letter to a person at some distance. (OP, 239)

The poet who turns in that direction denies that "reality was ever monotonous except in comparison."

Disavowing old comparisons (and their shadows of magnificence) he tries to find the object beyond comparison. No doubt this is the "thing" that absorbed ideas for Williams or resisted them. The point is made by Stevens as if he had Eliot and Pound in mind. It is his own statement against the abstract psychological, even ideological "comparisons" of Prufrock and Mauberley, though voiced with a serious hope to be relieved of the burden of comparison.

> He (the poet) asserts that the source of comparison having been eliminated, reality is returned, as if a shadow had passed and drawn after it and taken away whatever coating had concealed what lay beneath it.[3]

On this basis one can understand the search for epiphanies of the "real," almost mystical in expression, the poet being master of its rites. Reality is provocative, Stevens wrote, we never see it wholly as it is, and

> There is inherent in the words *the revelation of reality* a suggestion that there is a reality of or within or beneath the surface of reality. (OP, 213)

With a sense of empowered mission Stevens could think of reality as revelation somehow strong enough to replace supernatural omens and symbols. "The great poems of heaven and hell have been written and the great poem of the earth remains to be written."[4] To write the great poem of the earth, in the modern context, meant to call on neither religious aid nor pagan myth, nor even the sophisticated literary neo-Platonism that prompted the Romantic imagination. The modern poetry of dissociation, situated on the earth that is hard and bare, is written by the "companions in nothingness," by the "ancestor of Narcissus" and his descendants. In that world the threat is that "there are no rocks/ and stones, only this imager."

However transposed, denied, or affirmed, with on the one hand the loss of heaven and hell, and on the other, the possible regain of a poetically conceived earth, Stevens made a call to his imagination that his contemporaries could understand and share. One thinks of Joyce as perhaps the greatest of the poets of earth, without resources in the regions of heaven and hell nor desiring them. Eliot's most articulate and eloquent poetry was that of the loss of both earth and heaven; and for opposite gain of earth the suitable contrast is found in the strong voices of D. H. Lawrence and Williams. But Stevens' mind on this issue seems the most concentrated, the most clarifying, as he addressed himself to the "necessary angel" of earth as the important messenger. Referring to the "angel of reality" (in "Angel Surrounded by Paysans") he wrote to Sister Bernetta Quinn.

> This is clear only if the reader is of the idea that we live in a world of the imagination, in which reality and contact with it are the great blessings. For nine readers out of ten, the necessary angel will appear to be the angel of the imagination and for nine days out of ten that is true, although it is the tenth day that counts. (SLTR, May, 1952)

We consider again a paradox: angels of the imagination teach partial or exclusive loves and loyalties. The angel of reality, on her tenth day, brings everything. To explain, Stevens would give us a poetic parable. In "Notes Toward a Supreme Fiction" (part 2, sect.3) Stevens describes the statue of a dead general caught in stone or metal, at a moment of his "final" funeral when the music halted and his horse stood still. This rigidity made the general seem absurd and changed his true flesh to an inhuman bronze. The lawyers and doctor(s) approach to dissect and analyze, and they conclude that there never had been, never could have been such a man. For all the analysis of both monument and flesh, the General was rubbish in the end. And so efforts to halt the music and order the whole are destined to be absurd, even as in the preceding strophe the President would ordain a bee to be immortal, or would place apples on a table while a barefoot servant adjusts the curtains to a "metaphysical 't.'" The sound of reality is the "booming and booming of the new-come bee," the actual bee. Confronting inhuman bronze or metaphysical apples, it is the "golden fury" of spring that "vanishes" the question "of death in memory's dream." The "mind" is a metaphysician in a world of vital things and must be called back by a "booming and a booming."

The angel of reality is in flight always. In dedication to a localized truth like the view outside his window that was antidote to nihilism, Stevens could come with almost equal readiness of belief to the "mere air," nearest of the near. Writing to Renato Poggioli who requested comment on "The Man With the Blue Guitar," Stevens describes the dramatic base of the poem and much of his other verse. Referring to stanza xx,

> I apostophize the air and call it friend, my only friend. But it is only air. What I need is a true belief, a true brother, friendlier than air. The imagination (poor pale guitar) is not that. But the air, the mere joie de vivre, may be. This stands for the search for a belief. (SLTR, 793)

The imagination alone can invent but it cannot believe. The imagination could never substitute for "reality," though its burden and its content might be the search, as he says, for a "belief." This is what reality must finally be called, a convincing apprehension of the world, an ontological belief, as whole or minimal at its base as "mere air," and joined inseparably at one end of its apprehended existence with a "fiction."

The Apotheosis of Nothing

If so problematic an "angel" as that called "reality" should be loved like an "inamorata" by poets it was because they belonged to a period understood as enduring a crisis of knowledge and belief, and the imagination, that is to say, the source of the basic forms and substance of culture, as Eliot understood it and in effect, Stevens, Williams, and Pound as well, was in crisis too. "The Waste Land" echoed long for many of Eliot's generation as the summary poem of a modernist myth of the end of days. In effect the poem would read "As if the world gave up/ The secret of its skeleton," but the one who speaks says..... "I was neither/ living nor dead, and I knew nothing." "Nothing" is the dominant surviving word in the midst of the passionate, supremely articulate echoes of old verse. It was "nothing" and "again nothing."

Prufrock's clarifying statement came earlier with "Not knowing what to feel or if I understand." Perhaps this is how one feels to dance "like a dancing bear, / Cry like a parrot, chatter like an ape." Was that only the voice of the incapable imagination, as Stevens could put it? Rather Eliot saw the threat differently; the enemy was not just the limbo of "nothing." There is something one knows, "The conscience of a blackened street/ Impatient to assume the world." A moral conflict was better than the empty cry of "nothing," and so the protagonist of nothing, as one may say, adds rage to frustration by giving a blackened conscience to the world.

Stevens' apostrophe to "nothing," "The Snowman," can serve in modestly ironic counterpoint. The poem starts with an admonishment, "One must have a mind of winter" and "have been cold a long time" to eventually come to the total subtraction of "nothing." It is important, for Stevens, to suggest the responsibility of a "mind" for this wasteland. Yet the absolute zero is strong in Stevens.

> For the listener, who listens in the snow,
> And, nothing himself, beholds
> Nothing that is not there and the nothing that is.

The finality is in one sense healing. "Nothing" can be accepted on those terms without great outcry. If it is possible to thought or the imagination, it is therefore an experience; perhaps others will come with it, or despite it.

Could "nothing" be the setting for what Stevens in "Notes Toward a Supreme Fiction" called the "first idea," and Williams "the source of poetry?" If it is a threat to the imagination, the threat is nihilism where personal identity, metaphysical faith, cultural reality have been expunged in the "conscience that haunts a blackened street." The "first idea" may only be a question. The problematic words, "first idea," "nothing," are at a center where modern (and postmodern) poetry and literary theory make their revelations, and where the thinking and practice of Stevens and Eliot join and depart.[5]

Significantly the same theme returns in the verse of Williams. I would propose that in deep commonsense fashion for Williams "nothing" is a term for death, and the "snowman" in his verse is only a corpse, although he might arouse angry, not mourning response,

> He's nothing at all
> he's dead
> shrunken up to skin

and mocking response:

> Put his head on
> one chair and his
> feet on another and
> he'll lie there
> like an acrobat—

and shame:

> just bury it
> and hide its face
> for shame.

The essential lines are these:

> He's come out of the man
> and he's let
> the man go—
> the liar ["Death"]

The question is who is the liar? The guilt is in both the dead and the living man. As in "Dedication for a Plot of Ground,"

> If you can bring nothing to this place
> but your carcass, keep out.

The guest at the funeral, whose emptiness of response reduces *him* to a carcass, is not fit company for the dead. It was essential for Williams that the interview with death be reactive discourse. One must bring something, whether grief or something else, and that begins entrance into the life of "capable imagination." [6]

But what is capable in the imagination as Stevens gave it sense? And what in the "figure of the youth as virile poet" does virility in the poet mean? Eliot's "Gerontion" was evocative in the context for such questions.

> ...Think
> Neither fear nor courage saves us. Unnatural vices
> Are fathered by our heroism.
> I have lost my passion: why should I need to keep it
> Since what is kept must be adulterated.

The echoing note, filled with passion, is of "the God Hercules" who "Had left him, that had loved him well." We hear the question, "Who clipped the lion's wings/ And flea'd his rump and pared his claws?" In the ultimate weakening the poet is condemned to sing "some worn-out common song/.../Recalling things that other people have desired." These are the sounds of defeat, which Eliot made into great song insofar as capability remained. April is cruelest for mixing memory and desire and this pathos registers itself better than passion. However, passivity receives the salute of the mock-heroic. The anti-climaxes of action are best reserved for the carbuncular clerk of "The Waste Land" whose caresses "are unreproved if undesired." He encounters no defense, requires no response, and touches the nadir of both action and desire.

The ultimate passivity is that of dying. "We who were living are now dying/ With a little patience." Climactic action in Eliot is a surrender as in martyrdom: "The awful daring of a moment's surrender," or alternatively a passive release, "your heart would have responded/ Gaily, when invited, beating obedient/ To controlling hands." The religious victory *is* a surrender. In "Ash Wednesday," for the Virgin Lady, one might "Pray for those who offend her/ And are terrified and cannot surrender." The prayer is "Teach us to care and not to care/ Teach us to sit still."

There may be salvation in entire impotence. One must acknowledge "Shape without form, shade without colour, / Paralyzed force, gesture without motion;" (HM) and yet "Between the idea/ And the reality/ Between the motion/ And the act/ Falls the Shadow" That grave shadow falls over verse and the modern sensibility, Williams might say, but for Eliot it had a different meaning. The ultimate paralysis of belief, with impotence of desire and imagination, offers still a "Shadow" which is a spiritual "everything" rather than "nothing." *"For Thine is the Kingdom."* The martyr to a desiccated will translates impotence into transcendent response. It was a mark of extreme necessity that belief should be pursued to its negative absolute, renouncing thought, passion, action, and tangible physical existence. The imagination's ghost has become a transparent nihilism and its mystical reversal.

In this context Pound's choice for the imagination's success is the paradigm of Malatesta, the warrior-artist, as the most virile, most literally the figure of capable imagination. The contrast with Eliot's profound figures of impotence is striking. Pound imagined climaxes of political-esthetic power, which in his treatment joined esthetic order with its source in natural strength. In this he expressed a definition of power that owes credit to Nietzsche and Emerson. Harold Bloom observes that power in Emerson is desire and will, very much in the sense of the "virile" and "capable" imagination. In that view the lost hero and noble rider is the imagination itself, resurrected, and called upon to do Quixotic battle for the "nothing that is not there" against the nothing that is.

We marked these apostrophes to "nothing" in Stevens and Eliot where both denote the reductive margin where reality dissolves, loses guide, outline, and measure, and must be found again. If we ask the major question, what is the affirmed reality in this reality haunted verse of the modern Americans, it is a craving bolstered by signals the poet invents, a craving both satisfied and energized for further craving, but always equivocal, always clearly aware of the opposing negative which encloses the modern sense of being. The context is a great silence, and when the word reality is discussed it must be understood as a communication which is dynamic in a dialectical relation treated against the alternatives of "to have or nothing."[7]

But what is it like "to have?" In "Thirteen Ways of Looking at a Blackbird" the poem imagines the blackbird against the landscape of snow both in its beginning stanza and at its end. In closure he sits motionless, at a center of time beyond past and future.

> It was evening all afternoon.
> It was snowing
> And it was going to snow.
> The blackbird sat
> In the cedar-limbs.

Essentially the blackbird is an accent of black against the snow, and when he begins to move, "the only moving thing," down to the center of existence, is his eye. The eye moves and the eye is seen, and its ways of *being seen* are versions of multiple being, not as object alone but object-eye, independent, absolute, and at one in all its metamorphoses, a new example of Emerson's "transparent eyeball." Thus the blackbird is an affirmative reduction of being, an absolute of the real world. It is that which *happens* and moves and sees, and its existence in a poem is a search for the source. What the blackbird represents, (a contradiction, since he is too much of all being to represent anything) may have been stated by Stevens in his "Adagia."

> Perhaps there is a degree of perception at which what is real or imagined are one: a state of clairvoyant observation, accessible or possibly accessible to the poet...(OP, 166)

The clairvoyance is in breaking the barriers between thing and thought, object and consciousness. In a letter Stevens wrote

> I have been trying to see the world about me both as I see it and as it is. This means seeing the world as an imaginative man sees it. (SLTR, 316)

His word for this way of seeing was "realization," as if to dismiss the over-confident and naive claim in the word "reality." Realization requires a double consciousness, a duality of vision. The sense of the real is formed by two images that partly deny each other, but are mutually anchored in concrete phenomena and the will to respond, or remain conscious. [8]

Realization is a value process, not just a truth process, and value is even more a product of dual consciousness. The noble or sublime have meaning only against the poverty of the real or the quotidian world. "Death is the mother of beauty," the poet writes, and if with "realizations" he wrests order from chaos, it is with the proviso that chaos must return. Dedicated to "The Hightoned Old Christian Woman," Stevens wrote of the changing of fictive things.

> This will make widows wince. But fictive things
> Wink as they will, wink most when widows wince.

There are heroic as well comic orders of belief, and the alliteration in this case is here to defy as well as welcome the fanciful in belief and disbelief. The fiction that knows itself is on the way to transcending itself.

Faced by the imagination, reality is a monster, conquerable, unconquerable, eternally at large. So Stevens writes in that most thematically telling passage of "The Man With the Blue Guitar."

> That I may reduce the monster to
> Myself, and then may be myself?
>
> In face of the monster, be more than part
> Of it, more than the monstrous player of
>
> One of its monstrous lutes...

The installed premise, more poignant than death as the mother of beauty, is the fact that it is an animal that plays the blue guitar, "On that its claws propound, its fangs/ articulate its desert days." Such is the existential drama at the source of poetry, and for Stevens the "monstrous" can be to know poetry as "a worm composing on a straw" while the north wind horns its victory.

There is another answer with zest to the Snowman in Stevens' "The Angel Without Doctrine."

> I am the angel of reality,
> Seen for a moment standing in the door.

....
I am one of you and being one of you
Is being and knowing what I am and know.

Yet I am the necessary angel of earth,
Since, in my sight, you see the earth again,

Cleared of its stiff and stubborn, man-locked set,
And, in my hearing, you hear its tragic drone

Rise liquidly in liquid lingerings,
Like watery words awash; like meanings said

By repetitions of half-meanings. Am I not,
Myself, only half a figure of a sort,

A figure half seen, or seen for a moment, a man
Of the mind, an apparition apparelled in

Apparels of such lightest look that a turn
Of my shoulder and quickly, too quickly, I am gone?
["Angel Surrounded by Paysans"]

For Stevens it is clear there was no other way to approach or affirm "the necessary angel of earth," that angel "without aureole or ashen wing, without mythical glamor," who bore only a revealed confidence, not the heavy weight of philosophies. Michel Benamou, however, rightly distinguishes this figure from angels or a god. "It is the quest not for a god but for a man....for reality....the center which it seeks is both reality and a self.[9] As Benamou notes, the affinities with the tradition of Whitman and Emerson are clear. The sense of reality and the sense of a self both begin at the same center; there is no world without a self for its legitimation of being. This is not imperial egotism or solipsism but a gathering of world selves which meet at the center, "straight to the word, / Straight to the transfixing object, to the object/ At the exactest point at which it is itself." The object seen transfixed at that point could be taken as a lesson in epistemology. Reality is not a generic truth, it is an individual truth appropriate to a pluralist and individualist culture.[10] If this is a view of New Haven, the poem goes on, it is a view through "the certain eye." But the "transfixing object" anchors and defends the way to the shared consciousness of selves; this is the subtle triangular track of poetry.

For the poetry of belief, a man, not an angel, emerges from a speaking self. Stevens said the ultimate that could be said on this in "The Well-Dressed Man With a Beard." One wonders, could the bizarre, seemingly irrelevant title be the act of singling out one man from the crowd?

If the rejected things, the things denied,
Slid over the western cataract, yet one,

One only, one thing that was firm, even
No greater than a cricket's horn, no more
Than a thought to be rehearsed all day, a speech
Of the self that must sustain itself on speech,
One thing remaining, infallible, would be
Enough.

A speech of the self, sustaining itself on speech, this may be the final reality achieved in the act of the imagination. The infinite value of that act is affirmed by the closing line of the poem, "It can never be satisfied, the mind, never."

The invocation of the angel in "Angel Surrounded by Paysans" seems to be a summary statement. To "see the earth again/ Cleared of its stiff and stubborn, man-locked set" makes the angel necessary. In that "too quickly, I am gone" we understand that the angel does not represent law or doctrine, nor plain determinist necessity. It is a visitation and a mystery, not sure of its welcome, and yet a form of redemption, though half-seen and composed of half-meanings. An apparition requiring light apparel, reality is not an imposed decree, but the object of a search and a necessity of the spirit, its partner, so to speak. Before coming to address the redemptive figure of angels Stevens made a harsher claim, referring to

> ...the fifth column of reality that keeps whispering with the hard superiority of the sane that reality is all we have, that it is that or nothing. Reality is the footing from which we leap after what we do not have and on which everything depends. (SLTRS, 600)

This is a clear concept, "reality is all we have," and yet it is the footing from which we imagine what we do not have. It sounds like a confession of faith and the note is even more emphatic in a letter debating the role of distancing abstractions in poetry and painting:

> That does not have to be settled this morning. It is enough right now to say that after a month of rain my wife's roses look piercingly bright.... while piercing was the word, it was, after all, a very slight sensation on which to make so much depend.

The repeated echo for Williams' red wheelbarrow on which so much depends is not fortuitous. The two poets were in profound agreement; it was poetry that was in concern and Stevens could interpret dependency to its ultimate degree. It was in the same setting that he wrote elsewhere of looking out the window at his wife's roses to feel "a force capable of destroying nihilism." The phrase should resonate for his readers who grasp the largeness of reference behind Stevens' view of poetry.

The Anti-Poet of Reality [11]

For Williams especially the energy in his writing would urge the angel's necessity. To achieve "reality" was to gain a shape; the imagination's "unique power is to give created forms actual existence."[12] He would resolve difficulties by asserting that reality is the quality of "independent existence," something that is the possession of nature as well as ourselves. In effect he argued always against the megalomania of absorption or the opposite schizophrenic dissolution of "things" into mere language or any trope of the imagination. No doubt the doctor-scientist in Williams could never accept that self-defeating premise.

What he seized upon in his poetry was no philosophic abstraction. He wanted a force that was sexual, more assertive than sensual. Such is "the wild carrot taking the field by force" in "Queen Anne's Lace."

> Wherever
> his hand has lain there is
> a tiny purple blemish. Each part
> is a blossom under his touch
> to which the fibres of her being
> stem one by one, each to its end,
> until the whole field is a
> white desire, empty, a single stem,
> a cluster, flower by flower,
> a pious wish to whiteness gone over—
> or nothing.

The conclusion illustrates that the epistemological drama is not absent, nor is it simple. The altercation is between " a white desire," "a pious wish," and "nothing." Williams was explicit on a patrolling insight for his work. "I am extremely sexual in my desires. I carry them everywhere and at all times. I think that from that arises the drive which empowers us all" (WSE, 311). As if to end debate, sexuality (like Stevens' image of the "inamorata") proved a certain link between imagination and reality, and countered other large and small threats of the dissociated mind and sensibility. In sex the body thinks, imagines, desires. The erotic is the poet's touch, everyone's touch, the touch of the eyes and sensations, and 'she, ' whether a weedy flower or Mark Antony's Cleopatra, is that with which one has intercourse in the world. The poet would say to himself, in lines from "The Botticellian Trees," write! "until the stript/ sentences/ move as a woman's/ limbs under cloth/ and praise from secrecy/ quick with desire/ love's ascendancy/ in summer—" In a sense his "angel" was too overwhelming, too absolute to be called "necessary." He knew it this way, as he observed in "Against the Weather" (WSE, 196), "A life that is here and now is timeless. That is the universal I am seeking: to embody that in a work of art, a new world that is always "real."

Such was the commitment, requiring "a strange courage" no doubt, that Williams shared with Stevens, though expressed through his own instruction to himself on behalf of immediate experience. His words are blunt in "Spring and All," "There is a constant barrier between the reader and his consciousness of immediate contact with the world."[13] So writing must work against the natural tendency of reading, which is toward the abstract, the generalized, the associational. In effect the reader must be forced to read in order to escape the condition of mere reading. To sum up, Williams borrowed from other manifestoes, like that of Vortex: "To refine, to clarify, to intensify that eternal moment in which we alone live there is but a single force—the imagination."[14] "The true value," Williams notably said for the imagination in general, "is that peculiarity which gives an object a character by itself. The associational or sentimental value is the false" (WSE, 11).

One is not sure if this is an esthetic or metaphysical need against the "easy lateral sliding" of association. One may drift toward a second-hand "beauty" perhaps, but also toward an inauthentic world of conventional signs and symbols.

> Metaphors and similes were in this respect a retreat from experience into the easy path of general likenesses, structures of translation and interpretation, with their ultimate source in cultural ideologies. The thing that stands eternally in the way of really good writing is always one: the virtual impossibility of lifting to the imagination those things which lie under the direct scrutiny of the senses, close to the nose. It is this difficulty that sets a value upon all works of art and makes them a necessity. (WSE, 11)

Implicitly what is involved is again the alienation of sensibility and mind. Like Pound Williams might be thinking of a general therapy for culture, which had become increasingly schizoid, and whose only doctor was the imagination and only help the missionary work of art. Thus Williams used the phrase, "a culture of immediacy," to describe the old local nativist America, a primary culture now corrupted by the pursuit of wealth and replaced by " a culture of purchase," "a culture in effigy."[15]

It might as well have been called a culture of abstraction. Even science was not concerned with "things" in Williams' sense of the word. In science particulars were important as they gained statistical quantity or as they illustrated general laws. The particular, however, could gain from poetry a resistance to structured abstract meanings and remain open to the imagination, as Williams defined it. "The particular thing...offers a finality that sends us spinning through space" (WSE, 292).

It is the implied alienation from primary experience that reinforces the tone in these words. There is apt correspondence in the use by Joyce of the word "epiphany" to describe his own way of approaching immediacy and its radiance. Williams liked another phrase for such correlatives, "luminous gists." In "Tract," for instance, Williams gives great play to stripping away the ceremonial conformities of a funeral in order to approach the reality of death. But reduced to the blunt presentation of a corpse, it is not the physical features of death that are at the center of the poem but the exposed response to it. "Sit openly to the weather as to grief " and the line has remarkable resonance with the invocation to "share with us," understood on the plane of the weather. Grief has no comfort but supports a moral sanity. One estimates that this is as good an illustration as any for Stevens' figure of the "necessary angel of earth."

The quarrel that Williams made with Eliot is instructive on this theme. In actual effect it was not Eliot's traditionalism that bothered him so much as it was the path of reduction in Eliot's verse. Without tradition, without a moral or religious understanding, for Eliot the "culture of immediacy" would be mere brutal chaos. In his verse the reductive imagination worked as true "anti-poetry," reaching the human animal, the urban wasteland, the metaphysical void. As if in fright Eliot would choose the conventions of behavior and inherited belief called culture. Williams saw this rightly as contradiction to everything he believed—that reality was self-redeeming, that the ugly and the violent were paths of insight, that the quotidian was the sharable world of human experience, and ultimately the coherence of meaning lay precisely in the renewal of contact with touch, taste, sight and smell. I imagine Williams might have approved Eliot's representation of Grishkin for her "feline smell...in a drawing room." It was Eliot's half-trip to the "center" that repelled Williams, a process which found only one direction to turn from nihilism, toward a transcendental faith and its calcified institutional expression. The revelation of faith in Eliot's poetry sounded curiously like nihilism, or it was opaque as the heavens since it seemed to require a martyr-like extinction of earthly being. Meanwhile, to Williams, it looked like the mere cultural loyalties of an imagination in surrender of freedom. In that sense Williams was the most democratic of poets. The culture of immediacy he spoke of was that of his senses, the reality that of a man, the inner man or the outer, and ultimately perhaps a stranger, who could be known as simply and directly as the wheelbarrow on which "so much depends."

It is first of all clear that the attraction of the unbeautiful, the antipoetic, as Stevens called it, answers the need to assert *something* against nothing. To reduce ideas and valued experiences, or to delight in their decreation or deconstruction, is not to debate them so much as to find their function. It is to maintain the life of imaginative judgment that the romantic wishes to become the anti-romantic. Like violence in the apocalyptic mode it is an effort to shock sensibility into life and break with silence and a dead world.

The most direct unself-conscious use of this program for art probably belongs to Williams who believed in the power of the imagination to invade unexplored silences, unknown shocks of experience. In his declaration of creed he wrote "The processes of art, to keep alive, must always challenge the unknown and go where the most uncertainty lies." One could add that he was greater for his ability to challenge the known, or rather, the familiar that in its stale acknowledgements remains unknown. The necessary equipment was a capacity for dual vision to achieve the effect that Williams called tragic. "Masterpieces are only beautiful in a tragic sense, like a starfish lying stretched dead on the beach in the sun."[16]

In the effort to challenge both beauty and tragedy Williams' characteristic strategy is to accumulate a negative force to stress the sudden emergence of its antithesis. Thus these highly representative lines from "Between Walls."

> the back wings
> of the
>
> hospital where
> nothing
>
> will grow lie
> cinders
>
> in which shine
> the broken
>
> pieces of a green
> bottle

In a poem of this sort one understands best why Williams liked to dismiss punctuation. The fragment of glass punctuates for itself in a way that might escape formal language. Meanwhile the line breaks and the syntax force out the bare assertion, something said under pressure. The hospital is the familiar oxymoron, the place of affliction and cure, of death and birth. Cinders, in which nothing will grow, reduce all expectations, until eventually the green of a broken bottle flashes its signal. Picking among junk like an old beggar, Williams himself is the pantaloon Chaplin of Stevens' invention, the bearer of one gift of survival, or rather its minimal requirement, a distinct perception. When he wrote *Paterson* he did not forget to put his basis of inspiration in the foreground. "Embrace the foulness," he wrote, and its purpose was to "Be reconciled, poet, with your world, it is/ the only truth!"[17]

Thus Williams' deeper muse may have been not a city, Paterson, but his profession of medicine, as he suggests himself in the *Autobiography*.

> And my "medicine" was the thing which gained me entrance to the secret gardens of the self... I was permitted by my medical badge to follow the poor defeated body into those gulfs and grottoes....at such times and in such places—foul as they may be with the stinking ischio-rectal abscesses of our comings and goings—just there, the thing, in all its greatest beauty, may be forced to fly for a moment guiltily about the room.[18]

This is a fundamental passage of self-analysis between a poet and his work. What is that "thing," he observes, forced to fly about the room in that moment of discovery? "... its chief characteristic is that it is sure, all of a piece, and, as I have said, instant and perfect." The "thing" must be an epiphany of existence, its purity being a purity of perception, so much a thing that it is nameless. The word perfect also transcends its meaning; it exists, this thing, without value and measure. That is a rounded paradox. The more a thing is measured as good, clean, dirty, bad, obscene, the less it *is*. It becomes a concept, an abstraction of value. But the more it *is* independently of these value *judgments* the more beautiful and perfect it is.

Therefore the shock of the ugly, the deformed, the imperfect (now made perfect) is important. In the medical perspective it is an apprehension of life at precisely the moment when life is most transparently exposed to perception. What is foul is beautiful for that reason, the ugly and the foul having existential purity, they are what they are, no one wants to dress them or translate them into another medium. In a sense they are "perfect" because they are unredeemable, having achieved something like the immutability of the ideal.

It may help clarify this to refer to significant remarks by Stevens in one of his letters on the subject of "extraordinary actuality." If extraordinary enough, it has a vitality all of its own which makes it independent of any conjunction with the imagination." (SLTR, 411). He reemphasized the point in "Adagia." "In the presence of extraordinary actuality, consciousness takes the place of imagination" (OP, 165). In a letter to Henry Church, in discussing their project for a lecture series on poetry, it occurred to Stevens to propose Hemingway as the modern master for treating "extraordinary actuality."

> ...the anti-poet may be the right man to discuss EXTRAORDINARY ACTUALITY, and by discussing it in his own way reveal the poetry of the thing....the best man that I can think of for the job is Ernest Hemingway... (SLTR, 411)

Stevens was writing at a time (1942) when "anti-poetry" seemed to do the actual and extraordinary world the most justice. In this usage the ordinary is reserved for the everyday consciousness blurred by verbal abstractions. We infer that what is desired from "anti-poetry" is the unmediated impact of the actual, which arrives in its pure, or as Williams would say, its "instant and perfect" form.

But that "perfection" gains a voice and is not entirely self-redeeming, though the imperative of the "ACTUAL" makes it seem so. This is particularly true for Stevens as illumination arrives in later verse, in "Evening Without Angels." The first stanza asks "why the poet as eternal *chef d'orchestre*?"

> Air is air,
> Its vacancy glitters round us everywhere.
> Its sounds are not angelic syllables
> But our unfashioned spirits realized
> More sharply in more furious selves.

Therefore in the context of that which is unfashioned, and while the bare earth must be acknowledged, it is our own voice, "great within us," that calls for inspiration.

> Bare night is best. Bare earth is best. Bare, bare,
> Except for our own houses, huddled low
> Beneath the arches and their spangled air,
> Beneath the rhapsodies of fire and fire,
> Where the voice that is in us makes a true response,
> Where the voice that is great within us rises up,
> As we stand gazing at the rounded moon.

While writing this Stevens may have thought of the friend he first called "anti-poet," more committed to "actuality" than even Hemingway. When Williams addresses himself to the theme "bare earth is best," bareness takes on the most limited human condition expressed by "The Poor." The first lines express poverty as the anarchy of meaning and values as well as the bareness of possessions.

> It's the anarchy of poverty
> delights me, the old
> yellow wooden house indented
> among the new brick tenements...

and follows with the clutter of buildings and the motley dress of

> poor children...
>
> reflecting every stage and
> custom of necessity—
> Chimneys, roofs, fences of
> Wood and metal in an unfenced
>
> age and enclosing next to
> nothing at all: the old man
> in a sweater and soft black
> hat who sweeps the sidewalk—
>
> his own ten feet of it
> In a wind that fitfully
> turning his corner has
> overwhelmed the entire city

This is the minimum of possession but it is a claim on place, the right of place and with it, existence.

No poem does more to claim this than "Dedication For a Plot of Ground," the brief biography of his tough old English grandmother, Emily Dickinson Welcome. The word "lost" is repeated three times in the early lines of the poem, lost her husband, lost her daughter, lost her baby. These are the credits of the surviving poor, and they are supported by the verb phrases of victimization, "was driven," "ran adrift" "followed her husband." But the encircling circumstances are meant in fact to emphasize resistance, with thirteen repetitions for her firm role in the family, "fought for," defended against," "seized," "brought them," "domineered over," though what she domineered over finally was the grass plot where she now lies buried. All this is a confirmation of "living hard," with which she attains "a final loneliness." The phrase comes without irony, as if it were an apotheosis. It is as if she willed her own loneliness, wanting only this plot of ground for her reward.

It becomes obvious that no one was better equipped than Williams for writing memorials to the dead, or perhaps they should be called anti-memorials. Poems like "Tract," "Death," "To Ford Madox Ford In Heaven" record an obsession. In the last of these Ford is in "heaven" and heaven is described in his own terms as Provence, which was once made heaven by Ford's praise of it. What is strong in the poem is the theme joining two poets who meet in the heaven they have both invented. But in Provence it is the earth which is at issue after all. Such is the "heavenly man," Ford, not a saint, but with a grossness which is not like the world because the world stands for a certain efficiency, polished, well-made, the product of reason and practice. No, Ford is more earthly than the world, a poet filthy with the flesh and corrupt, who loved to eat and drink and whore and lie exorbitantly, thus closing a circle of perfectly reduced physical existence. A man of the imagination lies grossly, thank god, and the poet memorializing him calls it carelessness, "the part of a man that is homeless here on earth." Carelessness is magnificently understated of course; the grossness, the lying, the homelessness, are all part of the essence of Ford, out of which might come the only heaven to know.

Williams is drawing the portrait of the anti-poet as if to understand a way that the mortal filthy flesh can be redeemed in detachment, laughter, and the spirit within the grossness of lying. Implicitly this is an enactment of his theory of the imagination, which is, in turn, a theory of value. Value is not in some distant heaven but a part of the living fleshly creator. In the intrinsic thought of this esthetic its values are not to be understood in some resulting artifact, nor in a set of standards taken from a traditional canon, or from a culture of ethical-esthetic norms, but taken from an act of the imagination that transcends its history and its results. It would be a culture of value that transcends its own heroes and monuments. Inseparably it has the imprint of Ford, which in the act of creation, (or "lying") is a sort of "heavenly" force brought from gross substance. This is a reversal of ordinary Platonism; instead of the idealized beauty which the imagination serves, this beauty reflects its maker.

There is important summary value in another poem by Williams which says as completely as could be hoped what is at stake in the poetics of reduction. "These," a major poem by any account, must have been acknowledged by Williams for its powerful condensation of a life-long theme. It begins with the most abrupt treatment of reduction's nadir, a zero place in the season, ("the desolate dark weeks"), and a zero place in human capacity, ("when nature in its barrenness/ equals the stupidity of man"). It is a place beyond further descent as the poem engages with a sort of metaphysical double negative, the nothing beyond the designed limit of nothing.

> The year plunges into night
> and the heart plunges
> lower than night
>
> to an empty, windswept place
> without sun, stars or moon
> ....
>
> to make a man aware of nothing
> that he knows, not loneliness
> itself—

But there is still the margin of consciousness. There is, in that empty place,"a peculiar light as of thought/ that spins a dark fire/ whirling upon itself..." until in the poem's interruptions of thought, it kindles to awareness of the absence of something represented by ghosts that whine and whistle and long to be embraced. These are the ghosts of would-be experiences as well as memories, they are anything one wills, but they are still ghosts inhabiting emptiness. Briefly there is violence, "the flashes and booms of war." Can the ghosts that would be embraced call up violence? That is an appropriate effect, as we have seen, on a stage that has been set for loss, but here an echo is all that remains, in a "cold greater than can be thought." It is memory that defines absence, the something or nothing that is a ghost,

> the people gone that we loved,
> the beds lying empty, the couches
> damp, the chairs unused—

But emptiness is a provocation, and the poem explores it, turning the scene back, lower in deep consciousness.

> Hide it away somewhere
> out of the mind, let it get roots
> and grow, unrelated to jealous
>
> ears and eyes—for itself.

The rooted life that will grow is a metaphor for a life-giving thought isolated among ghosts in an empty world. The thought grows out of itself, "unrelated to jealous eyes and ears." The latter phrase may stand for contingencies, ulterior reasons and motives; the living thought grows, freed from anxious eyes and ears burdened with old thoughts and emotions. Either way the poem ends by invoking the reborn sensibility, "the source of poetry."

> In this mine they come to dig—all.
> Is this the counterfoil to sweetest

music? The source of poetry that
seeing the clock stopped, says,
The clock has stopped

that ticked yesterday so well?
and hears the sound of lakewater
splashing—that is now stone.

The source of poetry is in the field of absence, that mine where all come to dig. It is in the contrast of today and yesterday, directly facing the clock that has stopped, for its stopping is a powerful recall of its ticking. So the sound of lake water splashing is heard in the silence become stone. The poem is at the moment where the world ends and begins, no poem could do more to define the fall and rise of meaning, a definite disembodied spirit, where the imagination is afflicted and so rises into poetry. 'The poem reflects back upon itself as poem, it makes the claim of the imagination on time, place, person and mind which create a livable world of meaning.

Notes

1. *Aesthetics and Politics*, ed. Ronald Taylor (London: NLB, 1977), p. 41.
2. "Honors and Acts" (OP, 241).
3. "Two or Three Ideas" (OP, 213).
4. "Imagination as Value" (NA, 142).
5. I write later that Emmanuel Levinas the French philospher, who has weight in my discussion of Stevens' thought, presents a "first idea" which I think is analogous and instructive for Stevens' meaning as well as his own; it is simply "Thou shalt not kill," the commandment from the Old Testament. See chapter 17 and appendices.
6. I suggest at this point that the "capable imagination, reacting from nihilism," invents the future, replacing "nothing" with the fresh content produced in the free will of the "virile" imagination. I remind my reader that my political theme throughout is the contrast between the poets of two schools, one generally of liberal democracy and the other considered hyperconservative in the blend typical of the totalitarian era of the last century. I pursue the theme for Stevens in the following chapter.
7. To see a parallel intensity on this theme, the reader should explore Frost, as in "Bereft," "The Hill Wife," "For Once Then Something," "An Old Man's Winter Night," "Our Hold on the Planet."
8. Again I must insert a comment with a foreview of later discussion. What do Steven's own remarks on "reality," its "angel" and "realization" have to do with Steven's surprising engagement with politics? I would say it is a contribution to a civilized way of thinking about it. In a liberal democratic dimension it is neither relativist nor absolute in associating words and consciousness to reality (or truth). Call it the sophistication that rises from ambiguity, uncertainty, and even disagreement to good faith and consensus in thought or action. This may be in part what Emerson meant by a "double consciousness" and Keats by "negative capability." The question for Stevens is how the poetic imagination makes this act of mind possible, and what poetry tells us to do with highly conditioned belief, a "supreme fiction."
9. Michel Benamou, *Wallace Stevens and the Symbolist Imagination* (Princeton, NJ: Princeton University Press, 1972), p.84.
10. Benamou chooses a quotation from Husserl for gloss.

"The flux of living, my flux, as thinking subject, can be largely unapprehended, unknown to any extent of its past or future, it is enough to look at life in flux and actually present, for me to say, without any restriction and of necessity: I <u>am,</u> this life is, I live: *cogito*."
(Edmund Husserl, *Ideen su einer reinen Phenomenologie...*, [The Hague, 1950], p. 85).

11. One crosses paths with J. Hillis Miller's well-known and influential book, *Poets of Reality* so many times in this discussion that it would be unnecessary labor to footnote them either for agreement or disagreement, but Miller's general approach would be most interesting to students for contrast. In Miller's later work he was one of the influential leaders of the early "deconstruction" school at Yale.
12. *Imaginations* (New York: New Directions, 1970), p. 120.
13. Ibid., p. 88.
14. Ibid., p. 89.
15. "The American Background" (WSE, 146-48).
16. "Preface" (WSE, xvii).
17. *Paterson* (New York: New Directions, 1948), pp. 103, 126.
18. *Autobiography*, pp. 288-89.

13

The Imagination as Value

The Redemptive Imagination

When Stevens spoke of cultural crisis in "The Noble Rider" he described a failure in the relation between imagination and reality. The equation gave very large assignment to the imagination for the real world was in a climax of violence at the time he wrote in 1942. Actually he was viewing a very long history when he said, "Reality then became violent and so remains..." This was more than literal, a "spiritual violence" affecting everyone alive. As an issue for the imagination, Stevens defined what he meant when he said the threat was "direct and immediate" to the "sanctions that are the order of our lives" (NA, 22). With "eras of the imagination" and "the order of our lives" Stevens was referring to much more than the politics of revolution and world war. He would voice the commitment of poets in a time of crisis that threatened the valuing sensibility itself in its nature and function. That function, he said, was to meet the pressure of reality with "a violence from within that protects us from a violence without." In seeking to capture violence he was speaking for the gift of control and order in a time when intellectual habit gave most power to the fatalism of natural law and the blank force in events.

The result is a heroic understanding of poetry, though not sentimental or romantic; these latter effects were older diversions, which had their share in the increased violence of reality. For that reason poets had to become "Connoisseurs of Chaos" and the mocking title of that poem does not conceal its serious theme. If "a violent order is disorder," as one premise of the verse states, then we know we are at the line where order meets chaos. "An old order is a violent one," and "A great disorder is an order." The first suggestion is clear, as the order grows old it develops its own force of disorder. But how is a great disorder an order, as the second premise states? The poem gives itself up to dialectical contraction; a great sense of disorder is its own compulsion toward order in "a law of inherent opposites." But in the poem's intellectual detachment, "This proves nothing. Just one more truth, /...in the immense disorder of truths." But there, between order and disorder, so unresolved, the imagination has its existence. The poem does not argue this, but proposes an image, an eagle floating in the sky, "for which the intricate Alps are a single nest." The eagle in its purposeful life presides over the impossible crags and break-ups of the mountains. A flight like the eagle's flight is recommended to the pensive man who exists in the midst of a violent order now indistinguishable from a great disorder.

In another view violence itself is in the origin of poetry. Most explicitly, in "Poetry is a Destructive Force," Stevens traces the source from "what misery is, / Nothing to have at heart./It is to have or nothing." But the thing to have, this poetry, is beyond a misery, or a misery which acts like "a lion, an ox in his breast,"..."breathing there." A lion of consciousness is sleeping in the sun and "it can kill a man."

Confessing willingly, Stevens can assign poetry to its instinct for destruction, "in the land of war."

> It is not the snow that is the quill, the page.
> The poem lashes more fiercely than the wind,
> As the mind, to find what will suffice, destroys
> Romantic tenements of rose and ice.
> ("Man and Bottle")

But as always in Stevens a creative reserve is protected, or in fact, liberated. In the mind's "great poem of winter" there is a center that destruction only concentrates.

> ...More than the man, it is
> A man with the fury of a race of men,
> A light at the centre of many lights,
> A man at the centre of men.

In these few lines Stevens forms a master theme of his poetry and his poetics. To discover in the wars of the imagination "a man at the centre of men" is to affirm the source within the ruined tenements of rose and ice.

Thus Stevens, absorbing the language of the apocalypse in his native poise of spirit, described the path of his imagination.

> ...How cold the vacancy
> When the phantoms are gone and the shaken realist
> First sees reality. The mortal no
> Has its emptiness and tragic expirations.
> The tragedy, however, may have begun,
> Again, in the imagination's new beginning,
> In the yes of the realist spoken because he must
> Say yes, spoken because under every no
> Lay a passion for yes that had never been broken
> ("Esthetique du Mal," viii)

Most ambitious in tragic reduction, "the mortal no" forces "the imagination's new beginning," it becomes the starting point, the tragic shaken realist seeking "the mother of beauty." All "no's are major in implication, serious beyond their reference, even these three in the title of "No Possum, No Sop, No Taters." The poem presents a winter scene in deep January, the very center of the realm of "no", where "bad is final in this light," and where "snow sparkles like eyesight falling to earth." "It is in this solitude, /..../It is here, in this bad, that we reach/ The last purity of the knowledge of good." The challenge is one of metamorphosis, where the imagination lives, as if the dialectic of no and yes were itself redemptive and almost automatic as a mode of prophecy.

The impulse is toward what Stevens called "the exhilaration of changes," the very spring of metaphor, as expressed in "The Motive for Metaphor," a shrinking from the "weight of primary noon, the ABC of being." The right condition is autumn or spring, the poem says, undefined and changing, as in autumn where "everything is half-dead," and in spring with its "half-colors of quarter-things." The snow zero of "The Snow Man" motivates change, the weather is there for start and so is the quotidian. The title in "The Man Whose Pharynx Was Bad" suggests that the "malady of the quotidian" leads to voicelessness, a disease of speech. The cure for the "malady" may be the dead of winter; if he could penetrate "through all its purples to the final slate," the poet might retrieve speech. The final slate is at the bottom of the real, the pre-imagined. From here speech and perhaps song begin,

> Out of such mildew plucking neater mould
> And spouting new orations of the cold.

The temptation of the reductive is strong for poets because the redemptive metamorphosis is a natural task of the imagination. In the medium of poetry it fills empty space or alienated substance with intimacy and recognition.

In another movement of reversal it is the particular that best absorbs the universal. Stevens writes in "Nudity in the Colonies," "Black man, bright nouveautes leave one, at best, pseudonymous./ Thus one is most disclosed when one is most anonymous." I take this to say that efforts to name, to give meaning to new substance, lead directly to pseudonymous identities. Moving below these is a particular, with the least attributes, that makes the deepest disclosure though it has the effect of the anonymous. The trip downward to the anonymous may require a path through disillusionment, a kind of basic ordeal of the reductive. The situation is defined in "The Man With the Blue Guitar" where we contemplate "That generation's dream, aviled/ In the mud, in Monday's dirty light/...the only dream they knew" (xxxiii). In that spirit the poet builds a redeeming principle. The song of the guitar is an un-singing really, as it invokes

> Time in its final block not time
>
> To come, a wrangling of two dreams.

> Here is the bread of time to come,
>
> Here is its actual stone...

The dream of time to come and the dream of the past may wrangle, both derelict in disillusionment, but in their wrangling there is the emergence of time in its final block, the bread and stone from which both dreams spring.

> ...The bread
> Will be our bread, the stone will be
>
> Our bed and we shall sleep by night.
> We shall forget by day, except
>
> The moments when we choose to play
> The imagined pine, the imagined jay.

Sleeping and forgetting are the surrounding dimensions of the song of the imagination, and its substance is mere bread and stone. The basic design suggests where the music begins and ends, but also that we *choose to play*, so redeeming both bread and stone. The poem suggests other choices, to run hysterically into the madness of space, to sleep and forget in an accepted solipsist dream, or to play the clown without reserve, ("He held the world upon his nose"), or to reduce meaning utterly to the bread and stone of time. In this context the guitar bears its poignant sound. "We choose to play"—and at that point everything else fades before the gift of the imagination. The redemptive act of poetry now functions for the "empty spirit in vacant space." Is it pure spirit that transcends vacancy and its own secular or earthly emptiness? We do not need and Stevens doesn't make such affirmations. The act of poetry is Cartesian evidence; I sing, therefore I am, and seek to fill space.

The object of poetic reduction is to find the start or end of the meaningful. At the border of nothingness, a realized "thing," firmly concrete, can have transcendental effect. In one emphasis the poetry of Stevens and Williams was conducted as if to discover consciousness where no consciousness was before, value where no value was felt before. The sense of being inhabitants of an empty universe provides important atmospherics in their work and that of Frost as well. As Tocqueville noted (and also Glauco Cambon, another perceptive foreign observer), the context is American.[1] The inverse of the same effect, made with the supreme confidence of another century, is found in Thoreau's obsessive search for reality, while undergoing a thorough demythologizing exercise to say, "this is, and no mistake." Stevens expressed himself in quite Thoreauvian terms in one of his letters when he described a project for himself in learning how to enjoy "mere being." He remembers a holiday at Miami Beach, "in an isolated spit by the sea, where it was as easy to enjoy mere being...as it was to breathe the air" (SLTR, 449). He often used "mere," "mere air," "mere weather," as if the word meant pure.

"Mere being" is a large quantity if it is the void that is being searched. This is the case for "The American Sublime," which tells us much on how to read Stevens. The protagonist, General Jackson, poses for his statue. The legendary rough rider in his artificial embodiment mocks the inept sublime, but carrying the mark of "barefoot" reality is still the American sublime. Posing for his statue, he knows how one feels, the diffidence within, the exposure to the "mickey mockers." But the mockery goes deeper, into "the landscape and all that," questioning the possible reality of "the place where one stands." One stands posing for one's statue, with an empty spirit in vacant space. The sublime may come down to the spirit itself in vacant space, but how? Where does one find the wine to drink, the bread to eat? Jackson is the poetic subject at the margin where spirit meets space, and where something must happen, as it may have happened long ago in the first creations of the sublime.

A Moral Realism[2]

In my view Stevens' primary expression of poetry's cultural importance remains "The Noble Rider and the Sound of Words." In that essay when he wrote of "the spirit of negation" he meant more than the specifics of cultural conflict and dissent but the spirit that negates prayer, desire, and poetry. Thus he could juxtapose negation against what he called the "romantic," which in typical ambivalence had become a term to describe valuation at its forlorn extreme of dissociated fantasy. For Stevens it was a term to be revived and appreciated.

In the context of naturalist thought to seek value or invent it, as characterized by the word "romantic," expressed an ineradicable need to live in the unreal world of grand fictions. Modern reality had become a hard "pressure" because it offered no compelling belief and indicated only "the absence of any authority, except force, operative or imminent," for the "sanctions that rule our lives"(NA, 17). He did not need to mention that like any other form of omnipotence, force could receive worship as well respect. Force in Stevens' language becomes the antonym of value; implicit in his mind was the distinction between value relationships and power relationships no matter how much they overlap. Value denotes an authority that springs from acts of the imagination, or poetic faith, and distinguishes itself sooner or later from the threat of force or the dictation of natural necessity. The "sanctions that rule lives" may use and express power, just as power may manipulate specific loyalties and beliefs, but the essence of the imaginative intelligence is to be able to distinguish. The pressure of the real world would blur the distinction or erase it. On the ultimate field of argument it was poetry (sanction and value) against power. We can estimate the large meaning of a poetics for Stevens in this context. It also suggests his politics if I might expand that word to follow where power can mean the "absence of any authority except force."

As Stevens saw the world when he delivered "The Noble Rider" in lecture, there was no questioning the authority of force, whether in actual war as Hitler and the Allies made war, or in class conflict, or in theories of economic power, or in the immediate evidence of the authority of the democratic mass. Reductive political thought meant the penetration of the superstructures of value to find their supporting force, implying of course reaction from an opposing force. We can interpret Stevens' words as follows: if value does not inhabit reality, or grow naturally from it, or be summoned to it by the imagination, then force backed by violence becomes the only driver of action. Unmasked reality is force, since inert matter is nothing, and the possibility remains that beyond the movements of energy, reality is void, meaningless.

It was indeed that possibility that motivated several of the manifestoes of the avant-garde; one must study the art theory of the early century to see the debate between force and value, as when Marinetti wrote in the Technical Manifesto of 1912 to attack "the poetry of the human." "We must drive man from literature and put matter in his place." The poetry of the human was the anthropocentric ("psychological" in Marinetti's term) poetry of the tradition, and the new art aspired to be in touch with the reality of matter and "absolute force."[2] Marinetti was no eccentric on the fringe of modern art. He expressed a war of great assumptions, whatever the ostensible targets, sentiment, lying, hypocrisy, Bouvardism and the bourgeoisie, a universal weak-mindedness that had come to stand for civilization itself.

Necessarily all this would have a link with political expression. The connection between Italian and Russian Futurism and the respective creeds of Fascism and Communism has been well supported, and Marinetti may have had the same relationship with Mussolini that Mayakovsky originally had with Lenin. At the same period of revolutionary upsurge there was the significant linkage between Russian Futurism and Russian Formalism.[3] The conjunction is important because the Formalists preached another alternative to the poetry of cosmic force. Thus to generalize for emphasis, "the poetry of the human," was beset from two sides. One was on behalf of deep reality, the actual force that underlies the human cultural artifact. The other supported the poetry of pure order, of non-mimetic form, and as Apollinaire described it, the art of absolute imagination, uncorrupted by hypothetical or actual commands from the "real" world.

Stevens marks himself most clearly in his opposition to these two extremes. He could agree with Marinetti that civilization was in fact nothing but the "poetry of the human". He could say in "Adagia," "Eventually an imaginary world is entirely without interest" (OP, 175). But in very close order he also would say, "Reality is a vacuum" (168). A vacuum of value, perhaps, for at the same time he was convinced that "reality is the spirit's true center" and "the great conquest is the conquest of reality" (177, 168). The debate is characteristic, but the issue between reality and the imagined world was simple enough. Without each other they lost shape and definition. The imagination, in itself, cannot create a world in which to live. On the other hand, it was necessary to struggle against reality's hard force.

To be both "with and against reality," what was it if not to *live* in the imagination? But that was conditioned by a very strong thought. "Reality is the footing from which we leap after what we do not have and on which everything depends." Perhaps the ambiguity was in his thought when he wrote, in "Adagia," one of the richest of his gnomic utterances. "Poetry must resist the intelligence almost successfully" (OP, 171). The intelligence he meant may be the reductive mind that wars against the imagination's work, though in the broader sense he must have meant that poetry resists analysis, and that an *almost* success is good enough to save it. "As the reason destroys, the poet must create" (OP, 164). But to desert the footing from which poets leap is to confess a separation from the world of reason while giving the world up to mere reason. "The great poem " he said, "is the disengaging of (a) reality" (OP, 169). From what? From reductive reason, opaque substance, a destroying vacuum, a false and imprisoning abstraction, and at once and together, from what Stevens called "tainted romanticism." What he meant in expressing this precarious ground between the real and the imagined on which the true poet must stand was reflected in the words of Valéry. "The real, in its pure state, stops the heart....the universe cannot for one instance endure to be only what it is."[3] What stops the heart is the commonplace human world in its familiar ways as seen against the setting of empty space, unlivable, beyond instruments of the mind. Poetry was always in this sense the effort to restart the heart and rescue the sensibility. It was a base for inspiration. "...Poetry/ Exceeding music must take the place/ Of empty heaven and its hymns, / Ourselves in poetry must take their place."

The genius of poetry is a power that dominates life, Stevens wrote, even while completely aware that life was encircled by forces that resist mastery. This was the superior appeal of the arts in the age of naturalism. The music of poetry was "not merely verbal music, but the rhythms and tones of human feeling" (OP, 245). It is this power that defines the esthetic of the human. But in this case the esthetic moves beyond itself and becomes "instances of esthetic ideas tantamount to moral ideas." The ambition for poetry is therefore tremendous because it amounts to the self-definition of the human. "It comes to this that we use the same faculties when we write poetry that we use when we create gods or when we fix the bearing of men in reality"(OP, 216).

In "Academic Discourse at Havana," Stevens draws melancholy insight on a world defined by the decline of poetry's power.

> Life is an old casino in a park.
> The bills of the swans are flat upon the ground.
> A most desolate wind has chilled Rouge-Fatima
> And a grand decadence settles down like cold. (ii)

Above the casino, the cantina ends, the white moonlight silences the ever-faithful town. But a voice will not be stilled.

> But let the poet on his balcony
> Speak and the sleepers in their sleep shall move,
> Waken, and watch the moonlight on their floors.
> This may be benediction, sepulcher,
> And epitaph. It may, however, be
> An incantation....
> And the old casino likewise may define
> An infinite incantation of our selves
> In the grand decadence of the perished swans. (iv)

The lines express the poet-hero in Stevens' metaphysics of song. Above decadence, below cold moonlight, the song turns back to its source, not *in* the world but in ourselves, an "infinite incantation" of multiple selves in one poet.

> As part of nature he is part of us.
> His rarities are ours: may they be fit
> And reconcile us to our selves in those
> True reconcilings, dark, pacific words... (iv)

These are ideas of a poet in reaction to an age of disbelief. In Stevens' view the poet is dedicated to the satisfactions of belief, though not the doctrines of belief. There is an esthetic of belief which only a subtle understanding of it can propound. The primary belief, he would suggest, is that poetry serves great ends. "We must recognize this from the beginning so that it will affect everything we do" (246). He was even more purposeful on that scale in one of his letters.

> I think that the real trouble with poetry is that poets have no conception of the importance of the thing. Life without poetry is, in effect, life without a sanction. (SLTR, 299)

It was a phrase he liked to repeat and the negative helps his case. To imagine life without poetry is to conceive poetry's value. To imagine life without a sanction is to leave it sensibly dead. Indeed, Stevens was preparing to make grand assumptions for poetry when he said that in the age of *bassesse* we may be left without any sanctions except force. Sanctions are part of conscience and intelligence, and they have to be strong enough to resist either the anarchy or discipline of violence. The question Stevens would explore was the role of the poetic imagination in the *creation* of sanctions of value. For Stevens the *creative* center was not history and tradition, not biology and physics, nor the current environment and established culture. It takes poetry, as he thought of it, to touch the source of values apart from habits of obedience and the fear of punishment, and find pure discriminations arising from personal and immediate experience. The poetic imagination treats values as if they were new-born, becoming conscious as values and not something else. Since in its nature dogma is foreign to poetry old values return to the condition of hypotheses. They are supreme only as fictions, though that may be a difficult concept to maintain outside of poetry.

The culmination of this remarkable fervor was his plan with Henry Church to establish a chair in poetry at some distinguished university. This entailed what he called " a philosophy of poetry" and something like a creed. "There is no point to a chair of poetry unless poetry is a permanent value" (SLTR, 447). But it was obvious at this stage that the study of poetry was to be the study of value at its source. More than poetry was at stake, and he could not state the point of a crusade more clearly than he did a few years later in a letter to a student where he explicitly named the poet "the appreciatory creator of values and beliefs" (SLTR, 526).

The problem was that poetry, to take the place of empty heaven, must find substitute for the gods in "this (human) self."

> A substitute for all the gods:
> This self, not that gold self aloft,
>
> Alone, one's shadow magnified,
> Lord of the body, looking down,
> ....
> Alone, lord of the land and lord
>
> Of the men that live in the land, high lord.
> One's self and the mountains of one's land,
>
> Without shadows, without magnificence,
> The flesh, the bone, the dirt, the stone.

One marvels at the inspired presumption in that quiet voice. Here was biblical comfort and discomfort in Stevens' most serious and ennobling tone. Nothing lives without its shadow magnified, but the high lord of the land acknowledges flesh, bone, dirt, and stone. And he is alone. It is a curious ecstasy of the redemptively reductive spirit that lordship gains courage in the absence of magnificence. In "Repetitions of a Young Captain" he invokes a defense against the giant myths without body, abstractions, the incitements of war, the grand ideas.

> On a few words of what is real in the world
> I nourish myself. I defend myself against
> Whatever remains... (v)

In the world of imagination's theater, one character asks "secrete me from reality" and another hopes "that reality secrete itself." There in natural reality

> ...Green is the orator
> Of our passionate height. He wears a tufted green,
> And tosses green for those for whom green speaks. (vi)

This is Emersonian and Whitmanesque at a height in Stevens' own manner. We watch, however and an inspiration comes to the poet and his reader, a criticism of the aggrandizing selves and the many ranting selves that make a chaos.

Green is the costume, green is the illusion for anyone who likes green. Yet this is also the world of the myth-making great war where

> Millions of major men against their like
> Make more than thunder's rural rumbling. They make
> The giants that each one of them becomes
> In a calculated chaos... (iii)

But there may be redemption in the real and from such giants. The poem reverses the imagination's direction. "Secrete me from reality" is reversed by another appeal, as the poem ends.

> Secrete us in reality. It is there
> My orator. Let this giantness fall down
> And come to nothing. Let the rainy arcs
>
> And pathetic magnificences dry in the sky.
> Secrete us in reality. Discover a civil
> Nakedness in which to be,
>
> In which to bear with the exactest force
> The precisions of fate, nothing fobbed off, nor changed
> In a beau language without a drop of blood. (vi)

That is the added clarity; great fictions cost so much blood that the imagination itself can ask for a civil nakedness, a reductive truth, and the baring of myths and dreams makes for civility. This is not irony but a serious reversal of the traditional apology for myth. In a place beyond giant illusions, wielded by men against their like, in a "secreted," that is, a recognized reality, there is safety and recognition. In this sense the imperatives of the real are moral imperatives, and in this view modern poetry is "anti-poetic" on behalf of a greater realism than that of science, a moral realism. This may seem too large a jump to make, but I stress the poetic inspiration in such of his phrases as "a civil nakedness" and "nothing fobbed off" which communicate a necessary moral courage.

"An Abstraction Blooded"

As Stevens writes in "Notes Toward a Supreme Fiction," the fiction of poetries "must be abstract"; this, as I understand him, is not a redundancy since the fictive is always an abstraction from experience in some sense. It is not a contradiction but gives meaning to his stress on "reality," considered as the defense against abstraction working within the poem. In Stevens' view of the act of poetry, poems are exercises of perceived interdependence; the imagination adheres to reality, reality adheres to the imagination, or else both become "lost" in the nonsense of fantasy, or the blank sense of fact, or the alienated sense of abstract thought. Adherence is difficult, the marriage of these terms often perverse, and acutely subject to divorce. On the terms that Eliot wrote of Blake's honesty in regarding human nakedness, it became for Stevens a "civil nakedness" and his own theme to hunt out unaccommodated man, the "poor blind forked animal." The same theme finds Stevens writing one of the summary poems that suggest a significant dialogue between Eliot and himself.[5] "Mrs. Alfred Uruguay" presents a failed relationship as two partners of opposing need, the young man of "capable imagination," roughly dressed, who rides a horse, and the elegant lady who would strip herself of possessions and rides a mule in search of the real. They move up and down the mountain of the real without meeting as if it would forever be so.

In "Notes Toward a Supreme Fiction," a similarly obsessed lady of aspiration, called Nanzia Nunzio, approaches Ozymandias in the desert, a monument of ruined grandeur. "I am the spouse," she says, and then removes all her grand jewels and clothing.

> I am the woman stripped more nakedly
> Than nakedness, standing before an inflexible
> Order, saying I am the contemplated spouse.
>
> Speak to me that, which spoken, will array me
> In its own only precious ornament.
> Set on me the spirit's diamond coronal.
>
> Clothe me entire in the final filament,
> So that I tremble with such love so known
> And myself am precious for your perfecting. (II, viii)

This for Stevens may be the primordial act of poetry, nakedness demanding to become clothed in the spirit's passion. But Ozymandias, wise monument of poetry, puts her off as supplicant, as if he understood that she wanted to be clothed in a glory from outside herself, in the source offered by some ancient inflexible order." One reads and feels the suggestion of sly but deep irony directed at Eliot. The lady simulates a civilization decreating itself in order to challenge a god who has died. Clothe my nakedness, she begs. The answer is that of poetic faith.

> Then Ozymandias said the spouse, the bride
> Is never naked. A fictive covering
> Weaves always glistening from the heart and mind.

In his wisdom, Ozymandias transcends himself, greater as a ruin than in his former grandeur and "precious perfecting." In one of the "Adagia" Stevens says something equally provocative. "The mind that in heaven created the earth and the mind that on earth created heaven were, as it happened, one"(OP, 176). This is the imagination doing its work, creating the earth in order to have heaven. One reaches the place where poems begin.

There was a muddy centre before we breathed.
>   There was a myth before the myth began.
>   Venerable, articulate and complete.
>
>   From this the poem springs, that we live in a place
>   That is not our own and, much more, not ourselves (I, iv)

That margin reached in creative torment reminds us of another sentence from "Adagia." "The poet represents the mind in the act of defending us against itself" (OP, 174). In the later climactic passages of Stevens' great poem, Canon Aspirin is the protagonist of creation, roving between the imagination's angelic height and the earth's muddy center. He asks, what am I to believe, while the angel (not the necessary angel of earth) in his cloud, serenely gazing at "the violent abyss, / Plucks on his strings to pluck abysmal glory." Divided between himself and the angel, questioning the reality of both, ("Is it he or is it I that experience this?"), he still looks for a place of rest.

>   ...there is an hour
>   Filled with expressible bliss, in which I have
>
>   No need, /...
>
>   There is a month, a year, there is a time
>   In which majesty is a mirror of the self:
>   I have not but I am and as I am, I am.

The stoic resolution is another form of anchorage, as I am, I am—, in the search for a center. But in this proceeding one shouldn't forget the role of the guitar player, the Key West singer, and all such tune and word makers. In "Jumbo," the question is asked again, as if it had always a new answer. "Who was the musician..../ Who the transformer, himself transformed, ...

>   The companion in nothingness,
>   Loud, general, large, fat, soft
>   And wild and free, the secondary man,
>
>   Cloud—clown, blue painter, sun as horn,
>   Hill—scholar, man that never is,
>   The bad—bespoken lacker,
>
>   Ancestor of Narcissus, prince
>   Of the secondary men. There are no rocks
>   And stones, only this imager.

The secondary men are all men of mind, whose world has become and can only be composed of words and music. (Is "primary man" unreachable, beyond words, or is he finally "major man," the source of fecund imaginings?) These are the companions in nothingness who know each other through resemblances. The reality of rocks and stones descends and gives precedence to this imager, this lacker.

Yet to lack something is to begin to know it. The first unnamable idea must exist despite equivocation; "Say the weather, the mere weather, the mere air:/ An abstraction blooded, as a man by thought." A blooded abstraction is a marginal thought, passing into abstraction still "blooded" by reality (sometimes envisioned as "monster") bordering truth. Some of Stevens's strongest poems arise from this marginal place, offering a rich dramatic sense of death and its contribution to imagination's meanings. We have a sudden sharp vision of what "reality" must embrace, and what it loses when it vanishes at the edge of meaning. At the same time one realizes the redemptive work of the imagination, the sense in which it crosses over and *enters* reality and life. What is dealt with in existence are "potential seemings," experiences which are not yet artifacts of meaning, but which point to their origin and point to their ending. As "in the death of a soldier,"

> The more than human commonplace of blood,
> The breath that gushes upward and is gone,
>
> And another breath emerging out of death,
> That speaks for him such seemings as death gives.
> ("Description Without Place")

The ultimate challenge to "seeming" has to appear out of death itself, death being what it is. It is on this ground that the poet's task emerges as his commitment to seeming-being, in full realization.

The poet writing, the soldier dying, make an almost intolerable analogy, but yet nothing else will do in the "utmost will" for articulate speech. In "The Men That Are Falling" the poet is awake at night, without sleep, "beyond despair" and "staring steadily"

> At a head upon the pillow in the dark,
> More than sudarium, speaking the speech
>
> Of absolutes, bodiless, a head
> Thick-lipped from riot and rebellious cries,
>
> The head of one of the men that are falling, ...

Death awakes the speech of desire, and suggests what desiring means in a world of not-have, what "seeming" and "being" mean in a world about to vanish. Here then in an almighty seeming the imagination is finally at one with being. This is to provide the supreme fiction with its authentication. The clairvoyant state is one where the real world is given value, not value added on, but value at one with perception. In a state heightened by the intensity of both passion and perception, whereby the poet lives, the consciousness crosses over into being and this is the fullness of "realization." It is on this ground that Stevens speaks, as he sometimes does, of religion and poetry.

> Religion is dependent on faith. But aesthetics is independent of faith. The relative positions of the two might be reversed. It is possible to establish aesthetics in the individual mind as immeasurably a greater thing than religion. Its present state is the result of the difficulty of establishing it except in the individual mind. (OP, 166)

Implicit in these remarks is his own extension of faith to the esthetic communion that engages value with response, response with reality, a "whole amassing harmony." It is as if Stevens would ask, if the gods could incite faith why cannot the god-creating faculty have faith in itself? "It is the belief and not the god that counts," he wrote, and

> The final belief is to believe in a fiction, which you know to be a fiction, there being nothing else. The exquisite truth is to know that it is a fiction and that you believe in it willingly. (OP, 163)

This Jamesian thought is surely not meant as fanciful esthetics, however exquisite the pleasure, but how does one believe in a fiction? Is it because one believes in the believing, the poetry of belief? Again that is a self-indulgence, unless the verb participle, believing (and not substantive beliefs) presumes to be the higher truth because it is the irrefutable truth of a sensibility. If beliefs go on changing in the flux of poetries, no matter, the poetry incessantly reveals the larger truth of poetries, that is, that we live in a shared world of beliefs, creating and recreating our "natures" and our "realities."

There is a tautology here, but perhaps a necessary one. Being is intelligible, it *is* being *because* it is intelligible, reality supports the intelligence of being, there is no other reality. Early in the writing of *Harmonium* he writes the prologue of this theme. It again touches the margin of intelligible being with death mourned by a weeping woman.

> Pour the unhappiness out
> From your too bitter heart,
> Which grieving will not sweeten.
>
> Poison grows in this dark,
> It is in the water of tears
> Its black blooms rise.
>
> The magnificent cause of being,
> The imagination, the one reality
> In this imagined world
>
> Leaves you
> With him for whom no phantasy moves,
> And you are pierced by a death.
> ("Another Weeping Woman")

Death is the end of the imagination, and therefore the cause of inconsolable grief. Death, the mother of beauty, is also the mother of consciousness. "The one reality" of the imagination is sharpened by its ultimate negation. But there is a another paradoxical affirmation; "the one reality in this imagined world" is not the imagination itself but the imaginer, a weeping woman at a death, and left with that death as if it were the death of the imagined world. It is another expression of what I have called Steven's deep and lasting humanism, perhaps its ultimate positioning nearby an actual death.

What Stevens may have meant when he said," the ultimate value is reality" is this: faith is at issue not in considered doctrine but in the quickening percept, at the place in consciousness where the closest perception of the world reaches response. On the other hand if this leads to as many realities as there are poets (all imaginative persons are poets) that suggests a necessary pluralism. But the uniqueness of poetry is that it asks assent only to its act in being. "The poem is a nature created by the poet" (OP, 166). Can we have a nature independent of the minds perceiving it? But if nature is offered as a giant solipsism, many natures of many poets should be permitted to reflect nature as it is.

Literature then is the democracy of intelligent consciousness. It fills the world with sensible being, but does so on terms that are sharable, though not uniformly adoptable. The basis of civilization is the shared word which represents the shared world. Words are the intelligence of being. We are prepared to resolve all previous antinomies on the imagination's behalf by accepting that reality, as an angel, is inherently a moral figure. It comes to this in the end, Stevens' angels of poetry are also the angels of democracy at its deepest ground of psycho-ethical and philosophic evaluation. There a democratic community does not communicate on the level of doctrine or ideology, religious or secular, or under the supervision of infallible authority, but on the level of informal discourse, conversation, Platonic dialogue among individuals in images and words like poems for their sharable knowledge and power. That is true only in an ideal sense, of course, but that is what poetry can provide. There are in fact such high moments in the speeches of Lincoln and the poems of Whitman.[6]

Again, how does one transcend the limits of mind if existence in the mind is the only alternative to void? By the process of cumulative response implicit in the writing of poems, in the finding of what will suffice. "The poetic view of life is larger than any of its poems" (OP, 174). Just as an ideal democracy does not commit itself to constant images and fixed dogmas of belief, but rather to a process of consensus never terminated, never fixed, so does the poetry of belief. It is the imagination which sanctions freedom. But it must begin and end somewhere, be anchored in space and on the earth. That is where the "angels" appear and one must look for their appearance not in stones and dust, the air and winds, but in the human apparition and the sounds of words.

Postscript

As an afterthought and in conclusion for this chapter I feel the need to add a note here that has general application to the larger text. One of the challenges I faced in this writing was to show how poetry expresses politics while avoiding the obstacles that come with tendentious and simplified readings. The latter might be the result for example of attending, as in a previous distinction in poetry, the "monument" instead of the "man." Nor, obviously, is my thematic reading of selected poems intended as a final word of criticism or interpretation of the work of either Stevens and Williams and surely not that of Pound and Eliot. Nevertheless in the last few chapters of my book I find myself interpreting some of Stevens' poems as a master text for the relations between poetry and politics. With a series of remarkable insights, expressed in his poems, not in conceptualizing prose like mine, he produces informal doctrine for liberal and democratic humanism, or so I would argue in these four examples that embody central principles:

In the mind's "great poem of winter" there is a center that destruction only concentrates.

> ...More than the man, it is
> A man with the fury of a race of men,
> A light at the centre of many lights,
> A man at the centre of men.

To discover in the wars of the imagination" a man at the centre of men" is to affirm the source of inspiration, "a light at the centre of many lights", ... "within the ruined tenements of rose and ice," brief metaphors for the coming and passing of cultures. The two metaphors, I think, also represent perfectly what should be in the self-image of a truly multi-cultural society.

A motivation (in poetry and politics) is toward what Stevens called "the exhilaration of changes," the very spring of metaphor, as expressed in "The Motive for Metaphor," a shrinking from the "weight of primary noon, the ABC of being." The right condition is autumn or spring, the poem says, undefined and changing, as in autumn where "everything is half-dead," and in spring with its "half-colors of quarter- things." The snow zero of "The Snow Man" motivates change, the weather is there for a start and so is the quotidian. In the form of 'applied politics' there is not just tolerance but the strongest motivation for change.[6] The new is welcome particularly when the old and traditional appear where "everything is half-dead."

A major principle in the preceding pages is Stevens' view of the "tragic realist" as in *Esthetique du Mal* where the "'mortal no" forces the imagination's new beginning. This is tragic knowledge, the most serious knowledge, "as if the dialectic of no and yes were itself redemptive." The ability to endure and recover from failure and error is one feature of a self-redeeming humanism and *one* consequence is its welcome to "the exhilaration of changes. " But the deeper enlightenment is moral at the very center of the realm of "no." "It is in this solitude, /...../It is here, in this bad, that we reach/ the last purity of the knowledge of good." A sophisticated knowledge indeed for the democratic consciousness, but like poetry itself fruitful while possibly beyond adequate conceptual paraphrase.

As a particularly impressive text for my purposes Stevens writes in "Nudity in the Colonies," "Black man, bright nouveautes leave one, at best, pseudony-mous./ Thus one is most disclosed when one is most anonymous." I take this to say that efforts to name, to give meaning to new substance, lead directly to pseudonymous identities. Moving below these is a particular with the least attributes, that makes the deepest disclosure though it has the effect of the anonymous. The trip downward to the anonymous may require a path through disillusionment, a kind of basic ordeal of the reductive (democratic) mind. But here where the nude black man might be only a particle of humanity in his anonymity, it is the particular that best absorbs the universal. Moving below all pseudonymous identities (enlarged generalities or abstractions) is a par-ticular with the least attributes that makes the deepest disclosure though it has the effect of the anonymous.

Notes

1. Tocqueville, *Democracy in America*, p. 80. Glauco Cambon, *The Inclusive Flame*, (Bloomington: Indiana University Press, 1965), chapter 1.
2. *Selected Writings*, p. 87.
3. See *Russian Formalism, History, Doctrine,* Victor Erlich, ed. (The Hague, 1965).
4. Quoted by Frank Kermode, *Wallace Stevens* (Edinburgh and London, 1960), pp. 35, 38. As I write in my introduction I share much with Kermode in his fine reading of Stevens.
5. I have suggested a case to be made for an undercurrent quarrel with Eliot in Stevens' verse. It may be high comedy but it is plausible to imagine Stevens and Eliot arguing over the disposition of a "martyr's bones." If there were no issue between them why should Stevens wish to make "widows wince" in that early poem, "A High-Toned Old Christian Woman?" And why is not Stevens' "Sunday Morning" a tangential response to "Mr. Eliot's Sunday Morning Service"?
6. Much that I write in these two chapters, "The Necessary Angel of Reality" and "The Imagination as Value," does not inhabit the everyday working consciousness of democratic citizens any more than poetry is their favorite reading. I write for students and ideal readers and perhaps for an ideal democracy, and so must theorize and explain with illustration where it takes me.

14

The Dehumanization of Art

When the Spanish philosopher, Ortega y Gasset wrote his seminal essay on "The Dehumanization of Art" he was writing a theory of modern art that no doubt had influence on the mind of Stevens at the time he put down his own basic view of modern poetry in "The Noble Rider and the Sound of Words." What Ortega was feeling at his essay's inception during or shortly after the First World War may have its parallel with Stevens' mind in 1942.

They agreed on one basic theme, that art and poetry were undergoing "a pressure" from reality in violent manifestations beyond parallel in its effects upon art. As described by Stevens it was a failure in the relation between the imagination and reality: "The imagination loses vitality as it ceases to adhere to what is real"...and ...as we were traversing the whole heaven, the imagination lost its power to sustain us. It has the strength of reality or none at all."

Ortega in his essay implied a conflict between art and the capture of realism by other forces, science and technology in the pursuit of utility and wealth, and the general life of war and commerce. The effect he saw was the acute modern reaction toward a non-realist art which he described as a campaign against reality painted in human colors.

> Far from going more or less clumsily toward reality, the artist is seen going against it. He is brazenly set on deforming reality, shattering its human aspect, dehumanizing it.

True objectivists, realists, and even imagists shared in the dehumanizing project as if it were a cure for the primitive narcissism of the species, expressed in so many rich and satisfying anthropomorphic myths. Several modern generations were put into the position of regarding the known past with a kind of intellectual condescension. Reality was not reality while it carried the demeaning prejudices of homocentric illusion.

However, as Ortega revealed the matter, the modernist interest went far beyond the simple wish to correct the pathetic fallacy and thus know the "real" world. The battle against anthropomorphic vision became charged with antagonism.

> The question is not to paint something altogether different from a man, a house, a mountain, but to paint a man who resembles a man as little as possible; a house that preserves of a house exactly what is needed to reveal the metamorphosis....
>
> For the modern artist, aesthetic pleasure derives from such a triumph over human matter. That is why he has to drive home the victory by presenting in each case the strangled victim.[1]

In putting things so violently Ortega was presenting the "triumph" of naturalist realism as coming with a shock like saying that with God's absence or "death," man was dead, a point made more recently with vividness by Michel Foucault, and stated more humanely by Stevens as the loss of "confidence in the world," a confidence necessary for living in it. Certainly many of the avant-garde manifestoes in Ortega's time seemed to express the pleasure to be taken with strangled victims, atrocities of that sort. Ortega himself goes far in asking the question. "Why this desire to dehumanize? Why this disgust at living forms?"

> Should that enthusiasm for pure art be but a mask which conceals surfeit with art and hatred of it? But how...? Hatred of art is unlikely to develop as an isolated phenomenon; it goes hand in hand with hatred of science, hatred of State, hatred in sum of civilization as a whole. Is it conceivable that modern Western man bears a rankling grudge against his own historical essence?[2]

Certainly the last sentence persuades assent to its asking; the anti-humanism that seems connected with modernism (and post-modernism) can appear as a grudge against man's essence. Art that built a civilization could also imaginatively destroy one. To support the point, Ortega turns the question to its other side to see a radical ambivalence, the "disgust at seeing art mixed up with life" based on "respect for life and unwillingness to confuse it with art, so inferior a thing as art." Ortega knew of what he was speaking when he saw disgust and respect alternate in reaction to both life and art. The ambivalence on the larger canvas was expressed in apocalyptic moods of creation and destruction. The self-hatred of the species was only one effect of a great metaphysical disappointment.

To sum up Ortega's argument, modern art broke away from a traditional sensibility as if to see the world stripped of interpretation. Art as spirit without metaphysical attachment became a strange game, an esthetic played out on the field of the imagination, encircling itself and choosing to remain encircled. In contrast as Ortega made his point, the bourgeois artist of the late romantic century wanted to enhance his daily existence, wished to be human and that was all he wished. He betrayed his own anthropocentric interest by the banal investment controlling it. To break that complacency for the sake of "life" or "reality" was one gesture of opposition. But as the resources of naturalist reduction moved against the traditional means for interpreting life-reality, art had to regain its reason for existence. What would happen to art's magic priority when its fictions, whether realist or unrealist, became only fictions like all the others? Revulsion was aroused and deepened by the vulgar fictions used to control mass publics. Probably the rhetoric of politics and commerce did more than science or technology to alienate art from the pretension of mimesis. The acutely paradoxical result of realist goals, in either science or the quotidian life, was to de-realize (in Ortega's word) the imagination, and the issue of interest was how "de-realization" in the limbo world of alienated consciousness would accompany dehumanization, the loss of agency and stature for retrograde humanity.

De-realization was in the first place the product of the dissociation of mind and reality. As Ortega put the premise,

> We possess of reality, strictly speaking, nothing but the ideas we have succeeded in forming about it.... But an absolute distance always separates the idea from the thing...

And thus, as in modern art—

> we take the ideas for what they are—mere subjective patterns—and make them live as such...in short if we deliberately propose to "realize" our ideas—then we have dehumanized and, as it were, derealized them.[3]

Where "the thing" becomes separated from its idea the result must be its dehumanization, since all mimesis or "realization" bears the language of the human.

Ortega's words are most illuminating in a context where Prufrock and Sweeney dominate the human landscape, the first suffering his own de-realization, or mental exile, as the second becomes the object sign of dehumanization. Such terms come together briefly with the Prufrockian protagonist of "Portrait of a Lady"

> And I must borrow every changing shape
> To find expression....dance, dance
> Like a dancing bear,
> Cry like a parrot, chatter like an ape.
> Let us take the air, in a tobacco trance-

This is the true note of dissociation where a man, in sense of his own unreality, may borrow the shapes of animals, or else, take the trance of one or another drug. Oppositely one feels the distance or divorce so that what was dissociated must be contracted, the thing and its idea must become one, as Imagist doctrine and Williams would propose, or at least disown the traditional makeshifts of mimesis. In larger consequence facts, symbols, legends, narratives, even gestures and minor quotations, all became contracted into what Pound called "gists" (or winds from the Vortex) in the effort to bring full "realization" even to Pound's own extreme of monopolistic or imperial possession.

To view the work of Stevens and Williams we must invert Ortega's terms, or say that instead of accepting the distance between idea and thing they brought forth a new effort of "realization." In this they performed a distinguished service in stressing a counter-theme in modernism. Stevens could write, as if in sharp reversal, "...we seek\ Nothing beyond reality. Within it\ Everything..."

To use Ortega's language, instead of soaring they dived beneath, but they dived beneath the "poetical heights" not in order to leave realization behind but to restore it. It was not "anti-poetry" they sought but "the source of poetry."

Again to use Ortega's terms, realization was indeed and inevitably a process of humanization but both require, for Stevens, a dialectical or double consciousness. Readers of Stevens should keep in mind his words treating Verrocchio's horseman—"a form of such nobility that it has never ceased to magnify us in our own eyes"(NA, 8). That form haunts his verse, but the humanly invented figure of more than human size is essentially supported by the Chaplin clown, the monocled uncle, the fops and fantasists, the living ice cream emperor, and the dead Rosenbloom carried in mock cortege into the sky. The thing to say about the Stevens' hero is that he lives between the grotesque sublime and the grotesquely ordinary; he gains life from this ironic equation because the breach or distance is itself the basis of the "real" in life, though not perhaps in the precise sense that Ortega meant for "realization." It certainly could be the basis of *re*-humanization, a consideration that Ortega, with thought of Don Quixote, might accept. Comedy is the mark that one has known reality, pathos its confirmation. But that pathos in Stevens, the human pathos, is almost as articulate as Peter Quince, a gifted fool, at the clavier. One should note the surface similarity of Eliot's playing of Agamemnon against Sweeney. But that is a different irony, neither pathos nor comedy, with an important term missing between the non-human sublime and the sub-human debased. Those images contemplate each other but do not evolve.

Stevens' view of the "human pathos" strengthens in its affinity with Williams' human images. The "Poor Old Woman" with her plums exists at the nadir of the heroic imagination. But she surprises us with her intensity, so magnified with the taste of plums, so refined and clarified in that one "eternal moment in which we live." Finding that moment was Williams' project for poetry, and it is not only her moment that is memorable but ours as well in appreciating her existence. This is "realization" without doubt, and it rises beyond pathos in a world which might have implied question of her existence, or replaced it with a distancing abstraction, a "poor old woman."

It is true that Williams expressed a peculiarly salvationary statement on behalf of immediate existence, since like a reincarnate Whitman he assumed that the particular had universal value. In his later prose he spoke often of the artist *creating* the real world, but in his most compelling poetry it seems to be a matter of giving oneself up to it, as the old woman gives herself up to the savor of plums. Equally, the poet-persona gives himself up to her experience, and it is that empathy, more than the direct taste in her mouth, that the poem presents. This is true everywhere in Williams' verse; we have experience filtered through the senses of the poet, but not so much aware of him as we are of "things" brought to fusion with his consciousness. It is on that basis that we are willing to subordinate ideas; it is not to celebrate things, persons or a sensibility that his verse exists, but for a living "contact," and that offers the secret of its strong attraction.

Deconstructed Humanity

The poem is a "field of action" Williams wrote in his efforts to define "contact," the key word in his critical vocabulary which describes immediate experience. It is a word for response and joins subject and object, perceiver and thing or person more closely than any anthropomorphic metaphor. For Williams, as I have noted, that was an obsession which described how medicine supported the vocation of poetry. His passion to "gain entrance" to the "secret gardens of the self" contrasts significantly with the failure of "contact" for Prufrock or the protagonist of "Portrait of a Lady." To recall how Eliot once said that Pound's hell was meant for "other people," is to remember that alienation effect in his own verse as well, where being "other" is a universal effect. Gerontion and the depersonalized, multi-personed protagonist of "The Waste Land" are ultimately as inaccessible as the "Sybil of Cumae." So are Burbank, Sweeney, Cousin Nancy, Mme Sosostris, with no need to ask how much the poet wished to gain entrance into *their* "secret gardens of the self." It was Eliot's announced wish to forsake the personal, but he drew strong poetry from its absence and loss; as usual the negative is the source of his power. The immediacy of the person, or the lack of it, multiplies its importance precisely in the clarity of opposition between moral immediacy and alienated being.

Years ago at the height of Eliot's literary dominance F. R. Leavis (one major expositor of his work and critic contemporary) had written on the Quartets as sheltering "animosity against the human."[4]   Whether animosity is the right word may be uncertain but the anti-humanist strain (something deeper than a rejection of humanist ideas) in Eliot's work cannot fail notice today. Louis Menand, in his own recent study, emphasizes the debt to Futurism in the work of both Pound and Eliot, and describes the anti-humanist postures of Futurism and Vorticism in *Blast*. He points out that Pound made use of the machine metaphor in his Vortex because a machine makes a better analogy for the artist "precisely because it is inhuman."[5] Presumably it was desirable for its connotation of power but at its base was the same stark choice between animality and transcendence presented by Eliot. There was decided ambiguity in the use of the terms; in Pound's case the inhuman of mechanics and physics was preferred for the positive work of art, whereas the traits of the biological animal would serve negatively in a polemic and as an issue to attack cultural decadence. Of course the bias against Bleistein and Sweeney is transparent on those terms. Both Pound and Eliot used biological waste, disease and animality to define strangers and enemies that unmistakably anticipated the language of totalitarian racism.[6] How that language emerged in their poetry and their politics is a large question of modern history, but at its center is an "animosity against the human" against which ordinary secular life, on its own dehumanizing terms, had little resistance.

The theme becomes a springboard for studying the verse and thought of Stevens and Williams particularly in the aspect where their work was a challenge to Eliot's moral and literary ascendancy.[7] In the province of the imagination they shared the four poets faced a grave descent for humankind, and its common factor was what happens to human security under the attack of reductive or deconstructive reason. To repeat my theme at this juncture, modern poetry was haunted by the embarrassment of the pathetic fallacy, as well as the opposite threat of a dehumanized consciousness, intrinsic dangers in an age dominated by the intellectual standards of science and drawing favorite metaphors from the same source. Stevens' work shapes the contrast I would make, and he is most impressively a major poet because he understood the issue not only as the test but the inspiration of his poetry. He aimed to treat the intellectual danger with poetic means, confront the fallacy, and transform its pathos.

Directness can be a triumph. In defiance the human image penetrates nature, "celebrating the marriage of flesh and air," though it must end in the pathos of the human.

> This is how the wind shifts:
> Like the thoughts of an old human,
> ....
>
> The wind shifts like this:
> Like a human without illusions,
> ....
>
> Like humans approaching proudly,
> Like humans approaching angrily.
> This is how the wind shifts:
> Like a human, heavy and heavy,
> Who does not care.
> ("The Wind Shifts")

The "human" proposes an essential valuation, praise or blessing or heavy indifference. It is inclusive and inevitable as the sun.

> The sun, that brave man
> ....
> That brave man comes up
> From below and walks without meditation,
> That brave man.
>   ("The Brave Man,")

This defiant emphasis of the anthropocentric consciousness makes its powerful contrast with the force of Eliot's early verse, where Eliot contemplated Sweeney at his bath, or Bleistein underseas. Ethnic and racist prejudice even in their less extreme forms finds the universal stranger who always accompanies acculturated man. Culture, as I believe both Eliot and Pound used the term, became a word to lift the subject to a higher species identity, and I've called this a response to reductive naturalism. However, the four American poets I study were bred in the context of democratic doctrine that based universal moral equality and human rights upon the same unredeemed natural existence. This suggests a struggle with a moral necessity. The path to cultural or imaginative redemption became rigorous and conflictual, though intense in the energy we associate with classic literary modernism. Facing the crisis of the normative intelligence in its modern decadence, Stevens proposed (in his own reading of "Notes Toward a Supreme Fiction") that the incitement of the imagination depended on the freedom to aspire (like Canon Aspirin) even if only to reach "in the long run, a sense of nothingness, of nakedness.... But there is a supreme effort which it is inevitable he should make," that is, "if he is to elude human pathos, and fact...." in their finality and limitation.

It was on the same account of threatened "nakedness" that Pound and Eliot joined in their respective forms of escape from the human pathos, to make their respective ventures toward "a supreme fiction." Eliot's missionary essays on tradition and the beneficence of a class structure were efforts to bypass animality and its egalitarian fate of normless disorder. The depressing limitations of economic and democratic culture, brought to a modern pitch of development in America, could explain Pound's holistic esthetics and the devouring elitism that had its consequence in a reactionary political "fiction." He would say "There is no misanthropy in a thorough contempt for the mob. There is no respect for mankind save in respect for detached individuals" He acknowledged himself that his early scholarship in languages and literatures "keeps him (a poet) discontented with mediocrity."[8]   Such words declaring for an esthetic aristocracy confirm the search for the quotidian "malady," somehow to be transformed and reversed in the work of Williams. Stevens might have described Pound as the "old romantic," suffering from the romantic disease, but Williams wrote more vividly of his personal sense of the same alienating force, referring to Eliot and Pound as having the effect of reducing him to "somewhere low, among the reptiles, hidden in the underbrush, hearing the monkeys overhead" (WLTR, 312).

An alienation from the created species under the esthetic view could mark the difference between a "monument" and a man, that is, the difference between Malatesta's *Tempio*, which forms the inspiring theme of several Cantos, and Williams' Paterson where a city is personified as a man. In Pound the esthetic supersedes the ethical and in the strict sense takes the full normative function in the value added revelations of art. Whether conscious of itself or not, art could be hostile to the city Paterson as found, hostile to MacCullough, and it could take Canon Aspirin where he would not finally go. "What is divinity if it can come/ Only in silent shadows and in dreams?" is the question of Stevens' earliest major verse statement, "Sunday Morning." Or does it come only in "monuments," as found in culture and tradition?

It is fascinating to witness the debate between man and monument in the comparative study of Stevens' figure of Colleoni, the dominating statue in Venice, and Pound's view of Malatesta's architectural monument at Ravenna. But though he addresses nothing in stone, in Eliot's prose writing the "monument" is more sweeping and complete, including everything conscious and unconscious in the sense of history and traditional culture. This is as if to say that Hamlet and Polonius are much closer, more "real" to Prufrock than "the lonely men in shirt sleeves" inhabiting his street and the void. The parallel is found in Eliot's effort to depersonalize the artist creator. Inspiration itself is dependent on "a continual surrender of himself as he (the poet) is at the moment to something which is more valuable."[9] The accent on "surrender" is typical, and though it may be transfigured in the religious context the political implications are clear in the drafted edicts for art and poetry. The analogy surely is with the post-structuralist theory that claims to subordinate the personal author to something more valuable in the anthropological literary, political, and historical cultures within and behind language texts.

The contrasts with humanist and personalist values in the work of Williams and Stevens suggests that there is a confrontation in the historic sense among these four American poets. To recall the way Eliot distinguished protagonists in his poetry by quick pointed ethnic classifications, Sweeney the Irishman, Bleistein and Rachel Rabinovitch, the Jews, Hakagawa, a Japanese, amd Mme Von Kulp, of unmentionably complex origin, is to feel a powerful obsession. It breeds allusion everywhere so that even the pianist ("the latest Pole") in "Portrait of a Lady" distills his Polish essence through "his hair and finger-tips." Such classifications will have their authority when the personal subject retreats. In the long essay "Imperfect Critics" Eliot dominates the reader by speaking of the European intelligence or mind; what is negatively called "Eurocentric" today among embattled multi-culturalists was very much a salvationary matter to Eliot. The almost obsessive attention to the British, the French, the American in warning or commending subtitles, "A Note on the American Critic", "The French intelligence," all appear in the context of his attack on personhood and individuality in the criticism of art.

With "imperfect critics" the virtue exists in their group membership. "Every nation, every race, has not only its own creative, but its own critical turn of mind" (SW,47). Such secular abstractions of nation and race may have seemed the only refuge from the colder abstraction felt by individuals in the languages of industry, commerce and science. It may be that repelled by these classifications, Eliot's cultural conservatism was a maneuver to defend against constrictive forms much worse than the supposedly affective and humane English class hierarchy. The result was that Eliot turned to a secondary level of moral and spiritual relief, to cultural communities which could supply persons with ethical identities close to those of the traditional religious synthesis.

Culture became an obsession with Eliot in his own time because it could sublimate racial and national identities without destroying them and avoid the scientism of race and the destructive aggression of national states. Culture had at hand its traditional prophets and spokesmen in the arts and literature, so that the essence of culture could be transmitted in a cultural criticism of literature or a cultural poetics, which is in the end the best way of characterizing Eliot's approach to literature. Very much like current movements, the road was short to politics, since culture must be seen as the inclusive narrative and institutional expression of both politics and literature.

In his verse and criticism therefore Eliot was able to be both a pioneer and prophet of deconstructive literary modernism and the leader of a political, religious and cultural conservatism. For instance, in the face of his essay on tradition he seemed to endorse in his later essay on Blake "the eternal struggle of art against education, of the literary artist against the continuous deterioration of language." He attacked "the acquisitions of impersonal ideas which obscure what we really are and feel, what we really want, and what really excites our interest" ("Blake," SW,154). So stated, the individualist credo could have been produced by Williams. On the other side, however, as if reacting with revulsion from "what we really are," Eliot commented on "a certain meanness of culture " and "eccentricity of ideas" in Blake. Though Blake saw "man naked," he would leave him so, for what he lacked was "a framework of accepted and traditional ideas."

The sequence of ideas make a good portrait of Eliot's own dominant pattern of thinking. He deeply understood such "honesty" as Blake's and the condition of human nakedness. "Unaccommodated man" was the object of his own pursuit and in ultimate view he was in the same position as Stevens (and the poet writing "King Lear") in searching for the ground of human valuations. It should be noted how he and Stevens joined to bring literature to a unique role in modernity, as a recourse (after the supposed "death" of metaphysics) for the complex process of restoring the normative sensibility. Eliot's long polemic against humanism was in essence a protest challenging an inadequate defense against naturalistic nakedness.[10]

Notes

1.   Ortega y Gasset, pp. 21-23.
2.   Ibid., p. 45.
3.   Ibid., p. 37-38.
4.   See Christopher Ricks , *T.S. Eliot and Prejudice*, p. 207,for Leavis source.
5.   Menand, op. cit., p 144
6.   Anthony Julius's recent book on Eliot's anti-Semitism is fully documented and though his judgments may be disputed his evidence cannot be. One briefly treated but important insight reflects on the interchangeability of race and culture in Eliot's usage (*T.S. Eliot, Anti-Semitism, and Literary Form* [Cambridge: Cambridge University Press, 1995]).

7.   From Ellen Williams, *Harriet Monroe and the Poetry Renaissance,* pp. 95, 206.

8.   From C. David Heymann, *Ezra Pound: The Last Rower*, p. 10.

9.   "Tradition and the Individual Talent," *The Sacred Wood*, pp. 58, 52.

10.   A relevant note here is to say how accurately luminous Shakespeare's epithet "unaccommodated" is, and show well a poet can enter the field of cultural criticism or the life of man in culture   When dramatic literature (poetry, plays and fiction) presents the topic of "culture" for study the subject really is "the life of man naked or conflicted or accommodated *in* culture."

15

"The City as a Man"

As noted by Stevens there is much text for his outline of a poetics in the verse of Williams. Their friendship, both personal and literary, had its base in their ambition for poetry, their mutual agreement on its "importance," to use Stevens' word. If anything Williams' claim was stronger.

> On the poet devolves the most vital function of society: to recreate it—the collective world—in time of stress, in a new mode, fresh in every part, and so set the world working or dancing or murdering each other again, as it may be.[1]

His verse itself makes no such stated claim and as the words above suggest it is not a moral mission in the simpler sense, with good and bad set off from each other. Whether the world is set to murdering or dancing is a matter of relative and secondary judgment. Rather the world is set to discover itself in that rich field where the vital energies that create poetic value are stirred. Paradoxically the finality of moral judgment would throw a restraint, block a part of consciousness. In the "field of action" (for here consciousness and action do not seem apart) one gains a heterodox sense of values where opposites and subtypes flow into each other and become part of the vital whole.

An example of this transcendence of judgment can be found in "Pastoral," an early poem. The first stanza describes sparrows on the pavement, "quarreling/ with sharp voices/ over those things/ that interest them." The comparison is direct between "we who are wiser," who "shut ourselves in," and " no one knows/ whether we think good/ or evil." I read this as the important premise of the poem, we of the human order are shut in by its wisdom, whether for good or evil, which compares with the busy life of the sparrows for lack of vital interest. The second and last stanza simply offers a vignette of an old man who walks about gathering dog-lime in gutters. The humble action has purposeful meaning, demonstrating what it means to be shut in by higher terms, abstractions like "wisdom" or like those images of frustrated dreams drifting in the mind of Pound's Lady in her portrait. Though he walks without looking up and his occupation is the lowliest conceivable, yet "his tread/ is more majestic than/that of the Episcopal minister/ approaching the pulpit." "These things astonish me beyond words."

The reader, too, will ask where did this valuation come from? The poet is caught by surprise in his own reversal of norms. The energy of the poem is not in a hymn to the common and universal but rather in the push downward to the place where such an affirmative response might be most challenged. It either does or does not come, one might say, as if Williams were leaving it to others to make the discovery where it is not a matter of argument but a sudden epiphany. But how did the word "majestic" arrive? Why did the old man's tread arouse that response and how did the busyness of the sparrows join in? There are no words needed from the clergyman as a master of moral appreciations. By so much the minimal appreciations in the poem become transcendent. (One thinks of a tired Prufrock in that labor of distinguishing). This is affirmation in its simplest confidence, and the poet doesn't mind saying that it is kingly, perhaps "noble" in Stevens' sense. Of course the old man and the birds do not need to share this vision. The old man, in his tread, contains the latency for arousing such response, that is all that can be said, but it is a large amount for poetry.

One speculates whether Williams, if he had read Heidegger, would find Eliot guilty of the ontological sin, divorcing himself from the "poem of Being." In any case the following statement from Heidegger's "Letter on Humanism" can serve as an accurate gloss on Williams's struggle with Eliot:

> Thinking does not overcome metaphysics by climbing still higher, surmounting it, transcending it somehow or other; thinking overcomes metaphysics by climbing back down into the nearness of the nearest.[2]

Nearness measures distance from "Being" (or "experience" stripped of abstractions). For contrast Ezra Pound's large use of dominating terms like "culture" or "usury" must be "metaphysical" in Heidegger's primary meaning, though the latter had difficulty avoiding such terms himself when it came to his engagement with Nazi politics. If I understand Williams properly he is absolutely devoted to the "nearness of the nearest," and he would argue that Eliot's view of tradition, as well as all of Pound's belligerently abstract politics, needed either to be rejected or recreated in thought, but re-created on two counts. First, in the exercise of the free imagination, truly emancipated from the models of the past; second, in being inspired by closeness to such bare "reality" as exists in the form of a red wheelbarrow, for example. The key is immediacy, experience made accessible more in the styles of Thoreau and Whitman than Heidegger and Hölderlin, but with a special modern awareness of limitations on "confidence in the world."

For Williams it was not the sins of effete esthetics or the tired dreams of romanticism that made him expound reality. I would guess that much contemporary naturalist fiction must have frustrated him for its tendency to add quantities of documentation chiefly to illustrate political or neo-scientific abstractions. These were actually closer to Eliot's images of Bleistein, Rachel, and Sweeney that call up anthropological essences and ethnic stereotypes. Eliot's way to reduce abstraction was to oppose one essence against another, as Bleistein confronts Titian in Venice. The modes of poetry may confirm such orders of the abstract or choose to attack and dissolve their fixed shape.

Accordingly, and challenging all possible conceptions of the image, a poem like Stevens' "Thirteen Ways of Looking at a Blackbird" does its best to dismiss metaphoric essences, or rather, to multiply them until none is dominant and the sense of an authentic reading of "nearest" experience is achieved. I would describe Stevens' poem as quintessentially modern for in that poem we are at the intersecting moment where image and bird join each other in imaginative birth. The immediacies of perception in the poem give radiations of thought, but do not quite spell themselves out as thought. In a contrasting mode Williams pursues the immediate sensibility as if to its vanishing point bordering inarticulacy, as in "To a Poor Old Woman." The plain repetitions for woman and plum, "they taste good to her," transcend the effort to speak, beyond all metaphors, transcend sensation itself in the attempt to reach the primary sensibility. One could say for contrast that Pound and Eliot are generalists in poetry, accessible to essences traveling in time and seeking embodiment in words and images. The greatest departure from immediacy is a personification with all its political and cultural implications represented by Eliot's image of the 'jew' squatting on the window sill in "Gerontion," a vulture and a man, stressed as an abstract essence by the refusal of capitalization. The essential complexity of the effect in Eliot's poem, since the Jew, as an abstraction, clings to the image, is to double the strength on both sides, the generic Jew and the squatting bird of prey, and to obtain concept and image at the same time.[3]

In a curious, highly inventive sense, a collective memory speaks most strongly in "The Waste Land" and the *Cantos*, whereas in Williams' poetry memory seems to have no pertinence and is left behind. When the heroic past does appear, as in "To Mark Anthony in Heaven," it is brought down anachronistically to the poet's own immediate level: "Why did you follow\ that beloved body \....I hope it was because\ you knew her inch by inch\..." The only space dimension we know in the poem is that of "grass and clouds and trees" to join presence with "that beloved body" and with "Heaven." However, Eliot in particular presented historical and literary memory within the immediacy of experience and so brought memory into something much higher than pastiche, or imitation. Pound and Eliot convince us most when their open or hidden protagonists form a living dialogue with cultural memory. It is thus that their poetry is of a piece with their prose politics and cultural manifestoes.

The notion occurs that one might usefully recite "The Emperor of Ice Cream" in immediate response to reading "Hugh Selwyn Mauberley" or "Gerontion," those fragments stored against our ruins. Nothing could better reveal an important contrast in vision and temperament. Pound writes with offhand bitterness that Sappho would not tolerate the pianola, but it is a significant point that Stevens, in his poem, might easily have used it as proper background for the "roller of big cigars." The contrast in poetic paradigms would be even stronger in the work of Williams. The sharpest issue for Williams might focus on Eliot's lines in "Preludes," forming "a vision of the street/ As the street hardly understands." Williams produced his own vision of the street in *Paterson*, which in an early stage of inspiration he wrote as a specific answer to "The Waste Land." Like others at the time he read the latter poem most directly as civilization's apocalypse in the modern city. He knew of course that Eliot's later conversion cited the dependency of any society and culture on religious belief, in other words, if no God in the city, then only "the conscience of a blackened street/ impatient to assume the world."

In response Williams accepted the subject of an averagely dismal modern city, and brought its "conscience" to focus; as he wrote Robert McAlmon when he had already produced about one hundred pages, "Paterson (is) an account, a psychological-social panorama of a city treated as if it were a man, the man Paterson" (WLTR, 216). It was at least implicit that this was to be an epic effort to retake human possession. The city knows its "foulness" completely, but to say with Williams that Paterson is a man is to suggest that the human identity is the last term of reference and that "man" was irreducible to anything below or beyond himself. The religiously apocalyptic poet might believe that the city could be wiped out with "De Bailhache, Fresca, Mrs. Cammel," and "whirled /Beyond the circuit of the shuddering Bear/ In fractured atoms." Such destruction could be invited if the city were *not* a "man," or if it were condemned, like Sodom, under the power and justice of God. (To pursue comparison, the "jew" in Gerontion has had everything done to him to subtract his humanity and eject him from the "city" of man.)

As though by instinct *Paterson* was written to ward off the cultural apocalypse. It is a question of where the city lives, or how it is known—in religion or politics, in demonologies and ideologies, in spirit or matter, or rather than these, with the simplest direct report Williams could conceive, made out of himself, as local as can be, and yet in the most concrete universal sense of the word, " a man." One receives Williams' own conscious inspiration in the anecdote of the unfulfilled poet who writes letters to the author, charging him to give her as well as the city a voice and a language. It is a mistake to think of Williams as an "objectivist," with all that the word usually implies. "To copy nature is a spineless activity," he wrote (WLTR, 297). He wanted more than "a sense of our mere existence" among objects, and he writes everywhere as if there were an engagement with person and thing like that expressed by the immersion of the man Paterson in his city. In other words the imagistic look of things in poems is an action of the operative sensibility, not an arrest in thought. It "involves the verb: we then ourselves become nature" (WLTR, 297). He is in *effect* the most anthropomorphic of poets.

This of course is an understanding perfectly in harmony with his thesis on the poetic voice. He does not urge a neutral voice, or something approximating the purged vocabulary of science, strict as he may be about "ideas" or "lateral sliding" emotions. The sound of his verse is unmistakably that of his speaking voice, and his natural phrasing was a response to the realism of "things." Voice was dramatic in the work of Eliot and Pound, a monologue or dialogue addressed to ideas as much as things. One might assume that natural phrasing, for Williams, was meant to be the voice of objectified reality, but rather the effect in his writing is that of embracing the world with a single consciousness, like the man/woman of the city Paterson. In a letter to Pound, written in 1932, he said he wanted to take away the artificial music of traditional verse, accented and rhymed, and find a natural music, and doing so, find, as he said, the man/woman in the reader as well as the writer.

> ...today the words we write, failing a patent music, have become the music itself.... This blasts out of existence forever all the puerilities of dum te dum versifiers and puts it up to the reader to be a man—if possible....Without the word (the man himself) the music (verse as we know it today) is only a melody of sounds. (WLTR,126)

Purged of all sentiment these words put the emphasis on Williams' poetic faith. He speaks in this passage of the need to believe and not soothe that need with mere sound. To believe is to be, and "to be a man," which translates as an individual and not a species. Even the generic "human" cannot replace its representation by the word "man" which requires individual reference. There is a necessary complication here where the ultimate particular, "*a* man," expresses the ultimate universal. To Williams the belief forced by poetry is one which passes through and despite abstraction, artifice, and solipsistic dream. It finds the thing and it finds the man and thus reunites the divided sensibility, which was the issue among the modern poets.

Poetry rejects the truly alienated mind; that was the motive of his own poetry, to retrieve lost experience behind the fog of intellectual consideration. Very early Williams confessed that motive to Pound, writing him in the letter quoted above.

> Confusion of thought is the worst devilment I have to suffer—as it must be the hell itself of all intelligence. Unbelief is impossible—merely because it is impossible, negation, futility, nothingness. (WLTR, 126)

Against "the big believing corporations" he would replace "belief" with "focus," a focus on self and world that has the driving power of an obsession.

Addressed to focus, clarity, sanity, Williams' poems are acts of perception so sharp and insistent that they become acts of affirmation. But the affirmation comes in the capacity for response. This is explicitly conveyed in that striking poem, "Death," which gives a clear reading of the detestability of things that have no response and give none. The dead body has become less than a thing, really, it has most surely become something upon which nothing depends. Wheelbarrows, cats, flowerpots, are things which sensible response can touch, but death is immutable and, in the deepest way, unreal. The corpse is a "bastard" and "liar," for here is a man no longer a man whose form and meaning can evoke only anger and shame.

It is a betrayed lover who speaks. The poet is earth's paramour, wedded to reality, Stevens proposed, and the implied sexual dynamics, the deep synesthetic engagement, does exactly characterize Williams' verse. A well-known and favored poem, "The Botticellian Trees," accomplishes the expansive sexual design. The vital force is expressed in language, song, and the movement of the trees. "The alphabet of the trees is fading in the song of the leaves" and in "letters that spelled winter." Behind the song are "The strict simple/ principles of/ straight branches." But in addition, in the final phase of the poem, those principles blossom into the shape of a woman.

> until the stript
> sentences
>
> move a woman's
> limbs under cloth
>
> and praise from secrecy
> quick with desire
>
> love's ascendancy
> in summer—

The lines express the surprisingly large representational ambitions of Williams' verse. "To Mark Anthony in Heaven" matches the scale to include epic history and the kind of literary allusion he rarely used. However, the usual movement of an allusion is reversed. It is the mythic or historic Antony who disappears into a most fleshly passionate man, even his sexual being might be described as of the pure quotidian where all the romantic tragedy is focused as well as on its base in vital experience. Antony's secular power, his empire an abstraction far enlarged from its elements, is forsaken for the hypnotic attraction in knowing Cleopatra's body, "inch by inch." The synesthetic movement is directly sexual, encompassing a deeper than mental recall of that famous love. "Why did you follow/ that beloved body/ with your ships at Actium?" is the question, and the answer comes in the distillation of vital energy at the border of meaning:

> you knew her inch by inch
> from slanting feet upward
> to the roots of her hair
> and down again and ...
> you saw her
> above the battle's fury—

For students of contrast few poems give more insight into these matters than Williams' "Portrait of a Lady" which immediately draws itself up beside Pound's *"Portrait d'une Femme"* and Eliot's "Portrait of a Lady." There is a formal resemblance, all three written as dramatic monologues, but the respective ladies occupy different worlds. Pound's poem begins with "Your mind," and William's with "Your thighs," and the contrast, obvious as it is, controls the deeper effects of the respective poems. Pound (and Eliot as well) draw portraits of cultural incoherence, a "Sargasso Sea" of allusions in the lady's mind, and a richly described disorientation of identity and being.

There is more personal disengagement in Eliot's own poem, where the "lady" seems to dissolve into a misty afternoon tea mood, a Chopin-bred melancholia which has no foothold in either an actual relationship with the poem's speaker or her own past life. It is a literary consciousness based on echoes, calling up "an atmosphere of Juliet's tomb" and "My buried life, and Paris in the Spring." In the long dreamlike interview with no respondent she declares at last,

> But what have I, but what have I, my friend,
> To give you, what can you receive from me?

The poem is a portrait of de-centered existence, an essay in effective and personal de-realization, in the way Ortega y Gasset would have put it, or an example of the search "for an interior made exterior" according to Stevens.

There is of course a good deal more that needs to be said for all three of these very strong poems. I find it both urgent and useful to dwell on them since their contrast suggests so much to illustrate the dramatic role of 'culture' in the art of three of my subjects. In Eliot's "Portrait of a Lady," for instance, a longer and richer treatment than either of the other two, the dense background of culture in its higher as well as quotidian sense surrounds the scene and the consciousness of both the Lady and her embarrassed visitor. Personal disengagement is stressed by the fact that it takes place in "an atmosphere of Juliet's tomb" and where the "latest Pole" has transmitted the Preludes "through his hair and fingertips." Culture in its highest respected sense is lowered to comic reduction in typical Eliot manner, but "So intimate this Chopin..." reverses quickly to her own emotions and desires within a life composed "so much of odds and ends," the used and useless detritus of a personal culture. The narrator responds in his own mind with a dull headache and a refrain, Let us take the air, in a tobacco trance, / Admire the monuments,/ Discuss the late events,/

Correct our watches by the public clocks/ Then sit for half an hour and drink our bocks."

These are images to express a thinness or emptiness in the exterior and interior existence. The vivid note for this is in "I shall sit here serving tea to friends." He takes his hat, makes no cowardly amends, and will return to his own distance in unreal life, "Reading the comics and the sporting page. / Particularly I remark/ An English countess goes upon the stage. / A Greek was murdered at a Polish dance, / Another bank defaulter has confessed."

 The poem breaks with the visitor's thought, "and what if she should die some afternoon.... Should die and leave me sitting pen in hand." As if the poet himself had been the "visitor," he is remembering with pen in hand, still frozen from the real and unreal world, with death as the only closure. This is indeed a successful poem from Eliot's early creation, his own best illustration of what can be meant by dissociation and alienation.

Pound's "Portrait d'une Femme" presents the surface of culture as in a mirror of cosmopolitan society at a place where one might expect to have gained perfect intellectual and esthetic control over raw experience. But at the start this is a place in her mind like "our Sargossa Sea," filled like floating seaweed with Ideas, old gossip, oddments of all things." The Lady is more sophisticated but less interesting than the figures of pathos presented by Eliot, who after all give a dramatic human expression of desire and loss. Pound's Lady is one of the powerful and successful in society. "Great minds have sought you—lacking someone else." "You richly pay" but with "strange gain" of a dilettante sort. The end is sharper and angrier than Eliot's story of a double failure of mind and development. "No! There is nothing! In the whole and all,/ Nothing that's quite your own." In that respect the poem forecasts what is suggested by "cultural poetics," a major topic in the last two chapters of my text. I might say that Pound's Lady is not a human protagonist (or one who a responds in the double sense of poet-persona and subject-person as in Eliot's poem) but a sign, a carrier of cultural vacuity and failure where the actual focus is an emphatically declared judgment made from a cultural or ideological distance.

With almost indecent haste Williams in his poem would seem to provide an answer to Eliot's Lady. It comes within a similar disorientation, a poem broken with exclamations, fragmentary tropes and allusions to elegant art- Watteau and Fragonard

> ...Agh! what
> sort of man was Fragonard?
> —as if that answered
> anything...

Though even fancier than the allusion to Chopin's Preludes in Eliot's poem, this confusion of mind and imagery has been invaded by passion, and Watteau's painted slipper hangs from the same startling and unreachable sky as the blossoming apple tree, which in turn has the same overwhelming immanence as the lady's thighs. But what is most memorable in Williams' poem amidst the questioning of consciousness is the unimpeachable impact of the lower senses, as he resolves the helpless reach of mind, memory and emotion with "the sand clings to my lips—" a desperate clinging as one might take from the blow of a fall, or from the mental oblivion and physical truth of a sexual embrace. The last note comes with contrasting but appropriate delicacy, "I said 'petals from an appletree'."

It may be observed that Williams reduces poetic consciousness to a record of that which is its ground and thriving source. The same process of deconstruction in the contrasting poems of Pound and Eliot achieves significant emotion but finds a personal and relational void. Their poems are poetry with the full weight of its "treasure," its decorative allusions, its exorbitant claims, and poetry which then reduces itself for pathos, and finds irony in the absent relation between high poetry and its subject. But with Williams the possible irony, the poetry and its source are blended and become present with force like a blow, Agh! The speaker renders twice before becoming the softer "Ah" as if voicing inarticulate passion and forcing lyric sensibility to its physical source until he can state emotion with the contracted Imagist verse, "petals from an appletree."

In " A Sort of Song," Williams writes of saxifrage, the flower that splits the rock. The deeper thrust of analogy in the poem is to a snake waiting under weeds to strike.

> Let the snake wait under
> his weed
> and the writing
> be of words, slow and quick, sharp
> to strike....
>
> —through metaphor to reconcile
> the people and the stones.

This is the same poem that recites the formula, "no ideas but in things." But even like a snake striking and flowers that do violence to mere stones, things are no longer merely things; in vital possession the people and stones might be reconciled. The poet would be at the actual place of discovery, not a message carrier but the primal order maker. In reading Williams one sees an effort for empathic absorption as strong or stronger than the Whitman surge. He thought of this at times in a religious way, as he observed to Marianne Moore, who had noticed "an inner security" of some sort in his verse. He called it a "resignation to existence," the product of a youthful experience of despair, where "Things (had) no names for me and places no significance. As a reward for this anonymity I feel as much a part of things as trees and stones" (WLTR,

147). Anonymity as despair, despair as anonymity, are reversed to bring sub-mergence in total relationship, "a part of things."

What he meant by suffering from the loss of connection to names and places was illustrated by the enemy he found in the cultural establishment. It became fixed in his mind and in his poetry to resist the false trails followed by Eliot and Pound who were too full of "names and places." In a letter to James Laughlin, Williams declared that he would write *Paterson* in attack or defense against "those principles of knowledge and culture which the universities and their cripples have cloistered and made a cult;" he would make "the keg-cracking assault upon the cults and the kind of thought that destroyed Pound and made what it has made of Eliot" (WCWLtrs, 214). It is clear that he meant organized culture with its codes and cults, where the bigotries of secondary value systems, the order of established languages and prosodies, kings and bishops, old and new classicists, and spiritual translators like Pound all became targets for him. In the same letter to Laughlin he wrote, "If Stevens speaks of *Parts of a World*, this is definitely Parts of a Greater World—a looser, wider world where "order" is a servant not a master. Order is what is discovered after the fact, not a little piss pot for us all to urinate into- and call ourselves satisfied."

With that accent Williams was anything but a literary theorist, but it could be said he was a deconstructionist before his time, though of a special Ameri-can school that followed Dewey better than Derrida, to use a contrast made important by Richard Rorty. Williams wrote in another letter "art has nothing to do with metaphysics—I am aiming at the very core of the whole matter." By metaphysics one must assume he understood the meaning it has today in post-Heideggerian thought, that is, essentialist or foundational systems of thought that mediate consciousness and block access to immediate experience. How-ever, one need not grope for his meaning among philosophers for in the last analysis it can be referred to his poems.

A passage previously quoted from his autobiography gives as close a state-ment as Williams could make of his own inspiration. Williams remembers the schoolmates of his childhood, other "really vicious bits of childhood" now "dead of their excesses." These allusions, "vicious," "dead," were authenticat-ing marks of their presence to him. "They were there, living before me, and I lived beside them, associated with them....The thing, the thing, of which I am in chase. The thing I cannot quite name was there then. My writing...will not let me stop..."[4]

This is as if Williams were describing the birth of consciousness in himself. As the seeded source of Williams' coherent project in poetry it means to pen-etrate pose, dogma, and abstraction to acknowledge the "presence" or "face" of the "Other" in the high exposure described by Emmanuel Levinas, a phenomenologist who could be called a revisionist disciple of Heidegger and an increasingly important member of the "post-structuralist" school of French thinkers. "This immediacy, the thing, as I went on writing, living as I could," is the groping but intense language of Williams to describe something which renders what Levinas would call moral immanence. As poet-physician Williams knew the "face of the Other" very much in the way described by Levinas, "...the nakedness and destitution of the expression as such, that is to say extreme exposure, defenceless, vulnerability itself..."[5]

The best examples of that centralizing commitment relate directly to the moral and professional harmony between physician and poet. In "Complaint" it is past midnight in winter, and in the cold and snow the doctor is being called to the bedside of a woman in labor. "They call me and I go." he says, in stoic "complaint." "A great woman" is on her side in bed, vomiting. She is having her tenth child and the doctor greets this thought with "Joy! Joy!" At first this is ironic celebration but as the poem develops it mingles with something else. He evokes the night of lovers, "night is a room darkened for lovers"; and now the sun has sent "one gold needle" through the jalousies of their room. The scene does not encourage such associations, but the sunlight is insistent, enlarging consciousness. Joy is a complicated emotion, then, much the more so as the poem ends. "I pick the hair from her eyes/ and watch her misery/ with compassion."

The poem is a text on how much can be done with misery. Joy is in it for the brutal truth, the physical scene, the hopeless fecundity of the woman, the universal sexuality of the night and the sun, and for the simple inclusive response that can fuse with any of these without concealing their ugliness or beauty. It is not an intellectual or psychic complexity that is being presented; rather it is the poet expressing himself at one with "everything we are," a fusion of experience rarely achieved and close to that "sort of nameless religious experience" he described in his letter to Marianne Moore.

Notes

1. "Caviar and Bread Again" (WSE,103).
2. *Basic Writings*, p.231.
3. It might be described as a flight from allegory toward image and symbol and from there to the immediacy of person, living creature, or thing. Both Williams and Stevens carried the process as far as they could. A reader like myself might be accused of transforming the "blackbird" or "the red wheelbarrow" into symbols or signs possibly named "the real thing," or representing an abstraction named "reality." But before the critic's abstractions are expressed he is receiving an experience he is trying to describe or define. Such a sin against the immediacy of Williams' poem would be to insert thoughts about democracy, or a theory of its humanism into the reading text. The immediacy of art or imaginative experience is always resistant, even hostile to such "wisdom," which belongs to critical argument. My simplest answer at the moment is that poetry contains wisdom and is a form of subtle and complex thought which demands interpretation and inevitably receives it.
4. *Autobiography*, pp.288-89.
5. Levinas, "Ethics as First Philosophy," p. 83. Levinas is one of the least celebrated and most significant of French post-structuralist thinkers who came under the influence of Heidegger.

16

"A Peculiar Majesty"

The "Naked Man" and "Tallest Hero"

However boldly Williams pronounced himself in favor of the immediacy of "things," Stevens does not pour himself into experience in the same way. It is not he or the poem's speaker who is engulfed, it cannot be, for the poem is a demonstration of style, a way of bearing oneself in reality. He made this his strong point in the important essay published in *Opus Posthumous*, entitled "Two or Three Ideas." Though the gods were "esthetic projections," Stevens wrote, as images they reflected the "fundamental glory" of the men who imagined them. That is the nub, that the imaginations of men—alone in the universe and left there "to resolve life and the world on (their) own terms—shared in the divinity of their created gods. In this view almost everything Stevens wrote was a "re-humanization," resolving life and the world on human terms.

An intriguing aspect of Steven's mind is his use of the rabbi figure in his poetry, a pattern he was aware of and addressed himself to in his letters. He wrote to a correspondent in 1952,

> I have never referred to rabbis as religious figures but always as scholars. When I was a boy I was brought up to think that rabbis were men who spent their time getting wisdom. And I rather think that that is true. One doesn't feel the same way, for instance, about priests or about a Protestant pastor, who are almost exclusively religious figures... (SLTR, 751)

This was a significant effort to extract from religion its capacity for "wisdom" without being absorbed or encumbered by traditional religious and metaphysical narratives. The view from his side, I believe, might be disputed by rabbis, but Stevens reflects a sense of the way Judaism is a religion for living on this earth, addressed to a given people and circumstance, with a redemptive interest in everyday life.[1]

It is not that Stevens begins his thought with a strong sentiment on behalf of humanity, advanced in a world that lacked objects of piety. A clue to his mind can be found in that his testament on poetry makes use the word "noble" as if it might replace "beauty" or the "beautiful."[2] When Stevens was quite young and courting Elsie Moll, he wrote her an important letter that pointed the direction of his mind as a poet. From the French, he says, he was learning that "The torment in the man of thought is to aspire toward Beauty, without ever having a fixed or definite standard of beauty." This was a sentence for his journal, he said, to which he added words from Hamlet: "What a piece of work is man! how noble in reason! how infinite in faculty!" He went on to explain something fundamental for himself.

> ... I have lately had a sudden conception of the true nobility of men and women. It is well enough to say that they walk like chickens, or look like monkeys, except when they are fat and look like hippopotamuses. But the zoological point of view is not a happy one; and merely from the desire to think well of men and women I have suddenly seen the very elementary truth (which I had *never* seen before) that their nobility does not lie in what they look like but in what they endure and in the manner in which they endure it. For instance, everybody except a child appreciates that "things are not what they seem"; and that the result of disillusion might be fatal to content, if it were not for courage, goodwill and the like. The mind is the Arena of Life. Men and women must be judged, to be judged truly, by the valor of their spirits, by their conquest of the natural being, and by their victories in philosophy. I feel as if I had made a long step in advance: as if I had discovered for myself why Life is called noble, and why people set a value on it, abstractly.(SLTR,143-44)

The text suggests that the young poet was ready for the themes of his career. The important orientation is clear; the nobility of life lies not in beauty or any other excellent gift or faculty, but in valor of spirit, If men walk like chickens and look like hippos, that would be "the zoological point of view," which cannot hold. The "victory in philosophy" can only mean the "conquest of the natural being" or a victory over reductive thought. It is not that accurate knowledge or wisdom is overcome, but rather that it need not extend harm to the valor of spirit.

Readers will not question how readily the following remark from a letter written in mature life, as much as twenty years later, conforms to the achieved poetry as well as the formed character of the poet.

> The exaltation of human nature should take the place of its abasement. Perhaps I ought to say, the sense of its exaltation should take the place of its abasement. (SLTR, 295)

Written as this was in 1935 the principle, not a sentiment, can be carried to the time he wrote "Notes Towards a Supreme Fiction," and proposed "major man," as his universal protagonist. This was the supreme fiction over all, the one most necessary. As he put it with ardor in a question,

> Is it one of the normal activities of humanity, in the solitude of reality and in the unworthy treatment of solitude, to create companions, a little colossal, as I have said, who...are...assumed to be full of the secret of things and who in any event bear in themselves even, if they do not always wear it, the peculiar majesty of mankind's sense of worth, neither too much nor too little? (OP,207-08)

The statue of Colleoni, "The Noble Rider" in Venice, was much more than a little colossal or majestic. But that was for contrast. On the ground of his own poetry the less heroic statue of General Jackson, in Washington, was enough, for behind it there was the unmistakably rough figure of Jackson himself, standing barefoot and perhaps abashed in posing. That was in fact a "peculiar majesty." "Everybody but a child appreciates that things are not what they seem," and to achieve the bearing of nobility today one must bear such chronic disillusionment with courage. In the words of his verse such courage invades the bare prison cell of the world, observes man's bare skeleton and watches that skeleton dance.

> ...the skeleton in the moonlight sings,
> Sings of an heroic world beyond the cell,
>
> No, not believing, but to make the cell
> A hero's world in which he is the hero.
> Man must become the hero of his world.
>
> The salty skeleton must dance because
> He must....
> ("Montrachet-le-Jardin")

The imagination's courage returns to sing at that starting point.

> The skeleton said it is a question of
> The naked man, the naked man as last
> And tallest hero...

The man skeleton dreaming wakes from that old dream, "To project the naked man in a state of fact, / As acutest virtue and ascetic trove."

That was the project he shared with Williams, the project of naked man in the state of fact, and from that taking ascetic reward from imagination's angel.

> As facts fall like rejuvenating rain,
> Fall down through nakedness to nakedness,
> To the auroral creature musing in the mind.
> So lightly does assurance come as the poem itself disappears,
> And yet what good were yesterday's devotions?
> I affirm and then at midnight the great cat
> Leaps quickly from the fireside and is gone.
> ("Monchrachet-le Jardin")

She leaps and vanishes, the great cat of the phenomenal world, and the auroral mind confronts its own eclipse. That is the truly ascetic trove of possible affirmations, but such vanishings beheld are the gift of poetry, while the "facts fall like rejuvenating rain."

Where then is the "naked man" and "tallest hero" that was promised? In a poem of related thinking Stevens illustrates quite precisely how the furthest reduction moves toward the "subtle centre" of existence.

> ...if one went to the moon,
> Or anywhere beyond, to a different element,
> One would be drowned in the air of difference,
> Incapable of belief, in the difference.
> And then returning from the moon....
> And naked of any illusion, in poverty,
> In the exactest poverty, if then
> One breathed the cold evening, the deepest inhalation
> Would come from that return to the subtle centre.
> ("Extracts From Addresses to the Academy of Fine Ideas," vii)

Around that center "naked of any illusion" there still hovers the figure of "major man," now found in "exactest poverty." Who is this hero? He is the giant in the weather, he who first breathes the cold evening and can capture the phenomenal cat, or can propound the "first idea." Such terms, "major man," "exactest poverty," and "the first idea," are indeed major terms for Stevens, introduced and defined with important poetic explication in "Notes Toward a Supreme Fiction," the poem to be read closely and studied by every committed reader of Stevens' work.

In that poem he writes for his chief protagonist, "But apotheosis is not the origin of the major man." He comes rather from nearby McCullough, "lounging by the sea." McCullough is not the "major," the unusual hero, but that particular man who exists always below or beyond the idea of him. Accurately seen, he must be stripped of description.

> ...Give him
> No names. Dismiss him from your images.
> The hot of him is purest in the heart.

It is not by an act of faith but in the immediacy of his being that one cries, "He is and may be but oh! he is, he is." Naked of names and images, he takes value from existence, he is there in his core of being and lives beyond high slogans and generalizations of belief. Abstraction thus purges itself. A humanism purifies itself, its ground hot in the heart.

Yet "major man" is the exponent of the idea of man, abler in the abstract than in the singular, "more fecund as principle than particle." He has become a belief, and as the poet goes on to say, he is "the heroic part of the commonal," commonal being the word to condition any idea of the hero. This, then, is an "inanimate, difficult image." Who is it? How to see it? I repeat a climactic passage from "Notes Toward a Supreme Fiction."

> What rabbi, grown furious with human wish,
> What chieftain, walking by himself, crying
> Most miserable, most victorious,
>
> Does not see these separate figures one by one,
> And yet see only one, in his old coat,
> His slouching pantaloons, beyond the town,

> Looking for what was, where it used to be?
> Cloudless the morning. It is he. The man
> In that old coat, those sagging pantaloons,
>
> It is of him, ephebe, to make, to confect
> The final elegance, not to console
> Nor sanctify, but plainly to propound.

Why should this Chaplinesque figure be candidate for major man and not MacCullough? MacCullough has been drawn with aggressive particularity, lounging by the sea, absorbed in its washes, held in his own breath. MacCullough refuses to generalize himself, to speak for anyone else. His apotheosis is in his immediate unread being. But the man in pantaloons has been caught in imaginative vision, and lends himself to it. He is beyond the town looking for what was, where it used to be. Presumably he remembers, he is a dreamer, he wishes for major man, and in doing so he becomes the right election himself. This candidate has the pathos, he is already beyond himself. Despite the ascetic view of the poem, dismissing sanctity and comfort, to propound this humble figure is better than consolation. Of him one confects, invents, he is major in incipience. Before him lies a final elegance, since all values, whatever their elegance, must refer to him, slouching in pantaloons.[3]

I believe that it is not only correct to call Stevens a humanist, his writing helps define what the term could mean in modern use. However, he rebelled against its application to himself, as probably he would have rejected any classification of belief. Perhaps he would have said it would be humanistic to reject an ideology of humanism. Nevertheless, as he wrote in a letter, "It is a habit of mind with me to be thinking of some substitute for religion."[4] In the same letter he said, "Humanism would be a natural substitute, but the more I see of humanism the less I like it." What it was he disliked must be guessed, though he refers to its trivialization in the respect given to human pleasure and comfort, ("a baseball game with all the beer signs and coca cola signs, etc."). At several points in his letters he speaks of the confusion of humanism with mere socialism, which reductively affirmed the *average* interest of the mass collective (SLTR, 377-78). Sentimental humility was not a part of his respect for "major man."[5]

In a letter to Jose Rodriguez Feo, Stevens insisted, "The major men about whom you ask are neither exponents of humanism nor Nietzschean shadows" (SLTR,485). In a later letter to the same correspondent he referred to "Paisant Chronicle," as a poem to answer Feo's question, "What are the major men?" (SLTR, 489). The poem begins with a modest definition of a faith, the race is brave, the race endures, and thus "the chronicle of humanity is the sum of paisant chronicles" But the "major man" is not that sum.

> The major men—
> That is different. They are characters beyond
> Reality, composed thereof. They are
> The fictive man created out of men.
> They are men but artificial men. They are
> Nothing in which it is not possible
> To believe, more than the casual hero, more
> Than Tartuffe as myth...

The distinction Stevens wished to make was in favor of a poetic concept. The poetic theme is fictive man, the image, an artificial sign, and a character *beyond* reality, though composed of its elements. It was a belief, but an unrestricted poetic belief, an imagined ideal of any sort, at home with Tartuffe as myth, but meaning more than Tartuffe or any figure. Major man is a fiction beyond satire or reduction, beyond the self-attack of hypocrisy and delusion. Humanism as a specific commitment was vulnerable as Tartuffe is vulnerable. What Stevens wished to clear up was the independent status of poetry, apart from doctrinal and empirical tests of validity. The imagined was itself to be respected, and it was to remain the imagined, that is, fictive. Ideologies, one might say, confuse the imagined and the real, insist, at times with a utopist's violence, that the imagined and the real must be forced to fuse or co-exist. Stevens' humanism was indeed a pure humanism, which to be the work of the imagination (or what Williams called the "source of poetry") must be kept free from a tyrannizing commitment to particular realities. But he seemed to understand that for the human to be human it must also be released from aggrandizing utopist ideals, or imaginative *forms*.[6] It is the imagination itself, in *activity*, which is human. "The funeral pomps of the race/ Are a multitude of individual pomps."

The ultimate unity is that of the limit as well as the source, of fate as well as possibility. "They shall know the heavenly fellowship of men that perish." That ground of imperfection is enough upon which to base imagined values, even freedom and equality, for the imagined takes priority not as given but as finding "what will suffice." For the specific humanist ideal Stevens wrote, "Not as a god but as a god might be." The "might be" is everything possible, but here and now. "Might be" is the emperor of ice cream. The *only* emperor, king of the melting world of phenomena, he triumphs over his vulnerability. He is also king of the human spirit buried in the mundane world, banal or childish, but the agent of intense desire. Paradoxically he is also the emperor of *being*, not seeming, the most real of realities although seen vanishing at the climax of his power.

One must say almost at once that the emperor as such rules in the imagination and does not vanish. When Stevens put forward the contrasting example of the "noble rider" of brass or stone, he expressed its value in terms of the corresponding sensibility, the immediacy is that of a communication. He called it "a form of such nobility that it has never ceased to magnify us in our own eyes" (NA, 8). Nothing states more simply what Stevens thought was the problem presented by the disequilibrium between imagination and reality. The function of the imagination is not to give pleasure chiefly. It is rather to search out the response to "reality" in corresponding minds, and doing so, point to ourselves as it points to an imagined self and as it points to a created thing. The form magnifies "us," and a dialogue persists between "it" and "us." Whatever the particular features of Verrocchio's statue, it has established an audience with "a style of bearing themselves in reality." They do not make a copy or act like the Renaissance warrior, Colleoni. But in imagining him they imagine themselves; they exist at the contact point of the imagined and the real. The "noble" serves as an irreducible value term and Stevens matched poetry against reductive styles of thought that erased or inverted its measure.

> There is no element more conspicuously absent from contemporary poetry than nobility. There is no element that poets have sought after, more curiously and more piously, certain of its obscure existence. (NA, 35)

The hierarchical term in Stevens' language of poetic value is "noble" instead of something else because it points to character and is a human trait first of all. More than beauty it suggests an action, a process continued beyond itself where things are transformed in value. Values are never static nor superficial. They cannot be accessory or ornamental, and if they assert themselves as style, it is a style which permeates being.

> Style is not something applied. It is something inherent, something that permeates. It is of the nature of that in which it is found, whether the poem, the manner of a god, the bearing of a man. It is not a dress. It may be said to be a voice that is inevitable. A man has no choice about his style. When he says I am my style the truth reminds him that it his style that is himself. (OP, 210)

With the key phrase, "the bearing of a man," style now communicates as an existential reality. Bearing or style are terms to suggest the mysterious union of the imagined and the real, a part of predestined being.

Yet style is created, not given. The poet knows for instance that all gods are created in the image of their creators, and "he sees in these circumstances the operation of a style as a basic law."

> He observes the uniform enhancement of all things within the category of the imagination. He sees, in the struggle between the perfectible and the imperfectible, how the perfectible prevails, even though it falls short of perfection. (OP, 211)

In this meaning a style is impelled toward the normative, or the sense of the perfectible. The word has large not narrow application, and it comes close to what Williams meant by a favorite term, "measure." It is not so much a fixed standard as a capacity to measure things according to their value, to *discover* their value. In other words the imagination is never neutral, it always draws a comparison between images and words and things. Between better and worse it engages the sense of a value.

It is true that the style of the noble can easily suggest a Nietzschean standard, or the Pound—like vision of the warrior—artist. This is implicit in the choice of Verrocchio's Colleoni to represent the noble. To distinguish between the esthetics of order and the ethics of style is not easy. But here we are on the main ground of modernism, where art and fatal history converge. Most accessibly Hemingway, to Stevens, illustrated the noble as power, (as beauty was power for Pound), which creates order in violent reality. It is the esthetic of style, translated from a stoic bearing. But this style or bearing subordinates itself to its own conditions. It takes the features of violence, grants its own subjection to death in its power to inflict it or endure it, leaves no alternative to the desperate gestures of the hero. That style ultimately resembles that of the martyr, and is closer to Eliot than to Stevens.

A humane sanity in Stevens is observable in the distinction he makes between the actual and the imagined. But his use of the word "bearing" to translate style implies an accompanying reality that has not been obliterated. Style belongs to persons, not the world, but neither has the world remained untouched insofar as people live in it, or as it can enter their style. Stevens can refuse the absorption of man into hero which includes the fatal reduction of the man fallen from the hero, as well as the destruction and chaos that ends all gestures. In the presence of the gods or chaos, and in command of both as the poet writes, we move into the presence of ourselves, "as we wish to be."

Perhaps the imagination is the most beneficent of "angels" afer all. In "Adagia" Stevens declared what he would never surrender. "We live in the mind," and "the mind is the most powerful thing in the world," that same mind that "will never be satisfied" (OP,164,162). Such power is greatest in "The Idea of Order at Key West." Here there is the singer and the sea, two separate entities, as we seem to hear them. The song becomes transcendent for that separation and brings our preference; "It was she and not the sea we heard," and the song and its words are "of ourselves and of our origins." It is not solipsist song, though it is the song of ourselves, and the singer is ordering words of the sea, of the "fragrant portals." Portals to what, one wonders. To ourselves, to poetry, to the only sea we know, beyond mere "heaving sound"? There is an event, a thing, a body beyond her voice, and that thrilling certainty is in her song. She believes and sings for her belief in that from which all songs arise. Whether it is called mind or "sea" is no longer of fundamental consequence.

Notes

1.   A year later Stevens repeated this point with emphasis: "Frankly, the figure of the rabbi has always been an exceedingly attractive one to me because it is the figure of man devoted in the extreme to scholarship and at the same time making some use of it for human purposes" (SLTR, 786).

It is not my wish to make Stevens a champion of philo-Semitism. However, a contrast of the rabbi with Eliot's figure of the subhuman Bleistein points to a crucial difference not so much in specific prejudice as in a readiness to engage with "human purposes." In that sense I hazard the judgment that for Stevens Judaism was the more frankly homocentric of religions, and therefore more able to maintain the human interest after a forced retreat from metaphysics, or a disputed sphere of divinity.

2. *The Necessary Angel*, p. 12. "What I have said up to this point amounts to this: that the idea of nobility exists in art today only in degenerate forms or in a much diminished state, if , in fact, it exists at all or otherwise than on sufferance; that this is due to failure in the relation between the imagination and reality. I should like now to add that this failure is due, in turn, to the pressure of reality."

3. One should note promptly that in this aspect, a political theme that I have proposed stressing is indicated lightly in the word "commonal." A man of the masses, one of the democratic average, is the candidate for "major man"? Not exactly, but it is of him to "confect the final elegance" and most humble in his elegance, the latter word speaks for the ironies that play around the fictive creations and appreciations that must follow. Stevens has conducted the difficult and subtle task of defining a democratic humanism with a necessary bottom faith, or rather, an appreciation, and perhaps in his meaning a part of "the first idea" that followed from the " muddy centre before we breathed."

4. SLTR,348. The general point on humanism, poetry, and religion of course brings Eliot to mind, and Stevens makes the reference himself in his letter. The vigor of Eliot's attack on the Arnoldian position and that of Babbitt must have influenced Stevens in his own remarks on the subject. That he felt himself deeply opposed to Eliot seems clear in the context, though he does not debate him directly.

5. Frank Doggett aptly quotes one wry comment from Stevens' letters: "The chief defect of humanism is that it concerns human beings. Between humanism and something else, it might be possible to create an acceptable fiction" (WSLTRS, 449). That problematic "something else" would reject idealized fictions of "major man," which together with notions of the man-god become a defect of typical humanism. The acceptable fiction may point to "'the leaner being' moving in on the MacCullough-leaner because it is a more modest conception" (*Wallace Stevens: The Making of the Poem* [Baltimore, MD: The Johns Hopkins University Press, 1980], p. 100). This is very sound though the upshot may be that for Stevens humanism is not a faith or ideology but an imaginative search for the lodestone of appreciations and sympathy. The warrant is not for a completed or "supreme" fiction but poetry, or such fictions in the process of making. The justification of humanism lies in that process. This is one reason that I choose to refer to a democratic humanism, though Stevens never uses the term. The process is embodied in the commitment to free choice (election) and evolving forms.

17

The Sign and Presence of the Human

When Stevens began to plan in later life with his wealthy friend Henry Church to found a chair of poetry at a great university he must have felt that he had already written notes for a theory of poetry to be taught from that same chair. It did not need to be *his* theory, demonstrated by his mention in his letters that Eliot, or someone like him, would be the ideal candidate for the professoriat. Of course poetry was more than poetry, it was the normative imagination at its base, creating "the sanctions that are the order of our lives," which also indicates he may have recognized that Eliot's view of poetry, or literary culture, had the same broad reach as his own. But perhaps with sly irony he also understood that Eliot's thinking for how poetry should be read and written was the contrast with his own.

His extended correspondence with Church on the subject proves Stevens' seriousness, and the greater proof is in both his verse and prose essays. I propose that the elements of a subtle and sophisticated humanist poetics can be constructed from his writings and with more or less conscious collaboration from the work of Williams, particularly in his verse. Stevens was a humanist because the human universal was the source and theme of the "sanctions of our lives"; conversely, Eliot was not, primarily because he called on a supra-human source to endow the supra-personal culture of a species fixed by its history and tradition. To Stevens culture was already a poem, a supreme fiction imagined by men, that could be de-created and then recreated in a continuous series of poems and fictions. These issues have been summoned in my previous pages, but the following review may clarify in what sense Stevens was interested in the effort of someone, himself or another, to write a humanist poetics. Thus I will state some informal summarizing principles as if I were Stevens' active amanuensis. They are presented in italics, followed by discussion or illustration. A succeeding final chapter continues the hypothetical debate with Eliot's literary and cultural criticism while marking some aspects of a parallel argument with enlightening elements of post-structuralist or post-modern theory today.

*The ground of a humanist poetics was set by Williams like this: the poet in
a "field of action" is trying to make "contact" with human and non-human
reality. Stevens might define "contact" as follows: the poet, acutely conscious
of the abandoned self, speaks to his "companions in nothingness." The poem
offers a naked confrontation with "veritable and inhuman" reality. That "sophisticated man," the poet, in search of a "sufficing fiction" comes back to the
source. He comes and goes between matters of faith and ends up frequently
with "the headache of unreality."[1]*

In "Jumbo" Stevens invoked a "companion in nothingness" this way: "musician," "transformer," "prince of the secondary men," "ancestor of Narcissus,"
"bad bespoken lacker," and "this imager." Was he speaking for all poets and
were these humble ranks the only alternatives to being unvoiced and without
companions in nothingness? There is more explicit comfort for musicians in
the earlier verse of "The Idea of Order at Key West." "It was she and not the sea
we heard" offers an important inspiration of Stevens' poetics, as I interpret it.
Not nature, not "sea," but "she," the singer, gives ultimate voice to value and
meaning, terms which call on the sense of reality as an act of faith. Otherwise
the "veritable" and "inhuman" ocean offers only a naked confrontation.

There is always, as Stevens says everywhere, a function for thought and
imagination. In dealing with the role of Canon Aspirin in "Notes Toward a
Supreme Fiction," Harold Bloom first says that Canon Aspirin struggles to
find "the apocalyptic cure for our headache of unreality." Then he moves to
saying that "aspirin" belongs to Blake's "dare he aspire," and that canon
means "human self-definition" as from a previous poem. Canon Aspirin then
means:" the self-defining, self-describing human desire for a beyond, even if
that beyond turns out to be an abyss."[2]

Conceding the modest source of aspiration in the headache, if a canon is a
priestly functionary, the similar role is that taken by the rabbi described by
Stevens; "the figure of a man devoted in the extreme to scholarship and at the
same time to making some use of it for human purposes" (SLTR, 786). The
summary proof of those connections may be in Stevens' own comment on the
Canon Aspirin, of which the following is part.

> The sophisticated man: the Canon Aspirin, (the man who has explored all the projec-
> tions of the mind, his own particularly) comes back, without having acquired a suffic-
> ing fiction,—to, say, his sister and her children. His sister has never explored anything
> at all and shrinks from doing so. He is conscious of the sensible ecstasy and hums
> laboriously in praise of the rejection of dreams etc.

*Within the sophistication of an insecure imagination the exploring man in
search of a "sufficing fiction" comes back to the source. What will suffice
remains the question that comes alive at the source, which may or may not be
a sister and her children. That is one choice. But being pressed as near neighbor to the void the sophisticated man may simulate either romantic escape or*

a fall into nihilism. For survival's sake his poem may search for a source or sanction in animal nature or find itself blessed in reconcilement with "things as they are."

As the man with the blue guitar strums his note, the voice is that of a singing animal. "The blue guitar—On that its claws propound." Then what is the instrument and song for?

> A dream (to call it a dream) in which
> I can believe, in face of the object,
>
> A dream no longer a dream, a thing
> Of things as they are, as the blue guitar
>
> After long strumming on certain nights
> Gives the touch of the senses, not of the hand,
>
> But the very senses as they touch
> The wind-gloss. Or as daylight comes,
>
> Like light in a mirroring of cliffs,
> Rising upward from a sea of ex.

The poem aspires to become "no longer a dream" but "a thing/ Of things as they are..." How does reality return "rising upward from a sea of ex?" That is the "first idea" and part of the poem's work. There is a light from that "ex" rising upward and mirroring the singer. Prufrock's sea is different, one "in which we drown."[3]

The poem exists at the border of dreams and reality. The bridge between dream and reality is the "person" (subject, poet, or reader) who cannot be denied or excluded from the poem and whose imagination is the maker in "universal intercourse." It forms a process; there is give and take, borrowing and loss between dreams and reality. The poem highlights its source in the maker and finds the self.

To put things into place the poem performs a necessary music which requires "issue and return," an absence from reality and an "absence in reality."

> Poetry is the subject of the poem,
> From this the poem issues and
>
> To this returns. Between the two,
> Between issue and return, there is
>
> An absence in reality,
> Things as they are. Or so we say.
>
> But are these separate? Is it
> An absence for the poem, which acquires

> Its true appearances there, sun's green,
> Cloud's red, earth feeling, sky that thinks?
>
> From these it takes. Perhaps it gives,
> In the universal intercourse.

Reality in its "absence" surrounds the poem like a meaningful silence. "The universal intercourse" is a relationship of "give and take," and asserts existential being which comes to creation in that relationship. In observing the "universal intercourse," Harold Bloom observes that Stevens' supreme fiction turns out not to be poetry, "but as in Emerson and Whitman (and Wordsworth), to be a poet, to be a fiction of the self..."[4] This is true if we remember that a fiction of the self remains only a fiction, part of a dream, until it takes part in the "universal intercourse."

In Bloom's meaning the imagination that creates a world is the "man-maker" creating himself. Bloom has been the strongest critic to recognize Stevens in that role, proposing his mission in lines from "Chocorua to Its Neighbor"

> To say more than human things with human voice,
> That cannot be; to say human things with more
> Than human voice, that, also, cannot be;
> To speak humanly from the height or from the depth
> Of human things, that is acutest speech.

Though Stevens resisted being called a humanist, it is perfectly consistent with actual humanism to resist the label. His poetry's humanism is certainly not a regard for mankind in high moral or sentimental view. It is a need for the sensible world of meaning that is man-made, and high appreciation for the process by which it is made.[5] Therefore poetry and not something else may in the order of analogy support a secular faith which offers the space for persons in poetry and the poetry of persons.[6]

Because it is human in source the poem has an ethical bearing, not in fixed doctrine, but in what is basic to the knowledge of good and evil. The counterviolence of the imagination against the pressure of reality or its absence has ultimately an ethical meaning. The poem has its source in dialogue, as if it were made "for you," and features human interdependence. The protagonist in all poetry is the more than human human, leaner than life, whom we may call "major man." The act of recognizing him is a central act of poetry. A form of that recognition is to face the "human pathos" and dependency.

At one point in his deeply reaching letters Stevens defined the humanist poet:

> The extreme poet will be as concerned with a knowledge of man as people are now concerned with a knowledge of God. The knowledge of man is the knowledge of good and evil; the extreme poet has knowledge of good and evil." (SLTRS, 370)

He acknowledges the link with religion based on the observation that the *idea* of God and God are always the same. All paths into or out of metaphysics and ethics are set by the necessary life dialectic of judging true and false, right and wrong. The meaning of "good" and "evil" is brought down from superstition and yet re-awakened in force. Poetry in being close to experience is therefore closest to those terms.

The force of reduction and the dialectic of the imagination took Stevens finally to his own "source of poetry," in Williams' phrase. It is important that Stevens made the "knowledge of man" a matter of normative expression and not another anthropomorphic system. An explicit humanism extracts that normative factor from metaphysical God systems and rests its case on that basis. The man-God is not a concern; it is not a matter of straightforward idealization. In discussing "Notes Toward a Supreme Fiction" with Hi Simon, Stevens placed that condition upon his thought.

> The gist of this poem is that the MacCullough is MacCullough; MacCullough is any name, any man. The trouble with humanism is that man as God remains man, but there is an extension of man, the leaner being, in fiction, a possibly more than human human, a composite human. The act of recognizing him is the act of this leaner being moving in on us. (SLTR, 434)

The protagonist leaner than MacCullough though not quite lean enough is the "sophisticated man," Canon Aspirin, who is not, any more than McCullough, a personification of "major man." The latter, a composite "more than human human," might be, if found, the true hero of the poem. The Canon has praised the "rejection of dreams," has returned to "the human pathos and fact" and finds "in the long run" nothingness.[7]

The passages quoted above and in the footnote on this page are both from the same letter to Simons and are fundamental. They give an important gloss to what Williams in his own way meant in "These" by the unusually sweeping phrase "the source of poetry."[8] and they are a succinct help in characterizing the dynamic of a "humanist poetics; in the face of nothingness, a nakedness, there is an expression of the "human pathos" and dependency, recognizing MacCullough or his alternate, the Chaplinesque figure of "Notes," as emblems of the "human pathos." More immediately Canon Aspirin receives such revelation at "the side of the children's bed." And this in turn may be fundamental for the sign of the human in a "leaner being" which is the "extension of man." One must notice the humble site of revelation, at the children's bedside. This, like the reference to a "leaner being," emphasizes the effort to avoid abstraction. Poetry exceeds the limitations of mind (in myth and metaphysics) by basing itself in the "human pathos" at the point of "contact" with it.[9]

Bloom in his effort to point out Stevens' link with American humanism selects a passage from "A Rabbit as King of the Ghosts" where transcendental rabbit and materialist cat are in controversy. Bloom calls it a "major battle in the war between being-without-consciousness and consciousness-without being."[10] It is important to give special emphasis to the phrase "for you" in the same poem.

> The trees around are for you,
> The whole of the wideness of night is for you,
>   A self that touches all edges,
>
> You become a self that fills the four corners of night,"

Bloom accurately connects this to Whitman in "Song of Myself" and Emerson at the close of "Nature," ("Know then that the world exists for you. For you is the phenomenon perfect.") The major battle in the war between "being and consciousness" is not resolved in the intercourse of self and world but in the intercourse of self and self. "The sun no longer shares our works," and though "the earth is alive with creeping men" to stand and not creep requires an exchange of consciousness, the recognition of "human dependence" which perhaps resolves Canon Aspirin's cosmic headache. At that point the personal has anchorage, not solipsist isolation. Reality is "shared," and may be found in the "you" that marks an exchange in being and consciousness. There is more than the nostalgia of loss in these lines from the poem for that modest "Rabbit as King of Ghosts."

> ...the light is a rabbit light,
> In which everything is meant for you
> And nothing need be explained.

The statue that becomes a monument and a ruin gives an important theme to Stevens' poetics. The living person confronts the destruction of doctrine in stone. Monuments are abstractions of memory and history, of culture and the achieved imagination; their ruins illustrate natural deconstruction. The worship of the statue can displace the person, illustrate the displacement of reality by the imagination, and result in a form of dehumanization.

A survey of familiar reading brings up the jar placed on a hill which is like nothing else in Tennessee.[11] It is in fact a monument to nothing or a monument to dismiss monuments as the "snow man" is a form that freezes in warning of the "nothing" it is and will become. Again specifically that unstable monument of doom is matched by the equally unstable monument of joy in ice cream, whose emperor rules over a thriving commonwealth exposed like the "snow man" to the melting weather. In more detailed statement there is Mr. Burnshaw's ideological statue whose theme is "...Everything is dead\ Except the future.\ Always everything\ That is is dead except what ought to be." To be caught in the limbo between things that are dead and those that ought to *be*, the imagined future, is a perfect representation of the unreality of abstractions. There is a buried person, "barefoot and blank," who posed for General Jackson's statue in Lafayette Square in Washington. He would have known "The American Sublime,"

> The spirit and space,
> The empty spirit
> In vacant space.

"Vacant space" mocks the bathetic, poorly wrought imagination, that is, the work of art in its ultimate deficiency of source. On the other side is the example of the statue of Colleoni, the Renaissance warrior hero, a most impressive sculpture created by Verrocchio on a piazza in Venice. In "Notes Toward a Supreme Fiction," there is another grand statue of General Du Puy where his "true flesh" has turned "to an inhuman bronze" in "a permanence, so rigid\ That it made the General a bit absurd." And "yet the General was rubbish in the end." To explain this, in one of Stevens' great lyric moments he has the tourist Nanzia Nuncio confront Ozymandias, Shelley's fallen statue. All of romantic literature might be waiting for the old king's response. She is the spouse, the would-be bride of romance, and stripping herself "more nakedly than nakedness," she asks that she be clothed with glory. The response to that bride of romance would be critical; she should not to be condemned to nakedness before "the inflexible order(s)" of the past, nor will she be made insipid in perfection.

The poem is a "dream no longer a dream" that "gives the touch of the senses." It evokes that on which "so much depends," which "has no name" but is figured by earth, "my fluent mundo," where the protagonist of consciousness can say "I have not but I am and as I am, I am." The poem exhibits respect for reality- where things register their being in a dependency as deep as that of persons. Things register their being, the person registers his being in a dependency as deep as that which clings to the red wheelbarrow of Williams' revelation. A thing of mundane immediacy is the basis of the imagination's freedom as it expands to reality's limit. On the other side, at imagination's limit, there is "the remotest cleanliness of a heaven\ That has expelled us and our images..." "Phoebus is dead," Stevens advances in "Notes Toward a Supreme Fiction" at the start, "But Phoebus was\ A name for something that never could be named." Between nothingness and that which cannot be named, the poem exists and thrives.

> There is a project for the sun. The sun
> Must bear no name, gold flourisher, but be
> In the difficulty of what it is to be.

In the sun's project of discovery Stevens prepared for the great poem's deeply reached conclusion in the last stanzas of Part III. The Canon Aspirin, protagonist of the search, has once more moved from the nakedness, " a point, \Beyond which fact could not progress as fact," to another nothingness, " a point\ Beyond which thought could not progress as thought." He had to choose and he chose the whole "The complicate, the amassing harmony," of his own fiction. "He imposes orders as he thinks of them."

✽

The poem as it ends does not have an answer of the philosophic order for "the difficulty of what it is to be." The conclusion is more like a prayer and an appeal, "as I am, I am." To come to know "major man" is another such offering of ambiguous success. In correspondence the more inclusive "real" is no longer the sun but the earth. "Fat girl, terrestrial, my summer, my night." Earth is "familiar yet an aberration." She becomes "the soft-footed phantom, the irra- tional\ Distortion.... "the fiction that results from feeling." Despite these con- ditions the poet acknowledges a poet's kind of victory, a reclamation of naming.

> Until flicked by feeling, in a gildered street,
> I call you by name, my green, my fluent mundo.
> You will have stopped revolving except in crystal.

Crystal is both limit and form, and in the background we remember the criti- cism of mind and imagination that comes at the beginning of the poem: "so poisonous

> Are the ravishments of truth, so fatal to
> The truth itself, the first idea becomes
> The hermit in a poet's metaphors.

The faces of man and God are dramatic visualizations of the poem's source in humanized reality. The anti-hero of the quotidian comes forward to replace the hero's statue.

> If the imagination is the faculty by which we import the unreal into what is real, its value is the value of the way of thinking by which we project the idea of God into the idea of man. (NA,150)

With this as background readers can understand the actual grandeur of mission that Stevens gave to poetry. The focus of Stevens' incompletely acknowl- edged humanism is a struggle to engage the imaginative space once filled by the "idea of God." It was for him quite simply an obsession, but as fruitful as any in the history of poetry and religion. Williams pursued a parallel path according to his own temperament and style, but in result they were both poets who respond best to the questions raised by a humanist poetics.

Issues of important belief entail images of divinity, the right icons of wor- ship, which to provide becomes the task of the imagination. Pound could glorify a "monument," and Eliot occupy such monuments with the memory of culture; we understand with some excitement how the task for Williams and Stevens was to supply a counter theme and project. In chief the effort for them was to thrust past monuments and sculptured forms in order to see not the naked animal but the sensate and intelligent human face. If the poet is present in his verse, he at once asks for the presence of that face as if it were the mirror of his own, but more than that, as if it were the agent of intelligent "Being" which answers and corresponds with his own existence.[12]

In the paradigm among Stevens' major poems being mined for his thought one may find a glimpse of the ancient "forbidden" face that was sign for the "idea of God."

> A lasting visage in a lasting bush,
> A face of stone in an unending red,
> Red-emerald, red-slitted blue, a face of slate,
>
> An ancient forehead hung with heavy hair,
> The channel slots of rain, the red-rose-red
> And weathered and the ruby-water-worn,
>
> The vines around the throat, the shapeless lips,
> The frown like serpents basking on the brow,
> The spent feeling leaving nothing of itself,

In that ruined monument of a face we see the visage of a primeval deity appearing and disappearing within signs of the burning bush, a pagan coloring with a "frown like serpents," called up or called down by shepherds from hell and celebrated by children. The image is like a dream of shadowy fragments, discordant and ambiguous as the gods themselves were in their repetitions. When asked by Hi Simons for help in reading the stanza, Stevens replied with close application.

> The first thing one sees of any deity is the face, so that the elementary idea of God is a face: a lasting visage in a lasting bush. Adoration is a form of face to face. When the compulsion to adoration grows less, or merely changes, unless the change is complete, the face changes.... We struggle with the face, see it everywhere & try to express the changes. In the depths of concentration, the whole thing disappears. (SLTR,438)

In this we may perhaps see Stevens absorbing the Old Testament or that part of Judaism that attracted him. Stevens doesn't mention that men were from the first forbidden to look at God's face, just as they were forbidden to take His name in vain. In any case the passage comes as his own insight and as the "struggle with the face" it clarifies the ratios of struggle in the enterprises of the imagination, now approximating a search for divinity. It in turn explains the appearance and disappearance of the "angel of reality" whose absence is where nihilism threatens.

There is a simplifying lesson here for Eliot's poetic practice and spiritual career. Eliot's best poetry was written facing absolute absence, "nothing again nothing," and no one brought forward the penalty of disbelief so strongly. But that is where Stevens' poetry also flourishes. Belief without its support, poetry without a source for poetry— that is where the imagination is most alive, at the margins of its birth, or death. The early somewhat mystifying line from "Sunday Morning," "death is the mother of beauty" remains a sustaining theme in Stevens' later work.

If reality was a problem for modern poets searching for the face of man or God, the higher reality of God was a problem solved for Eliot who may have rediscovered His "face" in spirit but more concretely in the monument of His Church. Knowing God in dimensions that were both transcendental and immanent as well as practical, it was possible, indeed necessary to live with a system of secondary signs and abstractions that held people in an institutional order. It was a meta-culture, authoritarian, deserving a kind of worship, indeed one among supremely sufficing fictions.

In a modern world that daily deconstructed itself, the poets would find a void for the imagination to fill. "Absence" was a force, a "violence in reality," as Stevens could see it, a "pressure" which the imagination finds crippling, or, alternatively, the re-creative stimuli of poverty and pain. Williams and Stevens recognized the struggle and win credit and sympathy for their attempt to make it the realm of poetry. Williams' path was the stubborn pursuit of immediacy against all abstraction, taking joy finally from the immanence (the indwelling of value) of thing and person. For both Stevens and Williams neither God nor culture had precedence above these, not even poetry in its old measures and great lines had precedence.

The non-metaphysical "fat girl," earth, still revolving, could supply the need for Stevens. If it was a "presence" that the language of philosophy did not need, the language of poetry surely did. We might supplement by saying earth was not enough, and that finally what was needed could be provided in the poetry of consciousness by an icon of the conscious person, provisionally described as the "hero" in a verse statement that rounds Stevens' thought in "Examination of the Hero in a Time of War."

> Unless we believe in the hero, what is there
> To believe? Incisive what, the fellow
> Of what good. Devise, Make him of mud,
> For every day. In a civiler manner,
> Devise, devise, and make him of winter's
> Iciest core, a north star, central
> In our oblivion, of summer's
> Imagination, the golden rescue:

The imagination's hero is more sacred than shrine or statue, "a marble soiled by pigeons."

> The hero is a feeling, a man seen
> As if the eye was an emotion,
> As if in seeing we saw our feeling
> In the object seen....
> Instead of allegory,
> We have and are the man, capable
> Of his brave quickenings, the human
> Accelerations that seem inhuman.

Condensed in these lines there is a statement of literary doctrine, poet's theory perhaps rather than critical theory, "instead of allegory, we have and are the man." But more than that it introduces a larger doctrine, a matter of faith and necessity, devised, made of mud and of good. Stevens did his share in the exposition of that belief in the essays he wrote, particularly "Imagination as Value" and "The Noble Rider and the Sound of Words." However, the sense in the lines just quoted could have been taken from the contemporary French philosopher, Emmanuel Levinas. Levinas felt in summary fashion the same central impulse in the great canon of literature.

> I think that across all literature the human face speaks•or stammers, or gives itself a countenance, or struggles with its caricature. Despite the end of Europo•centrism, disqualified by so many horrors, I believe in the eminence of the human face expressed in Greek letters and in our own, which owe the Greeks everything. It is thanks to them that our history makes us ashamed. There is a participation in Holy Scripture in the national literatures, in Homer and Plato, in Racine and Victor Hugo, as in Pushkin, Dostoyevsky or Goethe, as of course in Tolstoy or in Agnon. But I am sure of the incomparable prophetic excellence of the Book of Books, which all the Letters of the world awaited or upon which they comment. The Holy Scriptures do not signify through the dogmatic tale of their supernatural or sacred origin, but through the expression of the face of the other man that they illuminate, before he gives himself a countenance or a pose.[13]

To me this could be read as a manifesto statement announcing the return of the old-new school of theory I've called "humanist poetics," and the chief matter for comparative study in my final chapters.

Notes

1. The last quoted phrase supplied by Harold Bloom's commentary on the poem.
2. *Wallace Stevens*, 205. Bloom here almost apologizes for excess as he notes, "As I am reading (Stevens) so minutely and madly..." An "aspirin" madness, then. I mean considerable praise in saying that Bloom meets Stevens at the point where, as he concludes in discussing "Extracts From the Academy," Stevens "becomes what criticism scarcely so far credits him with having been, a sage and seer, who chants persuasively a possible wisdom" (p.156).
3. Stevens' key terms in his informal theory such as "first idea" and "major man" are from "Notes Toward a Supreme Fiction" which Bloom has parsed so "minutely" but not madly for its instruction.
4. *Wallace Stevens*, p.206.
5. One can plausibly say that in modernity we distrust everything that is man-made - it is always at a considerable distance from perfection. That may be why the terms and principles of a genuine humanism are deeply distrusted. At that point many prefer nihilism, without compromise.
6. Allen Grossman, in his own contribution, as I interpret it, to a humanist theory of literature, stresses persons in both source and subject. (See chapter 18 following.)
7. "For all that, it gives him, in the long run, a sense of nothing-ness, of nakedness, of the finality and limitation of fact; and lying on his bed, he returns once more to night's pale illuminations. He identifies himself with them. He returns to the side of the children's bed, with every sense of human dependence. But there is a supreme effort

which it is inevitable he should make. If he is to elude human pathos, and fact, he must go straight to the utmost crown of night: find his way through the imagination and perhaps to the imagination. He might escape from fact but he would only arrive at another nothingness, another nakedness, another limitation of thought. It is not, then, a matter of eluding human pathos, human dependence. Thought is part of these, the imagination is part of these, and they are part of thought and of imagination" (SLTRS, p. 445).

8.   "Contact", as noted earlier, was a keyword in Williams' lexicon of poetic theory.
9.   Bloom, *Wallace Stevens*, p.137.
10.   "Anecdote of the Jar."
11.   I should mention again that "presence," in my usage is the so-neutral and ultimately nebulous term favored in the argument of post-structuralist, post-Heideggerian thought. The metaphysical "absence/presence" that begins the debate of deconstruction was the "idea of God" traditionally focused by Nietzsche and here stressed by Stevens. Should we not name a major theme of classic modernist poetry "absence?" Surely no one wrote more great poetry of the void, cosmic and local, public and private, than Eliot. There is an "absence in reality" Stevens wrote, leaving it to his poetry not so much to fill in as to give the frame, the imagination's necessity, that outlines the absence of metaphysical explanations and belief..
12.   Levinas, *Ethics and Infinity*, p. 117.

Part 3

Poetry and Politics

18

Cultural and Humanist Poetics

In much of this text I have been interested in the relations between poetic theory and cultural criticism and politics. That was an important engagement for Eliot and Pound and throws light on their role as avatars of literary modernism. In the best aspect it may be said that they returned poetry to major status in general thought and discourse. Stevens too moved toward cultural criticism in a time of crisis and change, and though his activity was concentrated in poetry, it was poetry broadly conceived as the valorizing imagination, "supreme" in its fictions. The aspiration was behind his tentative effort to help found a university chair for teaching poetic theory, and even to recommend "someone like Eliot" for the first appointment. Opposed as they were in principle it was their strong claims for the link between literature and culture that brings Stevens and Eliot together and points a comparison with much of contemporary critical theory.

At the same time I have argued for the sharp differences and implicit debate between Eliot and Pound on one side and Stevens and Williams on the other. This too is reflected in an extended argument today, particularly in the academy, between upholders of traditional humanistic studies and the proponents of post-modernism who have given a very strong cultural, historical, and political cast to literary theory and criticism.

Post-modern (or post-structuralist) literary theory made one feature its dissent from the "New Criticism," which had been rightly considered the product of literary modernism. This recovers an old battle in the memory of an older generation when the New Criticism was posed in reaction against social naturalists and literary Marxists during the decades of the twenties, thirties, and forties. In particular it reflects a parallel in the inner debate among the poets I study, and one that continues today between "post-modernists" and a diffuse group reacting against historicist and political perspectives very like that which featured criticism dominant in the thirties.

Certainly the New Criticism was born under the influence of Pound and Eliot, and it thrived in critical practice when dealing with the verse of Williams and Stevens. However, as a movement that came to rule in the academy the New Criticism left room for so many approaches to text, context, author, history, and reader response that it is impossible to summarize them under any one heading. Perhaps the principle that remains clear is the treatment of the text from a view of its autonomy as a text, the authoritative source of reading and interpretation. For valuation the New Critics were thought to be esthetic formalists, though I think that would have been a limited understanding of their work. Post-modern practice may seem to have begun similarly in the stress on language and the text, the important difference has been its assertive tendency to treat context (linguistic, political, cultural, and historical) as the matter of major interest in the work of analysis. In brief, the subtext of language and the context of culture have been given the greatest claim on power over the text. Now though the specific political alignments today are very different, characteristic post-modern views of culture and cultural identities quite resemble Pound's view of the link between cultural leadership and artistic power, and Eliot's view of the force of cultural tradition and its bond with the classic literary canon.

It then becomes apparent to most students that the categories of modernism and post-modernism largely overlap. Certainly the shades of change among the following are often not matters of sharp difference— semiotic and symbolic analysis, relativist and pluralist perspectives, the over-arching skepticism directed at language, action, thought and belief, the use of narrative and metaphoric irony, the practice of linguistic pastiche and parody. There is large commonalty in the critical and reductive treatment of cultural superstructures, and an absorbing spirit of cultural dissent, but I should say immediately that the differences that do exist are not a matter of shades but of major importance in my text. They are linked differences and converge on the theme of mimesis, the problematic of subjectivity and self, the problematic of reality and truth, the importance of text versus context, the determinism of language and culture, the role of the author and the issue of cultural narrativity, and the power and freedom of the literary imagination itself. My interest in this book has been in the ways in which some of these issues divide classic American modernist poets. But they also reflect the debate in contemporary theory directed to the binding relation between literary criticism and culture, the linking of a poetics with cultural politics, with politics in general understood as power relationships that have universal sway in the fields of knowledge, art, and social action.

Cultural Poetics and Culturalism

Though cultural dissent remains the heritage of modernism, the post-modern generations absorbed it with effects so large that it penetrated most of the major arguing themes such as inter-textual narrativity, cultural-linguistic dominance over the text, the overriding importance of group power conflict for dramatic theme and resolution. In a negative aspect cultural dissent was absorbed with effects so extreme that post-modernist generations have been accused of literary and socio-political nihilism, and ultimately, religious, metaphysical nihilism. This phenomenon illustrates how weighted the concept of culture had become with the role formerly held by nation, race, and religion. The basis for the excess and the critical response to it, must have been the same sense of anarchy in the areas of self-identity and community allegiance, and with the same negativity of analysis, the breakdown of social dialogue and confident communication. The large cause for the imputed nihilism was the shaking of the foundations of neo-metaphysical support for human language and culture.

The argument has classic clarity in the work of both Eliot and Stevens early in their careers. The poets believed that "confidence in the world," the ethical-esthetic motivation for living once rested on the sources Eliot proposed in the spiritual and traditional social order. Wallace Stevens responded (as if in thematic drama for my general text) with one of his earliest poems to be written and published, "Sunday Morning," as if to pose question and answer directly to Eliot. Were the traditional ghosts of the old "Palestine/Dominion of the blood and sepulchre.." now silent? The surrogate subject is one of those fine sensitive Ladies the three other poets of this text have seized for revelation in their "Portraits…" important for my theme (see pages – of this chapter). The Sunday of Stevens' lady in morning is both secular and profoundly thoughtful. Her response in argument comes in the ecstatically eloquent second verse.

> Why should she give her bounty to the dead?
> What is divinity if it can come
> Only in silent shadows and in dreams?
> Shall she not find in comforts of the sun,
> …in any balm or beauty of the earth,
> Things to be cherished like the thought of heaven?
> Divinity must live within herself:
> Passions of rain…
> Grievings in loneliness…
> All pleasures and all pains, remembering
> …These are the measures destined for her soul.
>
>   v
>
> She says, " But in contentment I still feel
> The need of some imperishable bliss."
> Death is the mother of beauty; hence from her,
> Alone, shall come fulfillment to our dreams
> And our desires…
>
>   vi
>
> Is there no change of death in Paradise?
> Does ripe fruit never fall? Or do the boughs
> Hang always heavy in that perfect sky…
> Alas, that they should wear our colors there,
> The silken weavings of our afternoons,
> And pick the strings of our insipid lutes!
> Death is the mother of beauty, mystical,

Within whose burning bosom we devise
Our earthly mothers waiting, sleeplessly.
                    vii
Supple and turbulent, a ring of men
Shall chant in orgy on a summer morn
Their boisterous devotion to the sun,
Not as a god, but as a god might be,
Naked among them, like a savage source.
Their chant shall be a chant of paradise,
Out of their blood, returning to the sky,
And in their chant shall enter, voice by voice,
The windy lake wherein their lord delights,

They shall know well the heavenly fellowship
Of men that perish and of summer morn.
And whence they came and whither they shall go
The dew upon their feet shall manifest.

                    viii
She hears, upon that water without sound,
A voice that cries "The tomb in Palestine
Is not the porch of spirits lingering.
It is the grave of Jesus, where he lay."
We live in an old chaos of the sun,
Or old dependency of day and night,
Or island solitude, unsponsored, free,
Of that wide water, inescapable.

And, in the isolation of the sky,
At evening, casual flocks of pigeons make
Ambiguous undulations as they sink,
Downward to darkness, on extended wings.[1]

Stevens' marvelous portrait of the contemplative woman of "Sunday Morning" would put the three ladies portrayed by Williams, Eliot, and Pound to
shame for relative barrenness of resources. The theme of finding a foundation
for living on a deeper, higher, more sustaining level than mundane biological
existence is the same—but the poetry summons stoic and courageous meaning
in such challenging closing lines as these: "Divinity must live within herself…"
"They shall know well the heavenly fellowship/ Of men that perish and of
summer morn/ And whence they came and whither they shall go/ The dew upon
their feet shall manifest./ … ; Death is the mother of beauty…. And again in a
stanza, "Death is the mother of beauty….a ring of men/Shall chant in orgy…Not
as a god, but as a god might be, /Naked among them, like a savage source/
…These lines evoke the powerful primitivist and pagan trends in modernism
particularly those of Dionysian and related myth. They function in exactly the

role we can think they had in the culture-lost or culture-lacking worlds of Western modernism and postmodernism. The lines repeated "Death is the mother of beauty..." have resonance for Stevens himself for what he called the "angel of reality" in its most heightened evocative sense, or so I would propose in later pages. They also communicate for me in Williams' phrase discovering "the source of poetry" in his poem "These." The last stanza as presented in its fullness I leave to the reader because almost every word in it offers embrace of what the philosophers call Being free of the hallucinatory transcendental spirits from Palestine. We are at the theoretical center of Belief in its largest sense and at the thematic center of comparisons in this book. It is the foundational support of "divinity," of "heaven," of earth itself, or all Being, or even a simple ethical humanism for Sunday rejected by Eliot and Heidegger as well as reflected in this shadow of a debate between a youthful Wallace Stevens and youthful Eliot.

Cultural Poetics

The common assumption between poetic theory and cultural criticism is that literature makes a formative contribution to an empowered culture of values. Conversely it is an assumption that literary works reflect a dominant culture and particularly the most powerful forces within that culture. For illustration here I shall refer to the postmodern theory that most intersects with my theme, in my view a thinking chiefly influenced by Michel Foucault in current expressions. In one phase its most direct manifestation has been known widely in this country under the heading of the "New Historicism." After collecting its affinities with other prominent schools including social constructivist, feminist, and neo-Marxist criticism, it may have seemed best to choose the more inclusive and appropriate name of "cultural poetics."

Eliot and Pound on one side and Stevens surely on the other would no doubt reject such labels and allegiances and I use them here on what may be called purely descriptive and hypothetical grounds. Of course the political analogies that exist today would seem most surprising to them. What was right wing with Eliot and Pound as cultural critics became left wing with Foucault and Jameson. However, if Eliot wrote some notes for a cultural and politically dominated poetics from the right, the literary Marxists of his day were even more directly the practitioners of cultural determinism from the left. Certainly in the politics of that time the extreme right and the Marxist left were both united against the liberal humanists in the center. It was not Marx or Stalin that Pound inveighed against so much as it was Roosevelt. It was not in Marxism but free-thinking liberal thought that Eliot found his chief intellectual enemy, just as that is true today among neo-conservatives and the religious right. Granting such complexities, I deal with the thinking about poetry and culture of Eliot and Pound on the assumption that basic notes of contemporary theory are expressed in their work. Differing as they do with Stevens and Williams on those same notes, the argument I arrange among them is relevant for understanding a present day argument between culturalists and humanists, an argument that distills its manifestation in politics, or I should say more accurately, a political ethos.

For the present generation of teachers and critics a unitary understanding of cultural poetics can be gained from a densely written volume of essays published several years ago and edited by Stephen Greenblatt, a leader in the contemporary school of the New Historicism, in collaboration with Giles Gunn, and subtitled *The Transformation of English and American Literary Studies.*"[2] The theme compares well with the powerful influence of most of Eliot's prose writings. For example, Eliot made at least three principles dominant in his literary essays and in his deliberations on the omens and challenges of modern civilization. The first of these was his emphasis on the foundational value of a cultural tradition, particularly as it enriched major works; it was in fact necessary for their creation. The second was the assumed detachment of the creative act from major personal interest and emotion; today this is expressed as resistance to individual subjectivity either to explain the source of art or the response to it. Third, just as there was in Pound's "rage" for literary and cultural order much more than a trace of naturalist determinism, bringing poetry, culture, and politics together, the even stronger amalgam existed for Eliot where religious authority would have made cultural power over the imagination almost complete.

As I see it the key terms for debate two or three generations later with the text anthology published by Greenblatt and Gunn question where to locate authority over texts and the reading of texts. The issue was translated by Michel Foucault when he accused Derrida at one point as personally wanting "sovereignty" over texts.[3] But who has authority if not its ultimate reader? The issue reached a logical result when Stanley Fish led his students to a vigorous concept of "reading communities" prepared to understand the text according to their interests and beliefs. It is profoundly consistent with a theory of literature that gave authority to its source in the historic and cultural ground from which the text arose. The ground on which it lands might have right to claim equal authority over what in the end is called its interpretation.

The rejection of authorial dominance in postmodernist criticism has been one of its most controversial principles, and used, with some error I think, to distinguish it from modernism.[4] One contributor to the Greenblatt-Gunn anthology put the revolutionary emphasis as "a disestablishing of the modernist image of the writer thinker," and "a development in the field that challenges assumptions about authorial autonomy, individuality, and artistic control inherited from the nineteenth century" (GG, 56, 50). Leah S. Marcus, who takes this view, is positive in giving its origin to Foucault, referring to his influential essay, "What is an Author." "The idea of 'the author' is not a transhistorical category but a cultural construct"(GG,46). Anne Middleton takes the point further: "As Michel Foucault observes, the author is an ideological product and acts as a 'principle of thrift in the proliferation of meaning'"(GG,27). This would seem to reduce writer and reader to receiving ideological messages from the past and from impersonal agencies of power. It would imply that the deepest "sovereignty" over the text is not that of the author, nor the most confident critic, but the anonymous and abstract power of history and cultural politics.

Perhaps that is at some distance from Eliot's discreet conservative views. Was he then and were all his works "ideological products?" Eliot would never have imputed less than full responsibility in an author over his written words and the content of his mind. Pound, too, would have said nonsense to Foucault's description of the author as a "principle of thrift" in the dispersion of culture. The author was of course a creator, not a product, and the well-principled legislator of culture. But the non-sovereign reader and citizen would receive the benefit. We can note the differences and still see a parallel in the suppression of the author person (or reader person) in favor of the inherited or recreated cultural context. The blunter determinism belongs to the contemporary New Historicists, as Professor Marcus writes further, "all interpretation is generated at least as much by the culture that has produced the critic as by the culture under scrutiny" (GG, 50). Thus reader, critic, and the author are instruments of cultural history, and if this is a circle that one can't get out of, it becomes inevitable that the significant source of meaning should be the last agent, the critic, particularly if he is disposed to be the culture critic. The problem would be how to escape the impasse when one sort of culturally determined consciousness in the critic collides with or attempts dominance over another culturally determined consciousness in the author. As usual when "determinisms" meet in collision the result may be decided by an immediate power at hand, as in the circumstance of the classroom, under the supervision of one teacher-critic. No one who has experienced a classroom would accept the consensus of a community as its best product.

Eliot was more of a cultural historian when he was sure that the mature classic embodied the values and forms of a rich civilization, these being the cumulative product of history. Pound, always the aggressive literary entrepreneur, thought in terms of the inventive imagination, expanded by the central role of the artist-statesman (or tyrant who was patron of artists) in the production of all forms, esthetic, political, and economic. That placed heavy accent on authority and equated creation with the vitalist sanction of power. Pound could surely have given agreement to this formulation for post-structuralist theory made by John Carlos Rowe:

> Literary deconstruction often offered a more ambitious, albeit elusive, political reward: to understand how a culture represents itself gives one access to culture's secret authority, transforming one into Shelley's fantasy of the poet as unacknowledged legislator of the world. (GG,194)

The frank statement may account for the drive and ambition of much post-modernist criticism; the "reward" of a higher politics is a heady one, and Pound himself desired it with as much seriousness as Shelley. Again, it is the modernist Pound one thinks of in these words of Rowe: "The primary mode of postmodern writing would have to be characterized as pastiche," and more important, that "language determines and shapes thought" (GG,187). Pound thought of art in the paradigm for the making of cultures and empires; Rowe could hardly be less sweeping when he proposes that "Like the postmodern experimentalists, the post-structuralists insisted on the fundamentally linguistic construction of social and psychic reality." The heraldic theme was this: "Every aspect of human experience became a 'text' — that is, a signifying system, including the acts of reading and interpretation by which we receive such texts" (GG, 189). Certainly this theme of the post-structuralists has its echo in Pound's treatment of the grand "text" of Malatesta's monument, the *Tempio*. When the power of the artist joins with the power of the artist's patron the imagination (in "linguistic construction") is sovereign, enforced in the concrete presence of Pound's Chinese emperors.

The ultimate issue is a power like that of Malatesta over *all* texts. The authority is again Foucault on this, as another contributor to the Greenblatt-Gunn anthology of postmodernism puts it: "I join Michel Foucault in viewing transgression and lawlessness as structural positions and as necessary elements in the fluid and contestatory scene within which power is defined and arrayed" (GG, 82). It would have interested Pound to find that cultural ideologies, and therefore a cultural poetics, base themselves on political engagement, though he would have preferred the reverse order of influence. The issues as a whole illuminate a resemblance to Pound's esthetic politics. "Postmodern politics," Rowe writes, "(is) a politics that conceives of resistance and social reform as dependent on a critique of representation." He goes much further with Pound in enforcing a naturalistic basis in art in the subsuming forms of "all human production."

> ....the economy of so-called natural production and reproduction would have to be considered central not only to any simple economic system but also to the more sophisticated economy of cultural production... Production, reproduction, and representation occupied the same "body," at once a physical discrete and textual body. (GG,199)

This language has close affinity to Pound's use of economics and is neighbor to Eliot's effort to describe the organic evolution of culture. The naturalist bridge between esthetic and ethical valuations and their political effects is evident even where Eliot speaks of his ultimate religious faith. In the last pages of his essay " Toward the Definition of Culture" Eliot calls himself "a student of social biology."

> An individual European may not believe that the Christian Faith is true, and yet what he says, and makes, and does, will all spring out of Christian culture and depend upon that culture for its meaning. Only a Christian culture could have produced a Voltaire or a

Nietzsche. I do not believe that the culture of Europe could survive the complete disappearance of the Christian Faith. And I am convinced of that, not merely because I am a Christian myself, but as a student of social biology.

Then you must start painfully again, and you cannot put on a new culture ready made. You must wait for the grass to grow to feed the sheep to give the wool out of which your new coat will be made. You must pass through many centuries of barbarism.[5]

If in Eliot's view of culture and his or anyone's view of a cultural poetics we have been or will be reduced by crisis to students of social biology and must endure "many centuries of barbarism," and if what I have quoted from the Greenblatt-Gunn text is a valid presentation of contemporary thinking about culture as the base in poetic theory, this is where one must begin to assert important distinctions. I direct these toward a humanist poetics, particularly as reflected in the verse and thought of Stevens and Williams. Their thinking gives precedence to imaginative process, poetic creation, not cultural forces and their effects. Where intimate and immediate experience is in the foreground, where the imagination has some defined precedence over or resistance to contingency and abstract causality, and where normative meanings have at least equality of treatment with historic process and institutional power, there the basic impulses of a humanist poetics might prevail. In his limited but definite sovereignty over the text the author might be called the protagonist of the imagination and his own creative will. We read for contrast this summary observation from the Greenblatt-Gunn anthology.

We usually call the human entities that live within and largely constitute society "persons," though we might more properly use some analytical nomenclature like that of narratology and label them "actants."[6]

The reduction of the literary text (or its expansion) to the ur-text of socio-cultural history is probably as far as one could go in the abstraction of discourse in the name of cultures. Under that heading it was exactly right to replace "persons" with "actants." The latter, as depersonalized agencies, have arrived in the process "through which societies define and maintain (their) structure(s)...and human entities." The "complex and contestatory" process in which this happens must eventually be politics (or in extreme resort, war) which under this rule would dominate and enclose all "texts" and the interpretation of texts, and of course all "actants."

It is here that what we call cultural poetics or humanist poetics move to broad existential meanings upon which in fact whole civilizations may rest. Let us say for hypothesis that in the theme of cultural politics (and poetics) social and biological group classifications like culture and race become the abstract protagonists of interest. I would like to propose for major distinction that humanist poetics and politics begin with individuals and the rights of individuals, and stress therefore freedom of choice, and the creativity of the imagination and personal will. We express this in ethics and politics, and recurrently in politics, as the rights and responsibilities of free agency in harmony with the laws and justice for all.

Humanist Poetics

I have hardly done justice to all the relevant matters that come under the heading of post-structuralist (postmodern) theory, nor to the theses presented under the heading of the Greenblatt-Gunn anthology and "cultural poetics," but my purpose is to narrow focus on the comparisons I have made in my earlier chapters. The sum of a contrast between humanist and cultural poetics is a critical perspective that for the former seeks emphasis on persons and things in their unique existence: persons, because they possess imagination and thought and are the receptors of sensible experience; things, out of respect for Williams' large claim that they belong intact within the sacred independence of the real world. Truth and the "real world," if still bravely naive terms, belong to a concept of mimesis and are "necessary" (as with Stevens' "angel of reality") because they anchor the imagination and open it to both its freedom and its responsibility. I emphasize this because here the differences with determinist and contingency theories have most application. The project is to restore both persons and the real world (as in what Stevens called "the motive for metaphor") to their traditional place at the center of literary discourse and invention. The question to be answered is how that place was lost when for contrast and mock inversion we have the recent communication technology that has made "virtual reality" a more interesting concept than "reality" itself.

If language structures are produced from large impersonal cultural communities, how are these to be defined? Communities and groups express a context and so the sensibilities of both writer and reader are to be understood in that context. Groups are determined by their social environment, their history or biology, and their position in the power structures of the cultural system of which they are a part. Most accessibly marked in intellectual operations, they may be ideological groups projecting a cultural past and chart for the future; they may be defined anthropologically as reading communities. Textual meanings (and values) are made determinate by group cultures, and whether overtly or covertly imposed, they are power communities most often defined in opposition to other dominant power communities, bourgeois capitalist, white, black, feminine, European, Christian, etc.[7] In any case a cultural determinism was suggested by giving dominance to language communities; the now collectivized act of creation was thus absorbed by large categories of group interest and conflict, essentially politics. Marking the strong influence of Foucault, the causal contingency that received the greatest respect was the abstraction of power, which is first to appear in manifestations of conflict among groups.

(One wants to ask important questions at this point, are culture groups, politically often called interest groups in America, anything more than that? That is, are they power groups not bound by organized ethical goals or commitments either to each other or to outsiders, not functional from within but chiefly in political power relations with a majority power and other sub-groups? What is the bond that unites them if not only a material grievance or need, a random appetite for the wealth and rank that reward power? These questions may have more relevance in the next chapter dealing with cultural politics but a poetics under that title can hardly avoid the glaring omission of primary human issues applied to literary subjects.)

In counter-definition, a humanist poetics and politics (inevitably converging here while concerned with imaginative freedom) holds the potential of being posed *against* external causality or contingency in all the ways of challenge, resistance, accommodation or defeat. From that point of view the critical systems that give dominance to cultural structures, or group monopolies of power, or the strength of historic contingencies, ignore actual literary dynamics and pass over dramatic structure in its old Aristotleian sense. One might say that they work against the grain of the literary imagination. As I made the point earlier a cultural group, a race, a nation cannot be made the protagonist of a literary form without drifting toward crude political allegory.[8]

Grand causalities in the naturalistic vein make poor dramatic agents even when worlds collide. I have previously referred to Kenneth Burke who, as a member of Williams' and Stevens' generation and its most profound literary critic, proposed a principle of literary form in a triad of dramatic development he called "purpose (motivation, intention), passion (conflict, action), and perception (recognition, new understanding)."[9] Their unity was "action" in the Aristotleian sense. I would call it humanist action for its stress on the personal theater of experience in all its terms; in *purpose*, expressed as the defining motives or character set of a person; *passion*, where such motives meets resistance from the scene and agents of the world; and *perception*, the consequent revelatory suffering or total response, which offers not reconciliation but a new fusion of conscious being on the dramatic terms presented. In this way Burke took possession of a literary theory that he called "dramatism." He enlarged its meaning in reference to philosophy and politics when writing about "the relation between drama and dialectic" in one of his early seminal works *The Philosophy of Literary Form*. He describes how in philosophic assertions ideas are developed by "cooperative competition" where opposition is invited in the perfecting of ideas. This is akin to the "agonistic development" Burke found in literary works. But thinkers and creators who put "the quietus upon their opponent (as in political dictatorships)... bring themselves all the more rudely against the *unanswerable opponent,* the opponent who cannot be refuted, the nature of brute reality itself."[10] In or out of politics the question is what happens to the dramatic (agonistic) structure of *free* experience when the power in "brute reality" is summoned to determine meanings and influence reading. It would prevent thought (and literary creation) "to mature through "agonistic" development," and thus be a form of fundamental censorship of the imagination. An *unanswerable opponent* is in control, whatever be its defined nature as blank violence, determinist history, or a group interest. Refutation can only be made by a rival force, equally strong in its claim on "reality." In the process, character and scene and ideas lose their hold on the action and are replaced by distant contingencies that have lost everything except their names, conceptual substance and real power. This may be cited as the method of reductively abstract history and politics which substitute groups as the protagonists of action. Burke prepares an indispensable concept for a humanist poetics where the true agents of meaning, the writer, the subject, the reader and critic, are all *answerable,* though still in some sense opponents. The answers must come from a protagonist in full freedom of thought and consciousness. Whether one believes in the general freedom of choice or not may be irrelevant. The writer of an imaginative literary work must write as if he does. A life of meaning is an agon, the work of art is an agon.

Humanism and Anti-Humanism

To appreciate fully the reactive call for a humanist poetics one should go to France where the quarrel began and where in a decade past an opposing group of thinkers attacked the anti-humanist themes in the work of Derrida, Foucault, Lacan, Lyotard, and the Marxist thinker Althusser. For the authors of something like a philosophic manifesto, Luc Ferry and Alain Renaut, the issue begins with Nietzsche and moves to Heidegger in his critique of "the metaphysics of subjectivity." explained as "a critique of the subject defined as conscience and as will, that is, man as the author of his acts and ideas."[11] Ferry and Renault do a large summing up by giving to Nietzsche two drastic conclusions that lead to the disappearance of the idea of truth, and the disappearance of the idea of the integrated self, or subject. These are basic among the issues raised by the debate with the anti-humanist theme reflected in postmodernist (or post-structuralist) writing.[12] The source in Nietzsche needs brief reference from *The Joyful Wisdom* the question, Nietzsche wrote, is "whether an existence without explanation, without "sense" does not just become "nonsense," whether, on the other hand, all existence is not essentially an *explaining* of existence..." The question itself would seem unanswerable because "in this analysis the human intellect cannot avoid seeing itself in its perspective forms and *only* in them. We cannot see around our corner.... The world... has once more become 'infinite' to us: in so far we cannot dismiss the possibility that it contains infinite interpretations." From this Ferry and Renaut derive (and criticize) the post-modernist Nietzschean theme, "there are no facts, only interpretations."

In a page or two shortly following the above pronouncement, Nietzsche addresses himself with characteristic ferocity to nineteenth century "humanism," based on the "religion of pity" or the "love of mankind." "Mankind! Was there ever a more hideous old woman among all old women (unless perhaps it were "the Truth": a question for philosophers)? No, we do not love Mankind!"[13]

It should be noted here that the fusillade from France was met with a singular lack of interest in this country, at least among literary scholars and critics, with the exception of one inadequately noticed book by Daniel R. Schwarz of Cornell.[14] His text was published about the same time as that of Ferry and Renaut, though it bases itself on his own work with fiction and sees the issues from the point of view of literary study essentially while occupied with debating the post-structuralist schools of literary theory imported from France. The same debate has existed in this country for some years, but like the French theorists, Schwarz goes quite far in defining humanist poetics against the background of explicit and implicit anti-humanist positions of deconstructionists and self-defined postmodernists. To view what anti-humanism means in literary theory at present Schwarz dealt with concepts of the de-centered text, authorless, and in a certain sense readerless, and in still another sense, without reference to reality or to clearly referred human subjects. He brings up the extremely large problem of mimesis and above all, the desertion of responsibility to the work and its author.

In this amalgam of ideas texts are considered to be language structures written and read by large impersonal communities and to have an indeterminate history and meaning. That is to suggest for many that meaning at the source being indeterminate, textual meaning at the end occupies an unwritten space to be filled by reading communities as they are led by their own histories, or as it may be, by ideological groups projecting a cultural past and cultural future. On the other hand it seems a deep reversal that an approach initially regarded as devoted to indeterminacy of interpretation and relativistic perspectives should have been so quickly borrowed and occupied by highly determinate and even narrow modes of interpretation characteristic of the varieties of postmodern cultural poetics.

In those years of conflict some critics accused the new wave of theory from France of literary and moral nihilism. The climax in that melodramatic effect had come when Foucault boldly asserted that "the game of autonomous language came into being in precisely the place where man had just disappeared. ....since then, literature has been the place where man has never stopped disappearing in favor of language. Where 'ca parle,' man no longer exists."[15]

In thinking of this apparent death-blow to humanism, the authors Ferry and Renaut observed strongly that .... communication (for example. philosophical discussion) must necessarily appear not as free debate among subjects responsible for what they say but simply as the sublimation of relations of force or, if you wish, as a euphemistic form of war...[16]

It is bizarre of course that this nihilistic note never seemed to reach the American venture into cultural poetics and politics, though the intellectual origin of deconstructionist and post-structuralist thinking was the same. One could say that the avenue to man's disappearance was diverted to revolutionary neo-Marxist thought following Althusser, or neo-anarchist libertarian thought following Foucault. Whatever the road taken the result has been a certain amount of confusion and contradiction, outright incoherence, in the post-modern stream of argument.

In any case the passage quoted from Ferry and Renaut on the "sublimation of relations of force" describes the serious moral and political dimensions of the argument. The negation of subjectivity, the reification of consciousness, the diminution of agents or conscious subjects in action or discourse, all these are points not only simulate war but challenge normative doctrines of human equality and freedom, and possibly the existence of civil society itself. It becomes clear that the anti-humanist critique centers on the dismissal of the central autonomy of selves. The reduction of "the subject defined as conscience and will" would effectively destroy what Stevens meant by the imagination and put all magnified "pressure" on the side of what he meant by reality, or what would stand for reality in the languages of science and politics. It would in the process eliminate the interest and meaning of freedom.[17] In systems where contingency is assumed to rule, freedom is a forgotten cause, a lost opportunity. It is at that level that the largest issues of debate in literary theory have to be understood. The rule of contingency, if enforced by the analytical mind, puts an end to notions of "the constitutive unity of mankind" or "the illusion of universality." The question is how much literature and the other arts depend on those notions.

Certainly a humanist poetics would demand the presence of authenticated human beings. The strongest possible judgment in its favor as a poetics could be taken from the contemporary French philosopher, Emmanuel Levinas. Levinas felt in summary fashion the same central impulse in the great canon of literature.

> I think that across all literature the human face speaks or stammers, or gives itself a countenance, or struggles with its caricature. Despite the end of Europocentrism, disqualified by so many horrors, I believe in the eminence of the human face expressed in Greek letters and in our own, which owe the Greeks everything. It is thanks to them that our history makes us ashamed. There is a participation in Holy Scripture in the national literatures, in Homer and Plato, in Racine and Victor Hugo, as in Pushkin, Dostoyevsky or Goethe, as of course in Tolstoy or in Agnon. But I am sure of the incomparable prophetic excellence of the Book of Books, which all the Letters of the world awaited or upon which they comment. The Holy Scriptures do not signify through the dogmatic tale of their supernatural or sacred origin, but through the expression of the face of the other man that they illuminate, before he gives himself a countenance or a pose.[18]

I read this some years ago as if it were a manifesto announcing the return of the old-new school of theory I've called "humanist poetics." Its new name is most useful in critical contrast against the equally fresh nomenclature of cultural poetics, viz., the anthropological (or archaeological?) and historical study of literature. Allen Grossman, poet and literature professor at Johns Hopkins, gave explication of his own significantly related theory of "person" and "name," in poetry. In his book, *Against Our Vanishing,* Grossman proposes several pre-mises:

> I view the world, and I think poetry by its very structures calls attention to the world, as not human; and in the presence of that world not human ....on that world poetry writes the name of the person....
>
> The distinction between person and self is that the *person* is value-bearing: the person is that fact in the world which we are not permitted to extinguish, which has rights. [and]...whereas selves are found or discovered, persons and personhood is an artifact, something that is *made,* an inscription upon the ontological snowfields of the world that is not in itself human.[19]

The words have remarkable eloquence from a long active teacher of poetry, himself a poet. Grossman affirms "the function of poetry which specify(s) the *keeping* of the image of the person in the world as its principal outcome." The goal is "keeping alive, across the abysses of death and to the difference be-tween persons, the human image"; or it is maintaining "the question of persons and the conserving of their value across time." The context for these thoughts remains the crisis of identity and value proposed by Eliot, Stevens, and other poets modern and post-modern.

> Poetry is situated upon the central crisis of our civilization-how do we know a *person* is present?—and suffers all the strains which we feel when we contemplate the precari-ousness of our visibility to others in this Postmodern world.

Like Levinas, Grossman's theme of poetry suggests a human ontology to re-place metaphysics, a "first idea" in consciousness which becomes with imagi-native effort the self-creation of persons and a world.

All this is context for the assertive reappearance of humanist poetics, the more assertive as I consider Stevens' strong endorsement in his own time and place. The implication of his own theory is that whatever the philosophic barrier between language and reality the literary imagination is still defined and made active in facing it. The creative imagination does not rest or remain long at home within an old enclosure, whether that is endowed by cultural inheritance or conventional language. Mimesis is a steadfast principle because it gives us a world to live in; the homocentric view of the creative act offers credibility to the imagination and defines it as formed by vectors of meaning extending from author to reader to world. The geometric image is an effective translation of a concept of objectivity and truth derived from the work of the philosopher Donald Davidson, a thinker with major influence on modern theo-ries of language and reality.[20] The "triangulation" requires three points, let us say two observers (reader and writer) and a "place," a "thing," or a person outside them both to support objective meaning, and to banish any one of them is to banish "reality" or what is needed to support it.

Davidson's exposition is perhaps the clearest a philosopher could provide to give backing to Stevens' poetics. Stevens would have us believe that poets question reality as much as philosophers who entertain the question. Two im-

portant values in writing are at stake. One is the motive to share experience
which receives acknowledgment in the reading. The other is the pleasure of
recognizing the knowable world and appreciating it in some fashion, just for
what Stevens called "an expressible bliss." Reality is not created or invented
(though Stevens sometimes speculated in those terms) but discovered (not
imposed, he writes) and recreated so that it can be understood and placed
within judgment and appreciation. Appreciation, invention, the sharing of
experience are all conditioned by a mastering phrase of ambiguity that appears in "The Idea of Order at Key West"; the listener in the singer's song
wonders if "it was she and not the sea we heard." But in the mingling of that
doubt was the poetry. The ambiguity I mention restores the sense of reality for
both singer and listener.

Recurrently in this discussion one comes across an insight that makes one
tremble for the human interest. I refer to the case of wholesale doubt of the truth
and reality of words and the report of experiences. Whatever the specific insta-
bility of reference the general ground of suspicion undermines the poles of
comprehension and communication, thus the anchorage of reason and sanity in
social existence. The sense of truth is the ultimate security no matter what
conditions are made on knowledge or the standards of truth.

The question Stevens knew was worth debating. Some might say that the
epistemological issue becomes irrelevant for literature or any art. Reality is a
trope like all the others. Maybe so but the "illusion" (another trope) of the
world's presence (or absence) is necessary to affirm the actual effect of *living*
with mind and senses fully engaged. Writing would be unintelligible, or
subject to anarchic interpretation which is the same thing, without a firm
consciousness of referability, or "presence." The reader is present, called up to
be present by the writing. The writer is present in that one existence is contingent upon the other. But a subject is also present if only to indicate outside the
margins of fantasy the *possible* existence of all subjects. These are in fact
existential needs. If it is a language, a culture, or society and history that
speaks in the text, how does one respond to it? A response always defines one's
existence as a person, and to assume that others read in the mind-set of a
subculture or another culture may abstract their existence entirely. How does a
reader abstract himself in the reading? The fact that "reality" or true existence
is an endless hypothesis does not lessen the *moral* as well as practical need to
affirm it. Words and reality and persons are dependencies. This demands a
response-ability beyond the responsibility of the critic to describe "what a
work says."

The suggestion that this is in some basic way a moral responsibility is made
by Lawrence Rainey in his recent book on Pound. He was himself viewing an
issue of deconstructionist skepticism. Was it important that Pound misused or
abused historic fact in the *Cantos*? Rainey found himself making a sort of last-
ditch defense of the validity of external fact.

...fact reenters the debate in a more virulent form, for every reader is painfully aware that *The Cantos* intersects with the salient fact of Western history in the twentieth century: the Holocaust. Indeed in the holocaust of fact enacted by criticism in recent decades, the fact of the Holocaust has been the only survivor.[21]

Presumably Rainey was thinking, with The *Cantos* as a literary example, of license taken with history, how a later effort might exploit the Holocaust according to radically relativist precepts. I would agree that the Holocaust may be one of the last historic *facts* that critical epistemologies and doctrinal skepticism must stumble against and find difficult to escape. The respect for fact is like the respect for moral equality in each individual of an abstract collective. Both supports went down before the confirmation of total destruction in violence.

It has been a matter of wonder for me to see how often Stevens' texts have had prophetic effect in this writing. The values of art and literature, resting on their metaphoric languages, were keenly at stake when Stevens wrote, "reality became violent," and when that "monster," "things as they are," had to be faced before creation was possible. To say that "reality became violent" would be a naively uncertain thing to say even with a bayonet at one's throat, if language skepticism could be carried that far. But Stevens said it strongly, even passionately, at a time of war and post-war crisis. The normative imagination has been haunted by concepts of false reality or false consciousness for as long as the word modern has possible application, perhaps since Descartes. In the ages of crisis in knowledge it was tempting to believe that "true" reality had only negative meaning in the denial of the inventions of human minds. What was culture and tradition for Eliot but that which anchored and controlled the natural "real" world in its reductive violence and animal emphasis? What was divinity if not the perfect recourse to a higher absolute "reality?" These are examples of the solipsistic alienated consciousness and Eliot was among the first to write of it when he expressed the surprising surreal image that opens "The Love Song of J. Alfred Prufrock."[22]

> Let us go then, you and I,
> When the evening is spread out against the sky
> Like a patient etherized upon a table.

No image could be more antithetical to likeness and be still true for the poem, highly denaturalized as the evening sky has become. The protagonist is made equally antiseptic and abstract just as his isolation is emphasized in the reference, "you and I." It appears through the length of the poem that there is no "you" and the dialogue is a monologue. In the apocalyptic sense all reality has disappeared, leaving behind only "a pair of ragged claws," an uneaten peach, and a dream of mermaids singing.

The question whether Pound was a forerunner of postmodernism is legitimate in those Cantos where the author vanishes and history itself becomes a serial text, its "gists" speaking for itself alone, the text of language, history, and a depersonalized memory having absorbed the world, author and reader. The triangulation that Davidson spoke of is gone, things seem flattened to the earth so that the quotes from the letters of Adams or Malatesta no longer seem theirs, or anyone's, not even for a subjective mind self-examined, nor for a dialogue invited with the reader. In a paradoxical sense "reality" has triumphed without mimesis or mediation, transcending the author's will or consciousness even as he dictates what its substance will be. But "dictate" may seem the right word once the hypothetical nature of metaphor has been removed. Even in the Bible God sometimes spoke and was heard in his own person, and sometimes the patriarchs and prophets dared argue with him. Did a deeper more inaccessible absolute exist within nature and in such abstract forces as the power of money and the counterforce of esthetic order?

One must risk summing things up. To find anchorage in the world, faced by the elusiveness of truth and reality, one tends towards the absolute; there is the absolute of natural fate and the force in events and people subsumed under the heading of *power*, there is the higher reality of the transcendental divine which includes both power and judgment, and there is finally and simply the acceptance of the man-made reality of culture, words on a page.

I have stressed the rejection of personal intervention and the self-surrendering acceptance of a higher reality in the work of Eliot. His way was transcendence, there was no other way out from being etherized on a table, or sunk like Bleistein beneath the sea and deservedly taken back into the protozoic slime. Though Pound might fairly be accused of a different violent extreme, he shared with Eliot an effort to position himself against one form of false consciousness, that of the post-Romantics. For with Pound, champion of modernism, the imagination of artists returns with greater virility of will to seize power for art in its own name, one way of reacting to the effect where "reality became violent." In a world of false consciousness and uncertifiable reality, power begins to substitute for knowledge and belief. As power it is "real," that is, enforceable, where nothing else has that assurance. It enforces itself in art and in Pound's strong pose of the esthetic in politics.

When Eliot sought backing for civilization in the naturalist theme of organic evolution, the preferred "reality" became traditional culture. Going deeper into the history of natural humanity and its link with culture Pound chose Malatesta. The face and posture of Sigismondo, not to mention Mussolini, can tell us one way a cultural order may find legitimacy. Critics and readers have noted Eliot's tendency to return to the "bang" from the "whimper" in describing the way the world ends. When the imagination is blocked by violent reality it begets a counter-violence in the apocalyptic imagination. By that I would refer to the super-heroics of martyrdom, though it might as well be called a super-passivity. The classic theme tells us that violence supports the sense of reality like nothing else. The greatest overt and subliminal expressions of violence are found in Eliot, including his plays, much more than in Pound, and the reason is precisely the hunger for transcendence, that is, for a reality made absolute. Spiritual transcendence needs support from martyrs in the struggle with reductive or illusory physical reality. Confronting naturalistic death the martyr bears its uncompromised cruelty. We are reminded of Rainey's point on the Holocaust as an ultimate "fact." The interesting thing is that writers cannot translate death into one of the "vocabularies" of metaphor satisfactorily, and when they try they succeed most in pointing to an opaque and unbearable reality.

Believe this or not as the reader will but years after I left my text's draft with the closing lines above I remembered the last stanzas of that remarkably expressive contemplative poem "Sunday Morning." and decided I had contradicted my own reading of Stevens' and Williams' poetry as in a phenomenologically humanist poetics. Death is an important subject in their poems and a representation of reality. In poet's philosophy without scaffolding of reason all phenomena are human and consist of life, death is real but without phenomena, "an opaque and unbearable reality" as viewed in prospect.

As example Stevens' poem treats the dramatic relation of Sunday's ghosts from a tomb in Palestine in their quarrel with a more or less golden earthly Sunday with all its non-divine pleasures. The tomb and its spiritual messages and particularly its victory over death reigns over the woman's mind throughout and demands response. The challenging reading comes twice before the end, "Death is the mother of beauty…" I read beauty to mean a different, not unbearable reality like that of the void, but another bearing the life sense of appreciations, even of the will to live, the "Everlasting Yes" which needs Death to be known and understood. But what does that mean? There are so many ways death has nothing to do with beauty. We say if it has meaning it pertains to poetic meaning. Perhaps it is what Rorty meant in the contribution of a "poeticized culture," or what Levinas meant when he spokes of the "trace" of God in the presence and revelation of the living human face.

Notes

1.   I have previously mentioned my early college youth attraction to all the verse and prose I knew of Eliot. That was later followed by an almost equal passion for this particular poem of Stevens, and later still in graduate work by devotion to all his work. I say this because the inspiration for this book has had a lifetime to nourish its effects upon my own writing and teaching. Before I read philosophy the poets were my philosophers, and so remain in this case with the exception of one I give myself liberty to treat in an appendix, Emmanuel Levinas.

2.   Stephen Greenblatt and Giles Gunn, eds., *Redrawing the Boundaries: The Transformation of English and American Literary Studies* (New York: Modern Language Association of America, 1992). [Hereafter referred to as GG.] The sweep of this collection of essays is represented by the fact that each of its contributors deals as an authority within the conventional period divisions of literary study. I take my

own use of the heading "cultural poetics" from an advertisement of the University of California Press when it published this text.

3.   James Miller in his biography of Foucault quotes one rebuttal to Derrida, charging him with "a pedagogy which gives...to the master's voice the limitless sovereignty which allows it to restate the text indefinitely." (Original source *Histoire de la folie a l'age classsique* [Paris, 1972, p. 603]. *The Passion of Michel Foucault* [New York: Simon & Schuster, 1993], p.121).

4.   It is more certain that postmodern poetics seems to eliminate individual agency on all sides of the equation for reading and writing. In theory the text seems to arrive and be received without passing through the hand and mind of a person. Of the modernists Joyce did most to disappear and become history, Ireland, Dublin, all of language and culture that was connected. But Joyce was a monster genius and agent artist, *sui generis*, present in all his styles and languages.

5.   *Christianity and Culture* (New York: Harcourt, Brace and Company 1940, 1949), p. 201.

6.   The fuller reference is this: "It is one thing to compare literature with the other arts (and disciplines) conceived as uniquely structured disciplines, and quite another to treat novels, paintings, buildings, logical treatises, legislation, and institutional regulations all as texts participating in the complex and contestatory process through which societies define and maintain the structure not only of their institutions but of human entities. (We usually call the human entities that live within and largely constitute society "persons," though we might more properly use some analytical nomenclature like that of narratology and label them "actants."), (GG, 88).

7.   It has been the source of question and confusion, how did postmodern literary theory develop as a critical method to create "cultural poetics" as its most influential offspring? In one general understanding deconstruction theory, as such, shifted interpretation away from reference to person and author, or any effective dependence on mimesis, leaving imaginative language to stand by itself except as it reflected the "narrative" texts of a culture or the subtexts of the individual and social psyche. One speculates that in part it was to fill a vacuum in historic causality left by the theoretical failure of nineteenth-century Marxism that such satellite schools of criticism as the New Historicism or the newest literary neo-Marxism were developed.

8.   I am not writing a polemic here and I am sure literary history is an indispensable branch of literary study and may have use of a discipline called cultural poetics; certainly that is true for the new departments of cultural studies. However, if in literary criticism as such characters, action (plot) scene, and thought become allegorical at every turn, what is the effect on the reader whatever his/her allegiance to ideas? The novel's theme will accuse itself for its mechanical effect on life and people. The novel's propaganda effect will be thin and decay as fast as the thinnest of all political speeches because it will bore and shame everyone with just average intelligence   Then what is the value and need for a cultural poetics? Usually a poetics is designed for the difficulties of reading not its simplicities. I have to confess that I have not read a treatment in cultural poetics of a novel like Malraux's *Man's Fate* or Dostoevsky's *The Possessed* or any lesser political novel and I seriously would like to hear of one. As it is I must think of it as a discipline best designed for histories and biographies, other more academic texts in psychology, anthropology, sociology and political science would hardly need a poetics.

9.   He taught this to his classes at Bennington College, where I was once his colleague in the Literature Division. See *Counter-Statement* and *The Philosophy of Literary Form* as the best texts for treating the fundamentals of Burke's theory.

10.   New York: Vintage Books, 1941, 1957, p.92.

11.   Luc Ferry and Alain Renaut, *French Philosophy of the Sixties* (Amherst: University of Massachusetts Press, 1990), pp. xii, 1-32.

12.   The terms postmodern and post-structuralist seem to have interchangeable use in the general discussion in this area. Postmodern has much looser and broader usage but since it is more familiar in this country in being applied to the topics covered I will use it henceforth alone.

13.   New York: The Macmillan Co., 1924, pp. 340-44.

14.   *The Case for a Humanistic Poetics* (Philadelphia: University of Pennsylvania Press, 1991).

15.   Foucault in *Arts*, June 15, 1966, quoted by Ferry and Renaut, p.98.

16.   Ferry and Renaut, p.18.

17.   A text published by Stanley Fish, influential as usual among general readers as well as academics, has the title, *There's No Such Thing as Free Speech: And It's a Good Thing, Too.* His work under other titles as well should be read for clarification as well as interest for the issues dealt with briefly here.

18.   Levinas, *Ethics and Infinity,* p. 117.See Appendix A for larger treatment of Levinas' thinking as well as the writings of Mikhail Bakhtin that have relation to humanist poetics. See also appendix c which treats the recent scholarly study of Michael Eskin of both Levinas and Bakhtin in connection with this aspect of poetic theory. At this point and wherever the reader feels the need for a definition of humanist poetics or the term "poethics" as Eskin uses it I refer him/her to appendix c (A Note on *Ethics and Dialogue in the Works of Levinas, Bakhtin, Mandelshtam, and Celan* by Michael Eskin. [New York: Oxford University Press 2000]).

19.   Boston: Rowan Tree Press, 1981, pp. 26, 14, 17.

20.   Frank B. Farrell, *Subjectivity, Realism, and Postmodernism—The Recovery of the World* (New York: Cambridge University Press, 1994), pp. 245-48. Farrell is a philosopher disposed to argue with postmodern thought. In his original text he presents Davidson's own remarkably apt explanation of "triangulation."

      If I were bolted to the earth I would have no way of determining the distance from me of many objects. I would only know they were on some line drawn from me toward them. I might interact successfully with objects, but I could have no way of giving content to the question where they were. Not being bolted down, I am free to triangulate. Our sense of objectivity is the consequence of another sort of triangulation, one that requires two creatures. Each interacts with an object, but what gives each the concept of the way things are objectively is the base line formed between the creatures by language. The fact that they share a concept of truth alone makes sense of the claim that they have beliefs, that they are able to assign objects a place in the public world. ("Rational Animals,"*Action and Events*, Ernest LePore and Brian McLaughlin, eds. [Oxford: Basil Blackwell, 1985], p. 480, referred by Farrell, op. cit.,p.118).

21.   Rainey, op.cit., p. 80.

22.   For the reader with interest in the theme and how it had development in my own mind I cite my first book *The Passive Voice*, published in 1966 and treating "The Solipsism of Modern Fiction" as outlined under that title in the first chapter. (Ohio University Press,1966).

19

Poetry, Culture, and Politics

From Culture to Politics

It is not by historic coincidence that the obsession with culture as a theme for literature and its criticism reached a climax at the time of the first great war. World War I, starting from political and territorial differences, came in propaganda or actual effect to be waged for the survival of European civilization. World War II had similar effect with much greater conviction for the poets I have treated in these pages. The sequence suggests that the penultimate political crisis is war, which finds its justifications where it can, at the heights or the depths of defensible reason. Eliot continued his own precedent in 1940, stating his faith in culture even to its metaphysical base: "The dominant force in creating a common culture is religion." It was logical to move from that point to say, "I do not believe that the culture of Europe could survive the complete disappearance of the Christian faith."[1] Within Eliot's comprehensive declaration culture met religion as the item of life concern, and both almost simultaneously met with politics, certainly the major arena of cosmic struggle in modern times.[2]

Eliot's claim for the saving of European culture seems absolute, but it is hardly larger in implication than Stevens' claim for bringing poetry into the saving of culture written in a letter to Hi Simon, one of the closest of his early critics and admirers.

> If poetry, "this base of every future," is really that, and if it is to be identified with the imagination, then the imagination is the base of every future.... Briefly, he that imagines the future and, by imagining it, creates it, is a creator of genius and stands on enormous pedestals. (SL, 2)

The contrast with Eliot's emphasis on the past is significant. Since Stevens in this letter was explicating "Owl in Clover" and arguing with his Marxist critics, the question of a political future becomes apparent and understandable. The equally significant parallel is with Pound's esthetic politics that found support from governors and tyrants who "stand on enormous pedestals." Knowing the apocalyptic crisis of culture, Pound, too, summoned poetry. He was the widely heard exponent of the modernist hubris for art (no longer art for art's sake alone) which he liked to express with informal abrupt-ness, "Man gittin' Kulchur had better try poetry first."[3] With more earnest dignity Stevens would make the same claim, acknowledging a question relat-ing the "fate of culture " to the "present position of poetry."

> It seems that poetic order is potentially as significant as philosophic order. Accord-ingly, it is natural to project the idea of a theory of poetry that would be pretty much the same thing as a theory of the world based on a coordination of the poetic aspects of the world.... Many sensitive readers of poetry without being mystics or romantics or metaphysicians, feel that there probably is available in reality something accessible through a theory of poetry which would make a profound difference in our sense of the world. (SL, 590)

In 1941 or thereabouts reality (the world) had become violent and what was needed was a theory of poetry that would in effect be a "theory of the world." Stevens was referring to his unfulfilled project for a theory of poetry, so very broadly defined, and a professorial chair to study it. It is with hindsight no surprise to see Williams endorse a similar project. During the debate over culture which had its impetus from Eliot's writing, Williams wrote one serial correspondent, Horace Gregory, "I think you and I should institute a research into the form of our culture..." With a confidence that matched Pound he had asserted earlier,

> With my knowledge and equipment, if someone should make me Professor of Ameri-can in one of our better universities, I believe that within a month I could push our literature and in consequence our culture ahead at least twenty years.

Inspired by both Pound and Gertrude Stein, he then proclaimed, "the tre-mendous cultural revolution implied by this interior revolution of technique..." The word revolution made a good mark of modernist excitement.

> It's the words, the words we need to get back to, words washed clean. Until we get the power of thought back through a new minting of words we are actually sunk. This is a moral question at base...
>   It can't be helped that the whole house has to come down. In fact the whole house has to come down....it has to be rebuilt by unbound thinking.[4]

The stimulus for this excess was probably his strong reaction to Eliot's conservative view of cultural crisis as well as, in his view, conservative poet-ics. Eliot "is for us a cipher. We must invent we must create out of the blankness about us, and we must do this by the use of new constructions." "On the poet devolves the most vital function of society: to recreate it—the collective world- in time of stress..."[5] Writing to Gregory he stressed,

> It is the poet who lives locally, and whose senses are applied no way else than locally to particulars, who is the agent and the maker of all culture.... But if the head, the intellect, on which he rightly calls for direction, contemns him,... then dynamite is the only thing that will open the channel again. " Eliot " being an expatriate, being a gifted

mind, being what he is, ...should be branded for the worst possible influence in American letters. (WL, 226)

This language of cultural combat and political revolution had of course its model in Pound. The incitement of his language in *Kulchur* is very strong.

Nothing cd. be less civil, or more hostile to any degree of polite civilization than the tribal records of the hebrews. There is not a trace of civilization from the first lines of Genesis up to the excised account of Holophernes. The revival of these barbarous texts in the time of Luther and Calvin has been an almost unmitigated curse to the occident.[6]

The passage is a good example of prejudice associated with abstract language; the great word "civilization" meets with the "tribal records" of "hebrews," the latter banished to lower case to emphasize the reduction to lower material or biological fact.

Disturbingly reactionary as that might seem today, it illuminates group prejudice as cultural outsiders become images to project the dread of cultural collapse. The fear raised by the "clash of civilizations" leads naturally to a central process of de-culturation projected in apt images of dehumanization as found or created in abusive treatment. Reductive language, reductionist acts are weapons of war and aim for extinction of the enemy. Williams wrote in counter thrust that poetry must act as *cure* for the associational mind, or for the tropes of prejudicial allegory. One thinks again of his own figure in *Paterson,* his "city as a man," a trope to end all tropes which descend from caricatured fragments of humanity.

It was inevitable that a debate so passionate on the subjects of poetry and culture in a time of periodic war should be linked to the most deeply partisan political conflict. Nevertheless it seems remarkable that two deeply commit-ted major poets with achieved identities, Pound and Eliot found it so natural and easy to move from poetry to culture and from there to what we would call activist politics today. Pound endorsed Fascism and Eliot made his early claim to be an English monarchist and High Church Tory, so much the Americans they both were, the first in his frontier radical spirit, and Eliot in his early outright acceptance of Europe as his cultural fatherland and England as his home.

Their history clarifies a definition. Cultural politics is holistic politics on behalf of large communities, whether nations or other sub-specie groupings. As poets, Eliot and Pound brought their politics from the defense of culture, or civilization, and they based themselves on the strongest criticism of the secu-lar, philistine, democratic and commercial culture of their original homes. Pound's esthetic standard and Confucian esteem for order in life and art looked for his ripest subject matter in that direction, and Eliot's firm belief that only a highly organized religion could give shape and moral fiber to a living culture gave him his discreet role as cultural evangelist in both Europe and America.

The consequence for my theme was that Pound and Eliot became deeply involved in the great twentieth century totalitarian challenge to liberal democratic politics. The implications were large. Could the state be made responsible for the whole goodness and happiness of lives, its culture of "sanctions and values," without becoming totalitarian? Was Marxism, for instance, an economic theory of politics or was it cultural? The deformed Hegelian Nazi certainly identified the state as embodying a culture and responsible for it. That ideal program was surely a greater temptation than defending racial identity to Hitler's followers, among them, Heidegger[7]. Eliot, on his own side, took as much inspiration from Matthew Arnold and Irving Babbitt as he did from Charles Maurras and *Action Française*, and though he insisted that religion was ultimately essential, in detail he was a vigorously holistic conservative who asserted cultural unity and authority as an overt goal of politics and this was the character of his frequent essays on politics in the *Criterion*.

Hindsight today suggests that the driving force in modern racism and nationalism essentially made itself known in cultural consciousness, not narrowly political or racial. German Nazism, it is generally understood, made the surprising but enormously successful synthesis of culture and bio-racism the metapolitical basis of its policies. Cultural politics at that extreme became the general acceptance of historical and naturalist determinism, moved toward thought police, and abolished quite literally the "rights" to life and liberty. People were manipulated and available to be manipulated. Why was that true? Perhaps it was because cultural consciousness reached more deeply with the Germans than racial or national identity. It touched past success and hope for the future more readily. Perhaps it was that they were in fact an army led by schoolmasters. But racial or biological determinism gave added security with the help of war. Hitler aimed for the secular redemption of the German people in the name of prejudice, order and power. The authoritarian impulse in cultural politics would purge humanity of its reductive human traits or the defined qualities of the flawed and inferior. War and euthanasia were Hitler's weapons of death offered in the name of evolutionary survival.[8]

The magisterial roles of Eliot and Pound in literary modernism followed according to their own ambitions, as they attempted the task of cultural oracles and teachers in ways that Arnold and Ruskin might not appreciate, but the theme is cultural failure. The accent is found in Pound's reiterations. "Democracies have fallen, they have always fallen, because humanity craves the outstanding personality. And hitherto no democracy has provided sufficient place for such an individuality" (PLE, 224). He writes this in the context of urging America to a renaissance of the arts where he counted on the indispensability of support from wealth. Reversing direction, Eliot made the same appeal for a hereditary aristocracy, in effect a clerisy under the sanction of the Church. In brutal fact their expressions in favor of a higher culture included strong traces of racism (or ethnic prejudice) and an allegiance to power and empire with backing from natural science, and in these crucial emphases they were in harmony with the totalitarian wave of the century.[9]

In his own voice Eliot announced a major life commitment in the *Criterion*, "Politics has become too serious a matter to be left to the politicians."[10] In his later poetry and his prose pronouncements Eliot writes as if he had really become the literary institution he describes in "Tradition and the Individual Talent," a medium for poetry and a culture, with a tradition speaking through him. The effects in his work seem *ex cathedra* and for his less appreciative audience he might sound like the Pope. In some respects he fulfills the prescription of present day literary-cultural critics who speaking with great authority, describe the text as a cultural artifact, whether expressing a cultural elite, an economic class or an empowered gender, all institutions reducing the individual writer to an half-conscious organ of communication, a cultural catalyst or medium.[11]

Ezra Pound, however, was able to speak in a more violent personal style for a similar theme where the author is raised to the status of cultural warrior, and his patron and protector typically in the form of Renaissance tyrant or Chinese emperor. But before that and fourteen years before the publication of "Tradition and the Individual Talent," Pound published "The Serious Artist" as his effort to "rewrite Sidney's Defence of Poesy." The empowering model for poetry and art was significantly the science of medicine, which included "the art of diagnosis" (called the "cult of ugliness" by Pound) and "the art of cure, simply summing up science, ethics and art in the "cult of beauty." Even then in 1913, Pound forecast his future career as political activist in declaring that art anticipated and laid the basis for ethics and civics in propounding "the nature of man" and "the nature of men when living together in groups" This was not a vague commitment, and as the years advanced Pound showed his temporary enthusiasm for the Marxist left in the twenties, though it was abortively coincident with his interest in Mussolini who began as a Socialist himself.[12]

Certainly his busy letters and manifestos to editors, publishers, patrons and other writers make him seem the master literary *entrepreneur*, handling the reputations of writers (mostly to their great benefit) as if they were commodities on the exchange or political constituents. He served literature well but fanatically confident in himself and confident in his estimate of others, insulting, hectoring, patronizing, and befriending, he was a tyrant at heart, and for a time very powerful. Above all his operations in the political arena were rashly confident and reductive. The following is characteristic from a letter written in 1934:

> We have got to clean up the economic mess; and your generation has got to understand how much of life can be cured by a very simple application of economic sense to reality...

> No one now writing can do anything of real interest unless they perform a few acts of mental hygiene. Mostly as simple as brushing one's teeth or using iodine on a cut.

One of his early followers in poetry was Williams, who, like others, felt both his beneficence and oppression. Though as a poet Williams learned much from Pound and was indebted for many acts of friendship, he knew his own cultural and political ethos very well and made the differences clear in his correspondence. Writing how some people have an innate power, Williams calls it authority:

> Pound has it in the evocative power he has over words. What is it? Damned if I know....To me it is an immoral quality. I suppose Napoleon and Alexander had it to perfection. It makes a man think he is better than anyone else. But unless he uses it for others, to make himself a servant in some sense for humanity, to man, to those about him who need him-he turns out to be a selfish bastard like Pound, like Napoleon...
>   I don't know the final answer but I do know that Ezra is just a self-destroyer when he talks as he has done to me of the Russians and the Spaniards and now of the Americans."[13]

This is interesting as a counter thrust from the same frontier of the democratic tradition which led to Pound's confidence in himself and his world-saving nostrums. The forthright thinking of Williams brought his moral proscription of Pound/Napoleon to confront the power over words in himself as well as Pound. There is confidence in Williams' poetic assertions, but always in the person speaking, never a generalized power, an omnipotence like that of history or the abstract omniscience of art. He expressed his opposition in an angry outburst like the following directed in a letter to Pound. "You deal in political symbols instead of actual values, poetry" (WL 249). Writing this way Williams was really making a claim for his own politics as well as his poetics of immediacy, bringing both into clear visibility. The immediate issue, of course, was the Fascism which had followed consistently from Pound's aesthetic politics as I've described it in an earlier chapter and less consistently perhaps, from his peculiar economic policy of anti-usury (or anti-Semitism). More directly Williams reacted to Pound's radio broadcasts from Rome.

> Ezra wanted to live, live fully, exquisitely at the peak of feeling, and to feel he was leading the others into a beautiful world of which he was the disciple. But Jesus, what did it lead him to? To an attempt to condone Hitler, to a completely unfeeling attitude toward the Spanish rebels, to real joy at the thought of Russians slaughtered by the millions at the time of Hitler's first success. If that's the end of his grand schemes then he's a plain dupe of his own vanity. I suspect him more and more. (WL, 213)

Williams saw that the error was in the coldly abstract political will that would sacrifice endless "human" content for the sake of the form. "The logicality of fascist rationalization is soon going to kill him. You can't argue away wanton slaughter of innocent women and children by the neo-scholasticism of a controlled economy program" (WL, 184). This was an insight from a politically liberal humanism as it in the end must be defined. For Williams it was linked to immediacy and free form in verse, what he called the new "measure." Pound's art became a search for authority and order, if not in traditional metrics than in quotation and translation, in the "gists," the ideas that became facts. These could be prejudices, sometimes paranoid abstractions that rose to the level of great effect in politics, like the Jew of usury. It was reification in reverse, where people became "ideas," and were dealt with as such.

The Search for Authority

On the highest religious level Eliot found the premise for authoritarian politics with the idea of God, and then with the "spiritual organism of Europe" which he said was indispensable to make people more than part of a material and mechanical order. "If (the spiritual organism) dies, then what you organize will not be Europe, but merely a mass of human beings speaking several different languages."[14] To avoid the simplification of a complex mind it should be noted that Eliot at one point warned against a danger in the thinking of his conservative dissertation subject, Francis H. Bradley: "His "words...indeed Bradley's philosophy as a whole—might be pushed, which would be danger-ous, (in) the direction of diminishing the value and dignity of the individual, of sacrificing him to a Church or a State" (203). This is a remark that belongs to Eliot's earlier mind and no doubt with his American education. It is note-worthy that the threat of biological and mechanical reduction, is one stimulus for Eliot's seeking the highest level of abstraction in the mystical and divine. A secondary height above reduction existed in the heroic and mythic contexts of reference used by Eliot and Pound in their verse. Williams' spontaneous reaction was to bring value response to the ordinary person and to the modern and imperfect secular world. It was also the response of Stevens in his serious interview with quotidian reality, and the discoveries of the secular imagina-tion. Together the poets asserted democracy as if strongly aroused to opposi-tion by Eliot in his search for divinity and the literary and mythical heroicism of allusion in his verse.

This later quarrel between Pound and Williams was particularly ironic since much of what the latter believed could be expressed in some earlier words of Pound himself, for so long Williams' mentor in verse. "Go in fear of abstrac-tions," Pound wrote in his testamentary statement for modern verse. He also said pertinently, "I am no more Mauberley than Eliot is Prufrock"[15] That was the ground perhaps on which he wrote his long essay on Henry James (1918) in great praise of a "hater of tyranny," a defender of "human liberty, personal liberty, the rights of the individual against all sorts of intangible bondage..."

> The whole of great art is a struggle for communication ...communication is not a leveling....It is a recognition of the right of differences to exist ....Kultur is an abomination....all repressive uniforming education is an evil." (LE, 296, 298)

In Stevens' mind the critique of teutonized *Kultur* was the substance of a critique of politics itself. In his case the poet, in distinction from the politician, became without paradox a sort of democratic hero.

> The role of the poet may be fixed by contrasting it to that of the politician. The poet absorbs the general life: the public life. The politician is absorbed by it. The poet is individual. The politician is general. It is the personal in the poet that is the origin of his poetry....
>
>   As individual he (the poet) must remain free. The politician expects everyone to be absorbed as he himself is absorbed. This expectation is part of the sabotage of the individual. (SL, 526)

What Eliot had to say for tradition, the "mind of Europe" and the impersonality of the poet comes immediately into contrast. When he wrote his critical essays he certainly did not mean to be the politician, and yet Stevens' words are most apt for a critique of Eliot's politics. In that respect Stevens expresses a political ethos as well as a poetics of the personal and individual. The first phase of the poet's problem, he says, is to reach himself. The second phase is "to maintain his freedom." To absorb the general life is to remain a person beyond group abstraction. To *be* absorbed is to surrender to large conformities or ideologies, and perhaps to end by translating everything into politics. I think Stevens suggests that this is not only an error for poetry, but an error and transgression *within* political discourse. "Life and reality, on the one hand," he wrote, " and politics, on the other, ...are not interchangeable terms." Stevens' "politics" could in this sense be described as a form of anti-politics. The paradox, however, may be considered an important characteristic of a truly liberal and democratic politics, a politics that distrusts itself, and exercises speech accordingly.

The political discourse of Eliot could conclude by elevating Church and State over persons, as well as the further institutions of a specified hierarchical and authoritarian culture. Williams would see that as a desertion of what he called the "local" (by which he meant "life and reality") and of what he thought of as true culture in its ever-making and unfinished process.

> Eliot is a maimed man. He fled the rigors of an American application, embracing the Church largely to cover up that.... "It is in the wide range of the local only that the general can be tested for its one unique quality, its universality. The flow must originate from the local to the general...." and "It is the poet who lives locally, and whose senses are applied no way else than locally to particulars, who is the agent and the maker of all culture. (WL, May, 1944, 224-5)

Cultural Politics and Democratic Humanism

I have been proposing that Williams and Stevens enriched acceptance of the democratic inheritance of America just as it can as confidently be said that

Eliot and Pound opposed themselves to it. One issue among others that haunted the youth of all four poets was the flight to Europe which eventually made Pound and Eliot exemplary expatriates. Stevens rather amazingly refrained from Europe all his life, despite his interest in the cosmopolitanism of his friends and his sustained attention to French art and literature. Williams, more exposed to the moods and interests of the literary avant-garde, seemed almost defiantly perverse in linking his life and work to the working-class town of Paterson, New Jersey, and its environs. The security if not the inspiration they took from their mundane occupations, pediatrician and insurance lawyer, have become familiar literary anecdotes.

It is true that expatriation can be as much the stimulus of the homeward seeking imagination as the outward bound. In their own problem of coming to terms with it Eliot and Pound reflect the culture of democracy. Tocqueville's lesson was prophetic in describing the burden of an artistic and intellectual elite, that is, the imagination's burden in the American democracy. To face average reality, a world without outlines or distinctions, and then create? To see beneath stale conformities the unheroic animal, or at best, the human universal which moves steadily and always towards its lowest common denominator, and then declare equality at the base? In this context one may remember Lionel Trilling's impressive generalization many years ago on the subject of modernist artists and liberal democracy.

> If we name those writers who are thought of as the monumental figures of our time, we see that to these writers the liberal ideology has been at best a matter of indifference. Proust, Lawrence, Joyce, Yeats, Mann (as novelist)—all of them have their own love of justice and the good life, but in not one of them does it take the form of a love of the ideas and emotions which liberal democracy, as known by our educated class, has declared respectable.[16]

Rather than a *love* for liberal democracy the question was what degree of hostility and rejection, and this takes a directly expressed form in the poets Trilling didn't mention, Pound and Eliot, and also a clearer form of affirmation (I believe one might even use the word "love") in the work of Williams and Stevens.

I understand the challenge Trilling's words give to my large undertaking in this book but I have already agreed to his characterization of literary modernists as indifferent or directly hostile to liberal democracy in assigning that role to Eliot and Pound. I'm not sure I agree with him on the basis of that hostility nor on the version of liberal democracy they keep in their targets. It is of course true that a large following of the modernist masters and the postmodern generations have been brought to accept extremely broad criticism of the general and political culture of the West in the last hundred years. But that may be a gift of the endowed laws and freedoms of the very same democracies being criticized or unloved. The passages that follow may help in distinguishing

what can be still appreciated in the old terms that became so strangely prejudiced by many sophisticated and unsophisticated in Trilling's time and ours—
liberal, democratic, and humanist.

Lionel Trilling, of wide influence and strong reputation in his time, was of
course the contemporary of Stevens and Williams and one of the satellite
critics attached to the New Criticism deeply influenced by Eliot. In his book
he examined high culture at the level most relevant to the canon of modern
literature read by students of the academic curriculum. He saw at the time he
was writing and publishing *Beyond Culture* (1961-65) the rise of what he was
one of the first to call the "adversary culture" in America.[17] It probably reached
coherence and strength with the anti-Vietnam war movement but it arose earlier with the so-called Beat Generation, more a literary movement, some of
whose leaders were his students at Columbia. He was by no means a friend of
the "adversary culture" and expressed a fear of its attack on "high" culture
itself (intellectual, esthetic, ethical) which proved prophetic. Here he was in an
ambiguous position for he found in his book that the great modern literary
creators he taught in his classes, Joyce, Proust, Mann, Lawrence, Gide, even
Eliot (to surprise younger readers of my text) were in effect the early mentors of
the "adversary culture" and enemies of the established culture:

> Any historian of the literature of the modern age will take virtually for granted the
> adversary intention, the actually subversive intention, that characterized modern
> writing—he will receive its clear purpose of detaching the reader from the habits and
> thought of feeling that the larger culture imposes, of giving him a ground and a vantage
> point from which to judge and condemn, and perhaps, revise the culture that produced
> him. (BC, xiii).

This is where a classic confusion or contradiction in modern concepts of
culture arises .It begins with thinking of culture in the Arnoldian sense of "the
best that has been thought and said" as distinct from the anthropological view of
the general culture and the modern view of pop culture which features everything
from the most mediocre and vulgar to the most interesting and obscenely criminal. In his own illustration Eliot insisted on including St. Paul's cathedral with
Epson Downs and cabbage dinners. The anthropological view, as I understand it,
does not stress mention of creative change and invention by gifted individuals,
able to stand "beyond culture" and *know* it, as for instance, Joyce attempted and,
most readers think, nearly succeeded. For the most part the anthropological view
would suggest it is an impossible effort. As Trilling puts it, "Yet of course this
total power that the strict definition of culture, in the large sense of the word,
seems to claim for itself can have only a mere formal reality. The belief that it is
possible to stand beyond the culture in some decisive way is commonly and
easily held. In the modern world it is perhaps a necessary belief..."

To be "beyond culture" in the same modern world could, I suggest be
described in many ways: as with outright revolution and anarchy, as giving

oneself up to Dionysian sexual anarchy, as sophistication expressed in comic satire, or in emancipation from average mediocrity and boredom, the outsider as wealthy hermit or snob, as jobless, homeless, transient, or criminal, or as simple depressive heading toward suicide and the outsider as nihilist. These can amount to total rejection of a culture, but Trilling reserved the most apt for the "adversary" he had in mind. "It is a belief still pre-eminently honored that a primary function of art and thought is to liberate the individual from the tyranny of his culture in the environmental sense and to permit him to stand beyond it in an autonomy of perception and judgment."

These are words that gave outlet to many, more than those who would be artists, particularly among the alienated young, naming themselves with the decades. Pound would have used stronger words, whatever his allegiance to Mussolini, and from the beginning he stressed the artist as rebel on his own terms, though I doubt if he could have accepted a "culture" scripted by some-one else. I assume Eliot could not have understood the term "beyond;" that was nowhere, or in what Stevens called "the chaos of the sun." In that respect he might be called a spiritual determinist. Where you stood in respect to culture was determined by faith. Certainly "The Waste Land" was not meant as a call to the rising "adversary culture."

Stevens and Williams were not always in unity of mind but in the essence they would have agreed on the modernist call to arms for art and thought. They might say in addition, however, that this was not the privilege of the artist or intellectual. It could belong to any citizen of an authentic democracy, for the imagination, which is both critical and inventive in its freedom, can always stand beyond the given traits or thinking of a culture. To them, too, the "adversary culture" would be a strange concept for there could hardly be anything in it adversarial that wasn't a part of the free dialogue of minds even when not already inscribed in its sacred monuments and laws.

Yet the war did come and was long in its coming and staying. The hyper treatment of the "culture wars" in the American media and in its politics began just as Trilling's book demonstrated an "adversary culture" and as if there were in fact two cultures at war. That reign of war terminology and hostile debate was increased by the famous or infamous speech that Pat Buchanan made at the Republican convention of 1988 where he asked the party to make total war on the Democrats on that neo-metaphysical stage while they were still fighting for civil rights for blacks and women The reign of warlike lan-guage was immensely heightened by Michel Foucault in the seventies and eighties. Writing from the left in politics he made the competition for *power* and therefore fateful conflict the theme words for understanding any culture and its institutions.

All this made dialogue in politics and culture distracted and dogmatic and prone to being ultimately hostile and violent. The language of power in the academic understanding of culture when combined by mysterious alchemy overt and covert ideological passion made the "culture wars" more angry and conflictual than ever. The effects were made world wide and dangerously so when Professor Huntington wrote his controversial book, *The Clash of Civilizations*, that predicted ultimate wholesale war between, as one example, Western Christian "civilization" and the Muslim Arab entity existing on the same broad level of a civilization. At the time I read Huntington's book I thought that the words "culture" and "civilization" had finally become the permanently active surrogates for national, racial, and religious identity, and with that must come the permanently hard climate of incipient war, known as cold war.

In the nineteenth century, German thinkers fused nation and *Kultur* in this way. We have seen how dangerous the word and the devotion to it as a mystique can become. Why has it returned with such passion in the recent three decades? Academic critics could point out that cultures, being what they are, are creatures of slow growth, change while having no laws, leaders, or formal process to govern change, that cultures are prone to change on mere contact with other cultures, as need and desire suit the peoples of culture. Those borrowings may of course include ideologies and political forms that are hostile, but cultures in their relative formlessness are actually more dependent upon free cultural trade, in that sense to be open cultures and peaceful. But academic discussion which does indeed favor a benign multi-culturalism as a general program, in fact focuses politically on militant and defensive cultural identity and finds that the typical relationship is that between hostile and oppressive majority cultures and minorities struggling to defend what they can from the bleak alternatives of restriction and unwanted assimilation.

What does the thinking of democratic humanism have to offer on this great test of its values? One might attempt a few ideas on the ground already covered. First, a universalist democratcy he will welcome the stranger to practice his own beliefs and life customs while assimilating his practical existence on the ground. As for his thinking about culture, his own and that of the new immigrant, the native democrat will believe something like the following:

A culture is not a creature with consciousness and imagination and freedom to think and act. The position beyond culture is a natural freedom when societies know freedom; to propose a change within culture is to be both in and out of the game," as Whitman writes in "Song of Myself," and he no doubt meant that as fundamental in a practicing democracy.

A culture is not identical with a race or nation and should not be their surrogate symbol.. Those who insist societies be inclusive in the way of multicultural states, are probably only insisting on democracy in the relationships of groups. Democracy *means* multiculturalism in almost the same degree that it means the autonomy of individuals and the pluralism of organized groups.

So long as language is not a real barrier the universal figurative nature of culture remains as a growing organism, absorbing, imitating, resisting supposedly foreign elements on the ground of cohabitation in a given space. Thus cultures are always changing, absorbing elements from each other if once geographically distant, borrowing eagerly with the power of the imagination, looking for the new, the useful, the enormously advantageous or pleasurable. But a culture is not fate. One isn't required to live or die for it or by it. To believe in the inevitable difference of cultures on the ground of biological-social differences is not being democratic at all but autocratic or theocratic or simply racist and nationalistic in their oldest vein.. Democracies which are universal in their welcome and social in readiness to meet other peoples, the stranger for instance, cannot be fetishized by the word culture and above all should be suspicious of its political use in identifying individuals and groups. It may not make sense logically, but an individual may identify his culture if he chooses but no one else can. That is to say cultures are subjective concepts and descriptions, voluntarily shared.

Finally, when the word war is used, as in culture wars, we must ask what cause is really at war? Is it a matter of a culture fighting for existence, expansion, conquest? Is it for salvation in heaven, a larger cause than survival on this earth, like the cause for which a suicide bomber dies? Is it because an antagonist trait, custom or belief has been embedded in a stranger nation's laws, or because culture traits are embedded in a religious metaphysics no longer susceptible to the laws of civil society or its constant negotiation for allowable tolerance and peaceful cohabitation? If an important culture trait has been embedded in a religion with values threatening other religions, or independent secular existence as such, then the democracy in which this can happen has already lost itself to the religious wars. The remedy for religious wars is to end the power of religious groups to wage war.

Democracy and Religion

The crowning secularism of American democracy, expressed in the separation of church and state, must be seen in the background of Eliot's campaign for a Christian culture. The Jeffersonian or Emersonian idealizing naturalism that gave so much moral impetus to the American democracy is also to be seen as the antithesis for Eliot's vision of unredeemed nature and unredeemed man in nature. Eliot's search for the spiritual life that counts on the annihilation of natural being in the emblematic form of martyrdom makes both "self-reliance" and "the pursuit of happiness" seem merely vulgar rivals for spiritual salvation and, of course, its antithesis. The ethnic prejudice not to be mistaken in his verse rejects the polyglot, pluralist society of late nineteenth-century America and his anchorage in cultural tradition reflects negatively on doctrines of change and progress, and more deeply, a distrust of the free imagination. Without flippancy one might suggest that Stevens' "first idea" is the reversal of Eliot's interest in "last ideas," that is, those that mark the sharp limit of death to secular and naturalistic thought. Eliot's rejection of humanism is the final touch for an anti-democratic creed without the anchoring premises of a humanism, which in turn cannot be dissociated from the doctrine of egalitarian human rights. The Declaration's universalist doctrine—that all men are created morally and politically equal—is the premise of a humanistic faith, and the search for its ground has, I believe, profound application to the verse and prose of Williams.

The more we speak of Jeffersonian humanism the more we remember its rejection by Eliot as the feeble third choice to his difficult alternatives: you must be a naturalist or super-naturalist, there is nothing else of significance. The consistent naturalistic fate to which he sentenced Bleistein and Apeneck Sweeney compares with the painful martyrdom of the saint. There is no place for Stevens'

"major man" or the "emperor of ice cream," or the virtues and happiness of the Declaration's citizen. Pound was even more absolute when, as in my earlier reference, he wrote, "Democracies have fallen, they have always fallen, because humanity craves the out-standing personality..." His strongest poem of cultural and political dissent, the first of the Mauberley series, makes a rounded judgment of loss and decline in one stanza:

> Faun's flesh is not to us,
> Nor the saint's vision.
> We have the press for wafer;
> Franchise for circumcision.

Pound's summary metaphors are quite convincing, particularly for the purposes of poetry, with the dramatic impact that makes much of the strength in Pound's verse and prose. Ironically, in their aphoristic concision, the lines above ring a bit like newspaper headlines to verify that Pound's strongest impulses underlying the artist's vocation were becoming political. Coincidentally the succinctness of the verse records the penultimate conflict between religion and democracy in the complex of thought shared by Pound and Eliot, Pound on deep modernist esthetic ground of the degradation of ritual and ceremony and discriminating values, and Eliot on his religious base.

On that level it was not mere hyperbole for Pound to condemn two damnable rituals with the franchise and circumcision. There is no disputing that Eliot shared his feelings in his early poetry In fact, as much as usury the franchise must have represented the antithesis to their artistic as well as political will. Where could the normative imagination that discriminates values find feebler inspiration than in the vote of a majority? The lines from "Hugh Selwyn Mauberley" point out the role of poetry in synthesizing the political sensibility on its cultural base. As I read, Pound's coupling of the Jewish ritual with the franchise has that significance. Anti-Semitism had several roles no doubt in

Pound's mind as well as Eliot's where it was even more brutally represented, but its equation here with democracy's ceremony and right may clarify things. Their verse arrived with the climax of anti-Semitism in America and Europe in the last quarter of the nineteenth century and the first decades of the twentieth. The rise of naturalist and apocalyptic thought coincided with the symptoms of an anti-humanist and anti-democratic age. We note the peculiar imagery and significance of circumcision, particularly as one might project it in the days when pagan vitalism faced the new rival religions from Judea and Palestine. The circumcision that dedicated the body to religious group membership must have had strongly ambivalent implications where a vitalist trend of thought was dominant whether it was regarded as physical defacement or the sign of ascetic repression.

If this was anti-Semitic prejudice it tells us much about important distinctions between Pound and Eliot in the precise imagery they used to express it. If circumcision was defacement for one, the Jew was the emblem for unredeemed nature for the other. "A lustreless protrusive eye/ stares from the protozoic slime." The stranger alien represented a species that carried the threat of naturalist leveling and violated both the religious and esthetic sensibilities. In social and political terms, the Jew (and other targets of group prejudice) threatened the sacral limits of racial, religious, national, and cultural identity, one or all of which had become for many the only way of escaping Darwinian primeval substance, "unaccommodated man."

Similarly the age of neo-Darwinian naturalism had much to do with the reaction from democracy and the universal humanism implied by the franchise. It may be that the multi-racial, multi-ethnic aspect of egalitarian democracy most aroused rejection with a real fear of drowning in the mass of mankind. Why should we think that the promise of equality is inspiriting for most people? It suggests rather the exposure to naturalistic death, where, unlike birth, there can be no ignoring human equality at the lowest level of existence. On the other hand, one is a natural democrat at birth, where equality *must* mean that of opportunity, the permanent chance to evolve in existence, a kind of guarantee of freedom in life and the "pursuit of happiness."

The thoroughly "American" poet, one in the mainstream from Whitman, would react precisely at that point. William's hostility toward Eliot was consistent from the first, though his responses mingled admiration with the almost visceral antagonism. In his own verse one may fancy that Williams walked with purpose down the urban streets of Prufrock's anesthetized city and through the "waste land," salvaging what was fixed for rejection by a temperament that had lost the will to live. Doing so he is the poet who reverses the implications of reductive descent, salvaging poetry in the form of "anti-poetry." In his own way he deals with the modernist art of broken images, and the art of unfinished forms that redeem ugliness by expressing it exactly.

The art of disorder, most impressively displayed by Eliot in "The Waste Land," could simulate the apocalypse, a poetic disorder serving as the weapon of a strong criticism on behalf of order. The project of order was more militant, of course, with Pound, who really could claim authentic credentials as a revolutionary. Even its avid defenders would admit that democracy was the politics of disorder. Pound's attack on democracy was explicit on that point, essentially adopting the Fascist formula. In detail, we have the exceptional man or hero at the center. Value in living depends on his force surrounded by the creators, artists and poets, statesman-philosophers for whom he acts as patron. The object is to create the paramount political form opposing itself to democratic anarchy or muddle. Order must be hierarchical; clarity of standards, lucidity of values are ideals of order. Pound's virile hero projects very specific qualities, and the intrinsic highest value is that of power. Order is power expressing itself effectively as control. If one concludes that Pound aims for an esthetic order in politics, it is an order based on power naturalism, sometimes expressed as the vital life in the distinctive hero. Esthetic order, so considered as the base of valuations, opposes itself to an ethical humanism that generates positive attitudes toward the fallen, the handicapped, the disabled, those who cannot add much or anything to the harmony and achievement of the state. It would discriminate between the ugly and the beautiful, between the weak and the strong, the brave and cowardly. Esthetics as the universal basis of discrimination would deny equality at every turn, and give sanctions to hierarchy and rank that seem arbitrary on one side and absolute on the other. Order and freedom, the ethical and esthetic, these are polarities held in negotiation or resolution in democracy's dialectic of weakness and strength that forms its history.

The Democratic Imagination: A System of Contradictions and Paradox

The ethical, the esthetic, and the practical seem to be permanently at war in the American ethos of democracy, and the resultant tensions make a rich source for the poets who have helped express that body of inspirational thought, particularly in the American writing that bases ancestry in Emerson and Whitman. When Williams called "the poet who lives locally....the agent and maker of all culture," he was making a conscious or unconscious recall of Whitman's pronouncement in favor of the poet, "The priest departs...the literatus..." The redemptive strain is in much of what both Stevens and Williams gave words to in the transitions they made between poetry and politics. Poetry was in their sense a higher politics, even in its critique and rejection of politics, as I noted earlier in the work of Stevens. One might go further and say that liberal democracy as such is anti-political in reserve since it is based as much on self-directed criticism as on its own affirmations. Stevens saw poetry as the medium for seizing awareness of concrete universals, where the particular and the general join in mutually self-correcting synthesis.

The imagination that is satisfied by politics, whatever the nature of politics, has not the same value as the imagination that seeks to satisfy, say, the universal mind, which in the case of a poet, would be the imagination that tries to penetrate to basic images, basic emotions, and so to compose a fundamental poetry even older than the ancient world. (NA, 144-45)

This is a statement that makes the essential case for poetic humanism and the echo from Emerson is strong. Equally so was the poignant appeal from Williams in the heyday of the American artist's flight to Europe.

No use for Stein to fly to Paris... The thing , the United States, the unmitigated stupidity, the drab tediousness of the democracy, the overwhelming number of the offensively ignorant, the dull nerve- is there in the artist's mind...She must resolve it if she can...
   How in a democracy... can writing which has to compete with excellence...be at once objective (true to fact) intellectually searching, subtle and instinct with powerful additions to our lives? It is impossible without invention of some sort... (WSE, 118, 119)

Williams is making a Tocquevillian statement, citing here the redemptive task of the imagination made necessary, an imperative in a democracy. It accounts for his obsession with quotidian reality, the latter a word that Harold Bloom called Stevens' fixation, and which Bloom regretted for its philosophic and poetic void of meaning. But what word would he substitute? "Reality" has to be a respected word for democratic poets and that I argue is a meaningful central description of both Williams and Stevens. Perhaps "reality" is a trope for the franchise, searching for the source of consciousness and the actuality of choice. Or again, reality is the name and premise for the existence of persons and shareable things, the world in which Williams grounded his poetry. Certainly it must be where the imagination begins with the "first idea," no matter how hard to locate, and the "first idea" is a necessary trope for freedom, the firstness being where free choice or inspiration have their beginning. In sum "reality" has to be respected even if it cannot be named or fixed in the primal flux, nor later traced in the flux of consciousness. It must be a respected word even though a fiction and even though the imagination searching for it refuses to fix it. Supreme fictions "must change," Stevens argued in his verse, for if all were imagination, or illusion, or trope, the imagination would be forced to stop at the strongest fiction, or the most beautiful and entrancing, and it must not be allowed to stop. Contrariwise the mind cannot stop at a reality, fixed and certain, for that way is dictation and authority.

The peculiar dialectic of the culture and ethos of democracy requires both reduction and transcendence. Reduction looks to the shared base, the common egalitarian substance of the peoples' humanity. Freedom evokes a hunger for the "absolute," or more simply the travel of the imagination to its furthest possibility and need. In democratic principle there is found the gift of self-transcendence. The person and the collective are held open to change; free criticism is imaginative transcendence of the given, the predetermined.

All of Stevens' so quietly passionate ruminations on the imagination are strong essays on behalf of freedom, and the endless open adventure human nature has with ideal versions of what is possible but not yet real. If nothing else the imagination gave release from the psychological burden of both natural and cultural determinism. Evolutionary determinism was real, biological truth was real, that is why the sense of truth required respect for reality. The imagination in a democracy invented fairy tales for children, myths that fed greed and selfishness in adults, prejudiced abstractions for the prejudiced. The imagination served freedom and progress, a necessary function for necessary angels. One could go on like this, reality was in the end, death, the imagination, life.

Williams, in his poet's claim on "life and reality," kept open the access to persons, to individuals otherwise locked in neo-scientific abstract categories. Immediate experience has always been the direction of thrust for self-adjusting democracy, where standardized myths, hysterical superstitions, lies and slanders, and violent actions are meant to receive their correction. It is not an inhibiting paradox to say that a democratic culture includes its severest critics, particularly in poets who give it important test and revelation. The measure of criticism is positive in the work of Williams and Stevens, with two essential principles of democratic humanism to highlight: the centrality of the person for interest and consensual judgment, and the command of freedom for the practical and intellectual imagination.

The Liberal Imagination

The broadest study of the four American poets treated in this text leads to the hypothesis that the relation between the poetic imagination and liberal democracy is not only interesting but fundamental on both sides. This confidence should be bolstered by the recent disquisition of a noted contemporary philosopher, Richard Rorty, who made the "claim that a liberal utopia would be a *poeticized* culture."[18] (Contingency in his title seems to be used to express events unwilled by humans whether accidental or caused in nature.)

In his view Rorty states that "The heroes of liberal society are the strong poet and the utopian revolutionary" (60) and he would "see the founders and transformers of society, the acknowledged legislators of her language and thus of her morality, as people who happened to find words to fit their fantasies, metaphors which answered to the vaguely felt needs of the rest of the society." These are claims that are ambitious and modest at the same time, founders of society who "happened to find" something to answer" to their "fantasies." But that one supposes is how authentically liberal thinking has to sound today. Rorty would probably allow Williams his poetic "absolutes," which are useful fantasies, since "liberal culture needs an improved self-description rather than a set of foundations" and since it is above all "a culture in which poetry had publicly and explicitly triumphed over philosophy, a culture in which recognition of contingency rather than of necessity was the accepted definition of freedom." Rorty adds dryly, "there probably cannot be such a culture," (40) but he would nevertheless still value poetry over philosophy in the culture we do have.

On this ground the differentiations made in the writings of these four poets may be found essential to the task of defining substance and style in the democratic imagination. Eliot himself would demonstrate that a consistently negative reaction from liberal democracy could be class and race oriented, elitist, authoritarian, and traditionalist. Pound shared temperament and conviction with him while reaching the extreme of Fascism with its tempting correlations of order and power. He was not converted by Fascism so much as being able to see it as the political fulfillment of his own long prepared views.

Did his poetic imagination follow suit? That cannot be forced into a simplistic equation. It might be observed, as Williams did, that the poetry of allusion, translation, and pastiche is authoritarian, the poetry of the ancestors. The modernist poetry of Pound and Eliot suggests an age of reactive transition with the imagination under siege, prepared for defense or attack. Its strongest mode is the irony of comparisons, though that can reach the heights with the aid of ancient symbols and myths, and equally matched, it can reach the depths of the reductive animal state. It calls on the power of metaphor to embody essences and abstractions. The part serving the whole, metaphoric prejudice translates quite easily into ethnic prejudice. Prejudice itself can be the bitter after effect of the reductive spirit striving to purge itself. There is a strong temptation for hero worship, and on behalf of order, a taste for the giganticism of power. A reactionary anger may seek the agents and agency responsible for a break with moral and spiritual values, the break with tradition and authority, the failure of heroism, beauty, and order. The enemy would be repeatedly found in the egalitarian and materialist culture that had been the target of the modernist avant-garde for more than a century.

If modernist art and literature absorbed the complex tactic of both extending the reductive spirit to its extreme and then attacking the degraded result, how does that engage with liberal democracy? The answer should be obvious enough. The leveling spirit abolishes discriminations and hierarchies of value, and would destroy the vocation of the elites who write poetry. The democratic ethos comes to terms with disorder or its threat, it comes to terms with plainness and mediocrity, and it must converse with "reality" in its most reductive aspect for, paradoxically enough, in pursuing the ideal of universal equality a reductive realism has no limit.

At the same time it would not inhibit the imagination in striving toward the heights. This may be another democratic contradiction. The imagination, in the Emersonian tradition and as Stevens and Williams understood it, is linked inseparably with freedom, just as a naturalist or supernaturalist determinism, we find historically, could be linked with totalitarian and authoritarian orders which instill obedience in their subjects. A democracy bred in naturalist scientific thought has a special problem with the imagination, just as the ideal of equality clashes with the ideal of liberty. Again, it could be argued that free market capitalism in its orthodox claims can be described as economic determinist and thus anti-humanist and that is a fair criticism of it when so treated. But it is also complexly self-correcting when it is assumed that the market's paramount guide and control is based on the free choice of individuals and therefore the state or some other agency accepts responsibility for social goals beyond the power of any automatic process like the market. Similarly, a democracy which accepts and affirms the principle of checks and balances and the franchise would seek to control and the means to resolve the inevitable conflict of power groups. It would reduce the respect for power as the operative principle in societies and their history. But that, probably Stevens would say, and Rorty would agree, is the right source of tension in the work of the imagination. Only a poet could truly refine the distinctions between contingency and necessity, or between power and values. In any case the argument points to the chief dilemma of a democratic system in leading freedom of choice and action toward an ethical and esthetic dimension beyond self-interest and the struggle for power. There I think Stevens would make his strongest claim for the role of poetry.[19]

I would pursue these generalizations from poetry and poetic theory to offer the conclusion that a democratic culture is a culture of discourse and dialogue and, as Williams used the phrase, a "culture of immediacy". If in this series of hypotheses, I claim that Stevens and Williams are truly poets of democracy they join in being ahistorical in the sense of denying the high authority of the past. Are they somehow extracted from history or nature's determining environments? No, but as in the Emersonian tradition, the poet traced in this outline performs on the level of presumed equality in a discourse with both nature and history. He reaches the immediacy of nature before acknowledging its dominance, before it crystallizes in causality and fate. The dialogue of *response* is the imagination at work, the imagination *is* response. The subject rejects fusion with nature, but while there is no subordination, neither is there aggrandizement of the esthetic or moral will. Freedom leads to a questioning and a discourse whose ground is reality and whose partners are found in the communities of discourse.

The poets of imagination's democracy would free themselves from totalizing formulae, from compulsory obedience to power or to supernatural authority. In effect they would find the true masters of culture in themselves, that is, in the "major man" of the species. The alternatives they would reject, (Williams in particular), would be to place everything into the forms of tradition, or to surrender everything to the higher determinism of transcendental revelation. They would reject the *"rage* for order," in essence, the esthetic will, or the will to power in more familiar reference.

Free choice empowers the democratic dialogue, where values are not a structure to be built and exchanged for other structures but part of a process in communication and consciousness, in authorship and responsibility for authorship, in responsibility for truth as well as fiction, and a conscience for understanding others.[19] Intentionality is accepted as a necessary assumption in discourse, and truth-reality is a warranted part of negotiation with all contingencies. The system, if there is one, is simply a discourse dealing in the free exchange of facts and value concepts, value experiences. It seems to be the field for poetry as Stevens spent years describing it. If the equation is imagination and reality, as in Stevens' preferred vocabulary, the two terms are indispensable and depend on each other for meaning. The dialectic, or dialogue,[20] puts into full play the person, for only persons can be free, and literary form requires the person of the author, the person of characters in action and thought. I might add, in poetic or literary form, the person of the reader. The point makes a clear recall that literary form is modeled from life and that in the end a humanist poetics in this aspect has linkage to a democratic system of free expression and the politics based on it.

As I've proposed, the deeper democracy in its sophisticated ethos takes its essential traits from literary humanism. On the whole one might describe that humanism as a recipe for poise in a turbulent world. Skepticism, irony, and the deconstruction of abstractions form one magnetic pole of Stevens' sensibility. On the other side there is the close lyrical attention to immanent experience. In that great attesting poem, "The Idea of Order at Key West," he blesses the rage for order, "the maker's rage to order words of the sea." "But it was she and not the sea we heard." The continuous dualism of mind and world, of ideal and real, implies the acceptance of conflict in an institutional order and the moral preparation for conflict. Founded on one resolving principle, the understanding of primary empathies and recognitions, "of ourselves and of our origins," that song in the poem supports the belief in the music *and* its maker, and that may be the secret of what I have called the philosophic poise of Stevens' verse. I have mentioned the essential poise maintained between the ideal and real and this is in all of Stevens' work though particularly where he asked where the "noble rider" can still be found.

What I have called the democratic imagination in its actual demonstration has been much more given to a plain sense of reality, utilitarian, mundane, mediocre in its claims on the world and its persons. Pound saw democracy as a threat to the imagination as a matter of course, and so did Eliot on a deeper basis, as a threat to spiritual existence. Williams and Stevens are perhaps best understood in their effort to reach and invoke the "angel of reality" in its lower being and bring it into a resolving relationship with the imagination. In a democracy the emperor of ice cream is a true emperor.

In licensed generality it might be said that Stevens writes the poetry of freedom while Williams the poetry of equality. That is no doubt too convenient a formula, but another would be that he writes the poetry of imagination and Williams the poetry of reality. At the most those terms clarify tone and emphasis. The imagination, Stevens wrote, *was* value, though it might have been simpler to say that the imagination *found* value. The imagination *is* freedom or is exercised in freedom, not bound to reality or to its lowest terms, but capable of imagining the highest terms, even the gods, without embarrassment. The democratic imagination would be guardian of the creative force in everyone, never absolute, never unforgiving, and never defeated, appreciating itself more than its creations. It was Emersonian in this respect, looking for the source of poetry in values, or values in poetry, and resembling idealists more than materialists.

In Stevens' writing imagination and reality form a polarity in counter-criticism to inspire speaking as well as poetry. Circumstance, fate, and power are all its subjects and, if you like, contestants in discourse and action, but the imagination holds them in its grasp. Ideally discourse does not surrender to the strongest reality, or to the bullying or seductiveness of the strongest imagination. Being bound to language it restores respect for language, speaks in discourse *for* discourse. Neither term, imagination and reality, has reason to exist without the other. Reflexive existence need not be offered freedom and that is why the age of naturalism has been so hostile an environment for intellectual democracy. However, it may be that when the pressure of reality is strongest in fact and reason, the imagination revives the use of normative language and gives it both license and substance.

The gift of the dialectical imagination is one of detachment and commitment at once, a peculiar combination which only the imagination can properly express since only the imagination can properly transcend the simplistic logic of the emotions and events. It can move the mind from any fixed point and make all comparisons in the open fields of possibility or probability. Commitment comes blessed with tolerance and detachment comes blessed with sympathy, as if the fortunate result were to ground all meaning in communicability. That mode of the imagination is redemptive; it is a way of thought that deals with antinomies that cannot have supernatural resolution, but yet escapes the hopeless alienations of conflict between right and wrong, good and evil, false and true. One does not have to choose between the perfect uselessness of dreams or the philistinism of survival. There is honor in truth, yes, but a greater honor in the critique of judgment that can be the prelude to the restoration of value.

If my theme has a moral conclusion it is one I have mentioned. The protagonist in the drama of poetry and life is not nature, not divinity, not history or tradition, and not a culture. It is "major man" wherever he or she is found.

Notes

1. *Notes Toward the Definition of Culture* (New York: Harcourt, Brace and Company), p.200.

2. All systems and parties met in the totalitarian spirit of war and the profound result in the revolutionary reaction of 1917-1920 in Europe was the totalitarian era of war and conflict and rule that lasted until 1989 and longer. What we call race wars, genocidal wars and culture wars are vestigial remains, we may hope.
3. *Guide to Kulchur* (New York: New Directions).
4. "A 1 Pound Stein," SE, p.162.
5. "Caviar and Bread Again," SE, p. 103.
6. *Guide to Kulchur*, p.330.
7. Of the large body of writing which connect Heidegger with politics, Richard Wolin's book, *The Politics of Being* (New York, 1990) and that of Julian Young, *Heidegger, Philosophy, Nazism,* (New York, 1997) are highly relevant to my discussion here, particularly in relation to the cultural politics of totalitarianism.
8. At that point we are dealing with historic extremes. The question it raises for cultural politics today is relevant for democracies since it has emerged so strongly in the so-called wars. How much role does a democratic government and the franchise have on issues of the bedroom and kitchen, on those that are the concern of religious and the medical and therapeutic professions? Should issues of law and government be separated from religion and personal, family and community culture so far as they can be, granted that they emerge constantly in laws of regulation and financial aid? . It seems the answer is simple. Example: If enough people want to read in a small town, there are enough to have a library. However, if a law is passed against libraries because reading is vicious and a crime then this may be an undemocratic intervention from a cultural or religious or just stingy sect or minority, the latter having succeeded in an act of power.
9. This was illustrated in a judgment made by Rene Wellek, that Eliot's classicism was "a matter of cultural politics rather than literary criticism." (Quoted by William Chace, p. 131 from Wellek *Concepts of Criticism,* p. 46-47, 357. Chace goes a bit further in saying "Eliot has redefined "classical" to mean "anti-democratic.") At this point such expressions no longer seem exaggerated or hostile to their reputations as poets and men of letters.
10. *Criterion* 6, Nov.1927: 386.
11. The culture critic today would stand for a clerisy, if not an actual clergy, a congregation of creators and interpreters of culture, in every way a ruling elite determining the ruling narrative. This could be a plausible consequence of years of dominance of cultural poetics and cultural criticism in the academy, a negative result for most, I believe.
12. *The New Masses* in 1926 printed an essay entitled "Pound Joins the Revolution!" based on his correspondence with Mike Gold. (December, 1926).
13. WLTRS, McAlmon, February 23, 1944.
14. *Notes Toward the Definition of Culture*, p.197.
15. Christine Froula, *A Guide to Ezra Pound's Selected Poems,* p.98.
16. *Beyond Culture: Essays in Literature and Learning* (New York: Viking 1965), pp166-67.
17. It could be pointed out that Trilling, writing in the center of the Columbia University student demonstrations in the sixties was writing in the midst of a third culture crisis since the first that preoccupied Eliot's and Pound's generation at the time of the First World War. If we conjure a less violent, less glamorous fourth crisis in the late seventies and early eighties when postmodernism raised its flag in this country we would have the more or less normal cycle of generations and wars every twenty years. History will no doubt examine the Bush era as still a fifth.
18. Richard Rorty, *Contingency, Irony, and Solidarity* (New York and Cambridge: Cambridge Univesity Press, 1989), p. 65.

19. In my appendix I treat passages from the work of Emmanuel Levinas to suggest how this humanist philosopher finds foundation for ethical roles in a free and secular society.
20. The importance of "dialogue" as a theme word for the interpretation of literature, particularly fiction, has been made central in discussion in recent years and my appendix includes a brief treatment as expressed by Bakhtin and on his own terms Emmanuel Levinas.

Appendix A

The Ethical Humanism of
Emmanuel Levinas

Emmanuel Levinas belongs to the very prolific French generation of think-ers and critics of language and culture who in the last quarter century have had great influence on the study of literature and other humanities disciplines. The example of Michel Foucault, previously discussed, is one evidence of that. The implicit debate between them has profound meaning for the intellectual life of the new century and becomes a striking asset for my purposes in the illuminating contrast Levinas forms with Foucault. The latter a most impor-tant intellectual resource for the school of "cultural poetics," and Levinas, in my mind, the necessary philosophic reference point for a humanist poetics in the frame presented by Stevens and Williams in my text.

I can't give full justice to Levinas' thought here since it is beyond my unspecialized philosophic powers and outside the limited space I have, but I hope that with some vital notes from his last book, *Entre Nous*, with its acces-sible summary of his life work, I can outline an ethical humanism which has immediate relevance to anything that can be said about a humanist poetics. So far as I know, Levinas never confronted literary texts directly at any length, but a remark he made in one of his published intellectual dialogues suggests that a theme statement for his whole work applies with special emphasis to the classic literary canon:

> I think that across all literature the human face speaksor stammers, or gives itself a countenance, or struggles with its caricature. Despite the end of Europocentrism, disqualified by so many horrors, I believe in the eminence of the human face expressed in Greek letters and in our own, which owe the Greeks everything. It is thanks to them that our history makes us ashamed. There is a participation in Holy Scripture in the national literatures, in Homer and Plato, in Racine and Victor Hugo, as in Pushkin, Dostoyevsky or Goethe, as of course in Tolstoy or in Agnon. But I am sure of the incomparable prophetic excellence of the Book of Books, which all the Letters of the world awaited or upon which they comment. The Holy Scriptures do not signify through the dogmatic tale of their supernatural or sacred origin, but through the

expression of the face of the other man that they illuminate, before he gives himself a countenance or a pose.[1]

At the center of Levinas' thinking is something like an hypothesis in the form of a parable of primeval times. A man, newly created or found, and possessing a consciousness and the freedom that goes with it, lives in a space filled only with *things* and animate beings until he meets a human person like himself who seems a rival for the possession of the same space.

> The meeting with the other person consists in the fact that, despite the extent of my domination over him and his submission, I do not possess him. He does not enter entirely into the opening of being in which I already stand as in the field of my freedom. ....Everything from him that comes to me in terms of being in general certainly offers itself to my understanding and my possession. I understand him in terms of his history, his environment, his habits. What escapes understanding in him is himself, the being. I cannot deny him partially, in violence, by grasping him in terms of being in general, and by possessing him. The other is the only being whose negation can be declared only as like others of that total: a murder. The other is the only being I can want to kill.
>
> I can want to. Yet this power is the complete opposite of power. The triumph of this power is its defeat as power. At the very moment when my power to kill is realized, the other has escaped. In killing, I can certainly *attain* a goal, I can kill the way I hunt, or cut down trees, or slaughter animals–but then I have grasped the other in the opening of being in general, as an element of the world in which I stand. I have seen him on the horizon. I have not looked straight at him. I have not looked him in the face. The temptation of total negation, which spans the infinity of that attempt and its impossibility–is the presence of the face. To be in relation with the other face to face– is to be unable to kill. This is also the situation of discourse.[2]

I paraphrase: The other person cannot be possessed or overcome with power unless he is killed. The space that cannot be reached is his inner space of freedom. [I should note here the fundamental exchange with Foucault as I see it. Power is not a monolithic term, it has its rival, combatant, sometimes master in consciousness, freedom and ethical choice]. That other person can be seen on the horizon, and understood for his history, environment, habits but that is not the man in him, who is "himself in being." A freedom has met another freedom and that is the issue to be resolved between them, and it is the paramount issue for Levinas in constructing his basis for a human ethic. I can kill him, the way I hunt, or cut down trees, or slaughter animals but that is a defeat, the world made emptier than it was at the beginning. The key is in that confrontation, face to face, and the difference it brightly illuminates between a person and a thing, or between a person and an abstraction on the horizon. Things and people on the horizon are part of a general scene, a collectivity, a group until, if a man, we see his face. As Williams might say this is the immediacy of contact upon which "so much depends." But we remark at once that "a man" is far more on which something depends than a red wheelbarrow, and

Williams might certainly agree, although as we see later, Levinas too, has a welcome for the immediacy of "things."

> The fact that a relationship with a being is an invocation of a face and already speech, a relation with a depth rather than with a horizon– a gap in the horizon– the fact that my fellow man is the being par excellence, all this may appear rather surprising if we limit ourselves to the conception of a being, insignificant in itself, a silhouette on the luminous horizon, acquiring a meaning only by virtue of that presence on the horizon. The face *signifies* otherwise. In it, the infinite resistance of a being to our power is affirmed precisely in opposition to the will to murder that it defies, because being completely naked-and the nakedness of the face is not a figure of speech–it means by itself. We cannot even say that the face is an opening that would make it relative to a surrounding plenitude.
>
> Can things take on a face? Isn't art an activity that gives things a face? Isn't the facade of a house a house that is looking at us?... [W]e wonder whether rhythm's impersonal gait–fascination, magic–is not art's substitute for sociality, the face, and speech, at any length
>
> I set the signifying of the face in opposition to understanding and meaning grasped on the basis of the horizon .... (EN,10)

For Levinas the face is more than an icon, the whole being is there alive in movement and in speech unlike the figure on the horizon. It serves a relation in depth, "in opposition to the understanding and meaning grasped on the basis of the horizon." The latter is a conceptual figure, the face means by itself. Above all it signifies an ultimate "resistance of a being to our power," defies murder as well as closure in our understanding and power. Is this not a theme of poetry? And more, Levinas says, "Isn't art an activity that gives things a face," if only by way of being absorbed in a consciousness? All anthropomorphic metaphors have this impulse behind them.

> How is the vision of the face no longer vision, but hearing and speech? How can the meeting of the face–that is to say, moral consciousness-be described as a condition for consciousness *tout court* and for disclosure? How does consciousness assert itself as an impossibility of murder? What are the conditions of the appearance of the face, that is to say, of the temptation and impossibility of murder? How can I appear to my self as a face? Finally, to what extent is the relation with the other or the collectivity–which cannot be reduced to understanding–a relation with the infinite? Such are the themes that arise from this first challenge to the primacy of ontology. In any case, philosophical research cannot be content with reflection on itself or on existence. Reflection gives us only the narrative of a personal adventure, a private soul, incessantly returning to itself, even when it seems to flee itself. The human gives itself only to a relationship that is not *a being able*. (Italics mine, EN,11)

Here Levinas sets the boundaries for this ultimate concentration on the meeting between face and face. It is not the solipsism of individual consciousness in "reflection on itself or on existence;" neither is it the collective consciousness, a reflection from the horizon and abstract. These both might be called yielding to power from the inside, or to power from the outside, abstract and detached thought, and as it may be, institutions and laws.

The contrast with Michel Foucault''s theme on power is vivid at this point. The topic is large in its profundity and I believe that most significant issues in modern thinking and practical action take form in the writing of the two Frenchmen. Levinas is saying that when power acts upon the free person (free beyond his own choice) it must inevitably take effect within the sphere of his own freedom, must be confronted as the "face" confronts potential acts of force or violence. Levinas adds a different force to what effects meaning and action- it is an ethical force not borrowed from doctrine or habit on the "horizon" but immediate in its response from the ethical source. So far as I can see in Foucault ethics has no meaning separate from its use in the system of power to manipulate consent. In Levinas choice and ethical response is at least equal to and separate from both verbal doctrine and immediate threat of force. If it persuades it persuades authentically on a level as pure as a threat or actual blow.

In an earlier quoted passage Levinas says, "To be in relation with the other face to face–is to be unable to kill. This is also the situation of discourse." It is obvious here that Levinas is providing the necessary basis for discourse within moral consciousness and meaning. Discourse is a favorite term for Foucault as well though in most of his writing it seems to be a medium for the assertion of power or submission to it. In contrast Levinas insists that "The human gives itself only to a relationship that is *not a " being able*." The single existence is a life with the weather and things, where the rule is "being able," how to survive, to eat, to control and use, to make disappear, etc. The human adventure is not a personal and private narrative but a continuous dialogue with the Other. The power to kill is the ultimate exercise of "being able."

> The relationship of the individual to the totality, which thought is, in which the *I* takes into account what is not itself and yet is not dissolved in it, assumes that the totality is manifested not as a milieu brushing against the skin, so to speak, of living being as an element in which it is immersed, but as a face in which being faces me....Thought begins with the possibility of conceiving a freedom exterior to my own. To think a freedom exterior to my own is the first thought. It marks my very presence in the world. (EN,17)

Although Levinas makes very limited reference to his political beliefs, he leaves little doubt here that he is a democratic humanist in essence. Thought, planning, choice, freedom begin with "conceiving a freedom exterior to my own." The passage is a good elicitation of human beings *not* "dissolved" in nature, or made distant and abstract at the horizon. Nor is it the same as Heidegger's profession of immediacy in the capacity to know Being, or "being in general." Nothing takes precedence over the first knowledge of "beings" in the human and individual Other. It is possibly a good philosophic definition to support Stevens' use of a "first idea" and his protagonist "major man." The latter is removed from hierarchy, removed from names, collectives, generalizations, from the *horizon* of thought. It stresses the importance of individuals and suggests democracy's dialogue with itself, prone to generalized analysis of the crowd and yet its primary need to know and imagine individuals.

> Language , in its expressive function, addresses and invokes the other. The relation of language is not reducible to the relation that obtains between thought and an object that is given to it. Language cannot encompass the other: the other, the concept of whom we are using at this very moment, is not invoked as a concept but as a person.... He is a being beyond all attributes, which would have the effect of qualifying him, that is, of reducing him to what he has in common with other beings, of making a concept of him. It is this presence for me of a being identical to itself that I call the presence of the face. The face is the very identity of a being; it manifests itself in terms of itself, without a concept....
>
> As an interlocutor, he faces me; and properly speaking, only the interlocutor can face, without "facing "meaning hostility or friendship.... The particularity of the other in language, far from representing his animality or the remains of an animality, constitutes the total humanization of the Other....
>
> I recognize him, that is, I believe in him. But if that recognition were my submission to him, that submission would deprive my recognition of all value: recognition by submission would annul my dignity through which recognition has value. The face that looks at me affirms me. But, face to face, I can no longer deny the other: it is only the noumenal glory of the other that makes the face to face situation possible. The face to face situation is thus an impossibility of denying, a negation of negation. The double articulation of this formula means concretely" the "thou shalt not murder" is inscribed on the face and constitutes its very otherness. Speech, then, is a relationship between freedoms who neither limit nor deny one another, but reciprocally affirm one another. They are transcendent in relation to one another. (EN,32-35)

The comment on these passage for Levinas' own hypothetical poetics should begin with the following words: "Language, in its expressive function, addresses and invokes the other." To invoke is to know the "other's" presence in immediacy; "it cannot be reduced to a relation between concepts." There follow a set of limitations or proscriptions on thought and language which in paradox suggest what it is to be "able" or unable in the literary imagination. "Language cannot encompass the other:...the concept of whom...is not invoked as a concept but as a person....

> He is a being beyond all attributes, which would have the effect of qualifying him, that is, of reducing him to what he has in common with other beings, of making a concept of him. It is this presence for me of a being identical to itself that I call the presence of the face. The face is the very identity of a being; it manifests itself in terms of itself. (EN,33)

I must insert at this point what would be in Levinas" hypothetical poetics a deep criticism of Eliot's figure for a collective abstraction, "the jew crouched on the windowsill," or the jew/animal within Pound's abstract evil of usury.

There is this moral danger in using persons as metaphors which lead from poetry to personal and social dehumanization.

The presence of a person with his face is the whole person, immune to disintegration, resistant to destruction except in murder. "As an interlocutor, he faces me," that is with speech and a question, the question coming from his freedom, his unique otherness. This is the person escaping objectification and my power. Levinas would say it is a relation between two freedoms. It is not too much to say that it resembles the relation between author and text and reader. "The particularity of the other in language, far from representing his animality or the remains of an animality, constitutes the total humanization of the Other." Imaginative language can represent persons this way, in a transcendence of animal or thing or a concept.

The face-to-face meeting comes very close to illustrating what Kenneth Burke meant by stressing for his students in practical criticism the dramatic triad of "purpose, passion, and perception." Perception in the dramatic structure of Greek tragedy, which was adapted Greek ritual, represents a theophany. It is a recognition scene that transcends and gives resolution to the struggle that went before.

> I recognize him, that is, I believe in him.... The face that looks at me affirms me....The face to face situation is thus an impossibility of denying, a negation of negation. But, face to face, I can no longer deny the other: it is only the noumenal glory of the other that makes the face to face situation possible....Speech, then, is a relation between freedoms who neither limit nor deny one another, but reciprocally affirm one another. They are transcendent in relation to one another.(EN,34-35)

The word "transcendent" needs much more commentary for which I refer the reader to the larger work of Levinas and its study that has been growing in recent years. Here the connection with literature, a poetics, leads to the formal conclusion with "belief," a literary theophany—always something higher, always the elusive transcendence of material and reductive existence. Levinas is not writing about tragedy here, but his own words illustrate a communication beyond flat reality while expressing a philosophy of existence. One affirms the other, ("without hostility or friendliness"), and thus they come into a mutuality of being which is higher than the landscape of objects. Levinas has entered the area of thought from which the most important consequences in valuations and motives follow, whether concerned with poetics or politics or any other field of action or branch of living.

> In a philosophy that, in our time, credits the mind with no other practice than theory, and which leads to the pure mirror of objective structures—the humanity of man-reduced to consciousness—does not the idea of substitution allow for a rehabilitation of the subject, which naturalist humanism, quickly losing in naturalism the privileges of the human, does not always achieve? (EN,58)

When one speaks of human subjectivity, whether to affirm or deprecate it, one affirms or negates the possibility of freedom, and the form of what he calls "transcendence." He continues later to stress the human not the God experience, as if to answer Eliot's double objection to both naturalist and liberal humanism, the objection that humanism of any kind loses its ground without religious belief. In the following passages I offer what may be Levinas' most focused presentation of humanist belief.

> My view is opposed to the tendency (in)....contemporary philosophy that prefers to see man a simple articulation or a simple aspect of a rational, ontological system that has nothing human in it; even in Heidegger, the Dasein is ultimately a structure of being in general, bound to its profession of being, "its historic deeds of being," its event of being. The human is not the entire meaning of being; man is a being who comprehends being and, in that sense, is the manifestation of it, and only thus does he concern philosophy.
>
> Similarly, in certain trends in structural research, rules, pure forms, universal structures, combinations which have a legality as cold as mathematical legality are isolated. And then that dominates the human. In Merleau-Ponty, you have a very beautiful passage in which he analyzes the way one hand touches another. One hand touches the other, the other hand touches the first; the hand, consequently, is touched and touches the touching...it is as if space were touching itself through man. What is pleasing here is perhaps that nonhuman–non-humanist...structure in which man is only an aspect.

This refers to the temptation of the non-human, essentially its appeal to a universality, an infinity of Being where it is difficult to make the Human central, that is, central to all meaning and yet escaped from human solipsism.

> In the same distrust with regard to humanism according to contemporary philosophy there is a battle against the notion of the subject. What they want is a principle of intelligibility that is no longer enveloped by the human; they want the subject to appeal to a principle that would not be enveloped by concern for human fate....
>
> I mean to say that, in consciousness (in the relationship with the other) thus conceived, there is the awakening to humanity. The humanity of consciousness is definitely not in its powers, but in its responsibility: in passivity, in reception, in obligation with regard to the other. It is the other who is first, and there the question of my sovereign consciousness is no longer the first question. I advocate, as in the title of one of my books, the humanism of the other man.(EN,112)

What is involved here is a form of transcendent belief which in Levinas' mind pairs itself or reproduces itself in the pattern of religious belief by its own mode of transcending biological egocentricity. The movement of the meeting between self and other is a transcendence of self-interested survival expressed by the keyword "responsibility"—to express one's life "not in its powers, but in its responsibility...an obligation with regard to the other." That is the beginning of an ethical system, the alternative, as he puts it in meaningful hyperbole, to murder, and in response to the command "thou shalt not kill." It is the beginning of discourse and the address to life's meaning which comes from the fact there are two in communication, the fact of language and speech.

> [T]he order of meaning, which seems to me primary, is precisely what comes to us from the interhuman relationship, so that the Face in all its meaningfulness as brought out by analysis, is the *beginning* of intelligibility" (EN,103)

If I end here parsing the wisdom of Levinas for the study of literature, I should repeat the point that the New Historicism or the new Cultural Poetics and possibly other branches of post-structuralist theory may be moving against the grain of the literary imagination. By transferring attention from the immediacy of experience, the communication between "faces," one might say, transferring that dramatic scene of imagination to the "horizon" of concepts, interpretations, edicts of cultural analysis and discovery—it has reversed and stalemated the imagination in its work, thus falsifying the text in its actual writing. That brings up another point I have already made, it may be that literary theory as practiced in most quarters today has no deeper instruction to give the writer or reader of fiction and poetry than principles of structural meaning found through a language dictionary, psychological thesaurus, a cultural and historical encyclopedia, or their equivalents. But the text in its lifelike complexity and immediacy of meaning, more like the shock image of "the face" than the abstract "horizon" of identities and concepts that Levinas speaks of and rejects in the effort to give final justice to a classic imaginative literature.

Notes

1. *Ethics and Infinity* (Pittsburgh: Duquesne University Press, 1985), 117
2. *Entre Nous*, trans. Michael B. Smith and Barbara Harshav (New York: Columbia University Press, 1998), pp. 9-10 {Hereafter EN.).

Appendix B

Bakhtin and the American Poets

If there is to be a formal organized presentation of what I call a humanist poetics, I believe that the thinking of Mikhail Bakhtin will have a primary place, along with the indispensable contribution of Levinas and the insufficiently noticed American philosopher-critic, Kenneth Burke. Both Levinas and Bakhtin play an essential role in the post-structuralist debate in theory, Levinas belonging to the French group of influence, though contrasting deeply with both Foucault and Derrida. Bakhtin in his concentration on the "prosaics" of fiction has most relevance in making parallels with the American poets, and I use his work here to make another condensed statement for what a humanist poetics might need for understanding. In this limited space I borrow from the cogent summary written by Gary S. Morson and Caryl Emerson in their book, *Mikhail Bakhtin: Creation of a Prosaics.*[1]

The first among several points of harmony between Bakhtin and the American poets would be what Williams called the "culture of immediacy," a phrase for the literature he valued against all forms of abstraction. Morson and Emerson wrote the following in their first synoptic chapter, "He [Bakhtin] consistently opposed all ways of thinking that reduced the present moment...to a simple derivative of what went before." As he emphasized the "eventness" of the event.... he also insisted on the *presentness* of each moment."(M\E,46}

To be "present" was one dramatic and convincing way of opposing abstraction. This is emphasized in Bakhtin by way of introducing the key importance of quotidian existence: "Prosaics focuses on quotidian events that in principle elude reduction to "underlying" laws or systems"(M\E,32-33). The principle that enlarges the quotidian is its value for the ethical imagination. In this Bakhtin was thinking of Tolstoy. "Tolstoy develops the idea that real ethical decisions are made, and one's true life is lived, at everyday moments we rarely if ever notice"[2] Bakhtin describes how Levin and Pierre, as major protagonists, were both "troubled by the impossibility of grounding an ethical theory" (M\E, 23-25). The similar challenge appeared for Stevens in grounding a theory of the imagination. That the latter had ultimate convergence in ethics for Stevens is something one can firmly believe, though he himself would have been reluctant to say so since ethics itself implies a certain specificity and abstraction of doctrine. He might more willingly have accepted what Bakhtin called "dialogic communication" in its place, since the latter was ethics in process and not in doctrine.

In Bakhtin's conceptual considerations the most important activity is dialogue: "we cannot properly separate existence from the ongoing process of communication." In Bakhtin, *to be* means *to communicate.*" "To be means to be for another, and through the other for oneself. A person has no sovereign internal territory, he is wholly and always on the boundary; looking inside himself, he *looks into the eyes of another* or *with the eyes of the other.*"2 That fleeting appearance of something in persons, in himself, resembles what Williams called "contact," a positive hunger of the imagination and spiritual need; it should have correspondence with the important metonymy of the "face" in Levinas' thought, matched in Bakhtin's use of the "eyes of the other."

The recognition of autonomy and uniqueness in others, as if the two were dependent on each other, commands the idea of selfhood. Morson and Emerson put it this way for Bakhtin. "There can be no formula for integrity, no substitute for each person's own project of selfhood, no escape from the ethical obligations of every situation at every moment" (M\E,31). That is a good way to characterize ethical immediacy as an effort to save the ethical potential that is threatened by abstraction. The latter term in its ethical effect Bakhtin called "theoreticism" where "particular people are reduced to counters, and their intimate and ethical relations to their actions are lost." The same was true for Marxist dialectics though with greater latent damage. "Dialectic is the abstract product of dialogue," Bakhtin wrote. As the authors discuss the difference, "from the point of view of dialogics...the world is a live event," whereas in dialectics it is a mechanism of conflict among forces and things rather than people (M\E, 57).

What would Stevens have taken from this and what does it have to do with the high role for the imagination as defined by him? We recognize "the world as a live event" and the dialogic "act of the mind" in poetry, a discourse in which even the snowman shares. An anterior statement for a humanist poetics can be gained from Bakhtin's book on Dostoevsky's poetics in discussing "The dialogic nature of consciousness. The dialogic nature of human life itself."

> [The person] invests his entire self in discourse, and this discourse enters into the dialogic fabric of human life, into the world symposium.[3]

It should not take much translation to see supreme fictions in that open-ended term, "world symposium." For Stevens this was the imagination's product, whose life-supporting consciousness was very close to what Bakhtin called truth. To Bakhtin "such a concept of truth is missing from modern Western thought," adding for great interest that so far only fiction approaches this "truth," and that the best novelists are far ahead of the philosophers (M\E, 60). It adds to the claim made by Heidegger that in imaginative letters there was a report of experience that moved beyond abstraction into true Being. Thus it was even possible that literary invention could defy Plato and take priority over philosophizing.

The universality of the theme was based by Bakhtin in the supreme value of freedom. He thought abstractions of law and necessity, of historic process and metaphysical truth would be deadly in their effect on creativity. He took much of this emphasis from Dostoevsky's "underground man," in the latter's rejection of the nineteenth century determinist utopia he called the "crystal palace." "Creation becomes mere discovery where laws are known or implied even if not known. Art and literature require 'the possibility of freedom, choice, and the genuinely new'" (M\E, 38).

That was the imagination's problem in modernity as Stevens saw it. The imagination served the sensibility of choice, and its exercise was in choosing what can be recognized as values. Its freedom was indispensable and yet much resisted in the age of naturalist and determinist thought. The Russian critic and the American poet shared a primary obsession as both recognized the pressure of things, the violence of power and the heavy weight of abstract politics in their time. Freedom in that modern context could seem absurd and only the visible face of chaos. But the imagination was as real as power, not its servant, and belonged to the world of "live events." "If freedom is possible, then ethical problems, always of central importance to Bakhtin, are also possible." "If freedom is necessary then responsibility is unavoidable" (M\E,38). If those words are true then the literary imagination can offer shelter and custom in the world of "things as they are," while containing the promise of liberation despite the weight of historical and cultural determination.

Leaving the texts of Morson and Emerson as well as Bakhtin I should add in my own comment that a single minded cultural-historical study of texts interrupts and blocks the traditional dialogue between author and reader. In fact so does the radical relativism which is one other by-product of post-structuralist theory. In such circumstances there are, strictly speaking, no debating opponents, answerable or not. By dialogue I mean a proper balance in the authority of each side for the control of language and meaning. When the author (of a text) is made subject to cultural-linguistic determinism, reduced to being part of his own environment of contingencies, the reader or critic must be similarly reduced or else take "limitless sovereignty" over the text, as charged by Foucault in argument with Derrida. The necessary skepticism and imaginative surplus of thought, in effect its freedom, are all on one side, that of the critic. It seems, for instance, that a sufficiently rigorous act of deconstruction could leave only a void of meaning, or it could leave a multiplicity of meanings that come to the same result. In fact the first reactive criticism to the concept of indeterminacy was that it would lead to interpretive anarchy or nihilism. What was gained by indeterminacy, some felt, was much better expressed in the Empsonian "New Critical" theme of ambiguity. Others, reacting to the implicit logic of interpretation, had a motive to join the most congenial reading community that could give them "sovereignty over the text." Curiously enough the way to master contingencies embedded in the text was to define them or support them. But the motive to do that is characteristically ideological. Thus what begins as a descent into indeterminacy can end at the peak of single-minded ideological determination.

Notes

1. (Stanford, CA: Stanford University Press, 1990) , 15-62. Hereafter referred to as M\E.
2. Taken from Tolstoy's essay " Why Do Men Stupefy Themselves."
3. From Bakhtin,"Toward a Reworking of the Dostoevsky Book" Appendix 2 in Problems of Dostoevsky's Poetics (Minneapolis: University of Minnesota Press, 1984), 283 -302.

Appendix C

A Note on *Ethics and Dialogue in the Works of Levinas, Bakhtin, Mandelshtam, and Celan* by Michael Eskin*

Almost all references here were taken from the introduction and first chapter, and many are direct quotations from the author's subjects in this dense and valuable analytic study. I hope the reader will find immediate relevance for my purpose to give philosophic background in the work of Levinas and Bakhtin to an understanding of what I call humanist poetics. Michael Eskin's book as a whole, however, is bound to become excellent preparation for study of the general subjects of poetry and language and poetry and ethics.

I should point out that this extended note is from a text I read two or three years after I finished my own manuscript (while it remained unpublished), and my view of the work of Levinas and Bakhtin and of a humanist poetics I have attempted in this necessarily complex discussion has not been revised. I can imagine the added support such a reading might have given me though my approach was different, more suited to literary study and criticism than the tightly woven philosophic analysis required by Eskin's subjects. I have highlighted passages where I was pleased to find close correspondence with my own approach.]

* * *

Michael Eskin's study of the seminal thought of Levinas and Bakhtin finds them sharing the foundational principle of dialogue in establishing the relationships between primary being (existence) and ethical and social being:

> Coming into consciousness in and through (speech) interaction with others and, thus, always already social, the human being may aptly be called the dialogic and, by extension, ethical being. (Eskin 1, introduction, hereafter E)

New York: Oxford University Press 2000.

And quoting Bakhtin,

> Given the dialogic character of the social *and* the social constitution of the ethical, the study of dialogue as a universal phenomenon permeating all human speech and all relations and manifestations of human [existence] falls into the domain of ethics...[and in short] everything that has sense and meaning. (E1, 5)

Dialogue here means speech, stressed as the language of response. Eskin writes in his second page that dialogue is not a literary genre, and in its narrow sense only one form of verbal interaction (E2,fn 6).

> But dialogue can also be understood in a broader sense, meaning not only direct face-to-face vocalized verbal communication between persons, but also verbal communication of any type whatsoever.

I would insert at this point that in linguistic and meta-linguistic discussion today Bakhtin and Levinas have argued the substitution of dialogue for a key term, narrative. This Eskin stresses with the important metalinguistic distinction between intersubjectivity and intertextuality, thus highlighting post-structuralist argument expressed in the work of Julia Kristeva and Michel Foucault on one side and Bakhtin and Levinas on the other. Though Eskin confines his direct study of theorists to Levinas and Bahktin, his work has high concern for my own distinctions between humanist and cultural poetics in general literary theory.

Eskin places the opposition this way:

> In contrast to influential post-structural conceptions of textuality, which undermine the (ontological) significance of the speaking or writing human being by valorizing the text's subject-constituting productivity (Eskin calls it in Kristeva the general replacement of intersubjectivity by intertextuality), the metalinguistic concept of text as utterance inevitably links each utterance to its author's active position in the "chain of speech communication."

The intersubjective, or dialoguist school of interpretation sees the inseverability of the text from its author, and is expressed by Eskin in its most positive form: "The literary work is, in its entirety, a real and unitary utterance having a real author and real addressees." This is to be straightforwardly opposed to what was mentioned at one time by Foucault as the "death of the author." (See my earlier discussion [chap. 18] of disciples of Foucault in the school of cultural poetics which in post-structural or post-modernist debate attends almost exclusively to the cultural *narrative*, imputedly the source of all texts.)

Eskin adds a point with Bakhtin: "The work, Bakhtin emphasizes, like the rejoinder in living dialogue, is oriented toward the other's response." This is individualized, personal in its reach and effects, voice and response, expressing the relation between author and reader. When a third person, or tenth, or thousandth has been generalized and given voice, in Levinas' view it moves to public (or political) narrative, oriented toward collective action and response.

Speaking from my own perspective here, the intertextual emphasis would severe communication from personal response and responsibility and perhaps finally from judgment; the text speaks for history, the social environment, culture as a force, politics as power, or it may give license to the most powerful readers of the cultural narrative and thus monopolize judgment. Interpretation blanks intentionality - or may assume it for the authoritarian critic's self. Perhaps it neutralizes all normative response, or response masks neutrality as pseudo-scientific politics. I have an example in my text where History writes within and through Pound's memory and reading consciousness, a political ideology speaks in verse as an epic of intertextuality. Or intertextuality covers itself in the consciousness stream of a persona, Prufrock or Tiresias, a curious device to cross between intersubjective and intertextual effects.

According to Eskin (E4) there is both similarity and important difference between Levinas and Bakhtin on the intertwining relations of existential being, verbal communication, and social being, and between ethics and in the end, "politics and poetry." The important difference has to do with foundational ethics and its role in poetic utterance.

> Bakhtin [E5,fn17] emphasizes the existential roots of human activity (including utterances) and argues for its fully responsible assumption by each individual. ...He defines Being itself as dialogue: 'To be means to communicate.'

(But)

> While Bakhtin elaborates an internal and external approach to utterances insofar as they are permeated by traces of intersubjectivity *and,* simultaneously, constitute and inform it, Levinas investigates dialogue on a pre-existential, pre-ontological level, that is, in Levinas' terms, on the ethical level: "Ethics is before ontology..." [AT,109].

According to Levinas, "dialogue [in the ethical sense], or more precisely...the ethics of dialogue [DD, 230] precedes and conditions dialogue as an exchange of rejoinders in the chain of speech communication." "[It]... is central to Levinas's understanding of ethics as pre-communicative and pre-verbal discourse directed toward the other..." *as a language before words, the original language.*" [E7,TI 104, iii]

Eskin interprets in extended quotation from Levinas ["Language," 115-119, his view of foundational ethical communication. Speech is more than an exercise of thought, and not

> "our participation in a transparent universality. Whatever the message transmitted by speech, speaking is contact....One must then admit that there is in speech a relationship with a singularity outside the theme of speech, a singularity who is not thematized by

speech but is approached. Speech and its logical work would then unfold not in the knowledge of the interlocutor but in his proximity....Proximity is *by itself* signification....This is the original language, the foundation of the other one, the precise point at which this mutation of the intentional into the ethical occurs, and occurs continually, at which the approach *pierces* consciousness, is the...human face. Contact is responsibility....This relationship of proximity...in which every transmission of messages...is already established, is the original language, a language without words, or propositions, pure communication" (E8) [The larger tract seems to be *En decouvrant l'existence avec Husserl et Heidegger.*]

I don't believe it is straining exposition to see an important gloss here on what Williams meant with his theme words "Contact!" and "immediacy" and even "no ideas but in things." For that matter, as Eskin and many others have commented, it is explanation for the essential "modernism" in modern verse. Thus arriving at the origin point of ethical communication in Levinas' thought Eskin rightly introduces his subject's important treatment of poetry.

Levinas emphasizes the signifying character of ethics in which interlocutor becomes 'all sign, signifying himself'(AQE, 31) Ethics, the language of proximity, is also called "Saying," as opposed to "Said"; "Saying [Dire] thus understood, is giving a sign...by turning oneself into a sign," and not the "communication of a Said [Dit] which would immediately cover up and extinguish or absorb the Saying" (223). The "condition of all communication" (82), Saying is[proximity [and] contact...before language, but without which language as the transmission of messages would not be possible" (32). It is... a "response preceding all questions" (47), "*signified* like an order in the [other's] face" (EN 161). [Earlier references here from (AQE, 75, 243](E8-9)

   Levinas (thus) singles out two particular modes of speaking -the philosophical and the poetic- which, more than other modes, bring to light ethical Saying. Philosophy is "called upon [phenomenologically] to reduce.... the Said to Saying" (AQE243, 278) insofar as Saying "can only be attained by way of the Said, which shows itself"(76). Philosophy, "being consigned to the *Said*... says that of which it is but the servant, which it, however, masters by saying it, in order to reduce , in a new *said*, its own pretensions"(200). Poetry, on the other hand, as "the first of languages," is itself "a modality (NP50) of ethical signification."(E9)

The distinction between Saying and Said is fundamental - and the issue can simply be put that poetry (or "poethics" in Eskin's usage) brings them together. "While 'philosophical speaking....betrays in its said the proximity which it translates before us' (AQE 261, E10) ethics 'bares itself in the poetic *said* and the infinite interpretation it calls for'" (263). Levinas brings the point further when using Paul Celan's work as example, (E10,fn 27) he defines poetry's ethical status "while simultaneously rephrasing Celan's dialogic conception of poetry as a mode of verbal communication. Insofar as the ethical contact with the other involves my 'turning myself into a sign' signifying the 'donation of the sign', that is, the donation of myself, Levinas implies both that I *am* a poem (in the ethical sense) and that the poem is I, when he depicts poetry in ethical terms as 'Saying without said.'"(NP 49)...Eskin follows these remarks with a broadly clarifying footnote (fn28 p 10) "While philosophy always remains a discourse on a subject, poetry does what philosophy is 'about'. Derrida's observation that Levinas' discourse.....(is)   a metadiscourse, underscores philosophy's incapacity to attain a pre-linguistic, pre-logical, ethical level of signification, which, Levinas suggests , is the prerogative of poetry (NP 50). In this rather convoluted discussion Eskin does well to take his source from Levinas' own words as much as possible. Ambiguity will always remain in the effort "to attain a pre-linguistic, pre-logical, ethical level of signification" an effort that becomes the shared responsibility of the reader.

Summing up, Eskin writes, "He [Levinas] clearly points out that it is Paul Celan's poetry in particular which *does* what he philosophizes." "The poem, defined as 'the fact of speaking to the other', precedes 'all thematization'" (NP53. E11,10). This could be a definition of humanist poetics in considering poetry as dialogue in a close sense; if Levinas found Celan as his poetic interlocutor, Celan, found the Russian poet Mandelstam (dead in the Gulag)as close literary correspondent or 'secret interlocutor'. "...Mandel'shtam's contention that poetry necessarily constitutes itself in and through [poetic] dialogue with a 'secret interlocutor' {MSSi.275} in 'posterity' (184) implicitly calls for the consideration of his own poetry as not merely oriented toward, but moreover, as received, understood, and retroactively constituted by (an) interlocutor(s) whose 'responsive understanding' (BSS 168-70,318) may in turn manifest and objectivate itself in (equally) poetic utterances" (E13).

* * *

In making this claim for poetry Levinas and his interpreter Eskin are philosopher critics acting as interpreters of the poetry of Celan, Mandelshtam, and I venture to say, the poetry of Stevens and Williams (in the context of my book), and what I have tried to say for a humanist poetics. In saying this I stress again the primacy of poetry as medium for immediacy and personhood and direct response-ability in both senses of the term. It is a dialogue in which terms and images are constituted and reconstituted, evolving and deconstructed, all changes posed against the fixity of concepts, images, ideologies, conventions, laws and beliefs - all that has been fixed in the Said and needs to be tested and renewed or re-known or rejected in the fluidity of the ethical consciousness, a purifying stream of Saying that can only be known in freedom.

It is not unusual for philosophers, modern and ancient, to give precedence to poetry over philosophy. What is equally significant here is the primacy given ethics, a double endorsement for what I call a humanist poetics. "Ethics is before ontology," Levinas writes in Alterity and Transcendence. One might add that even more assuredly ethics is before politics, which tends always to seek or pretend to seek a basis in the ontological. Levinas's stress is that it is antecedent to what Sartre called engagement, which was explicitly political. "'It (ethics) is in a responsibility which does not justify itself by any prior commitment [engagement] in the responsibility for the other....'" It is anterior to discourse (whether that of Heidegger or Sartre or Foucault), conceived as a practical, inter-subjective, consensus-oriented 'procedure' based on universalizability and informed by an universal or transcendental pragmatics..." In the 'ethical situation' even Sartrian freedom lacks primacy. "'This (ethical) mode. mode of responding without anterior commitment (engagement) is ...anterior to freedom'" (E21-22 AT 109, AQE162-3, AQE184)

In this way Levinas coordinates all normative systems or ontological structures on their foundational human base. "By positing the precedence of ethics over ontology as an explicit reversal of Heidegger's and (Sartre's) existentialism, Levinas underscores the interhuman significance of ethics as 'an irreducible structure on which depend all other structures'(TI77) including 'the structure of Dasein's Being' (SuZ 130), that is, existence."(E25) AEthics, Levinas reiterates, is an interhuman dynamic, which transpires in my concrete encounter(s) with the other(s)" (E26, AQE 223-39 .... In this relation the other 'calls on my response' and 'on my responsibility'" (TI 271, 229) On this ground Eskin brings up what Levinas always means to emphasize: "Levinas' ethical subversion of ontology must not be mistaken for any kind of 'mystical' or quasi-'mystical' endeavour."

If ethics precedes ontology, Eskin writes - ......"my comprehension of my own Being, and, consequently, my theoretical interrogation of my own existence always already occur against the backdrop of and within my relation to the other"(E26)....This is precisely what Levinas means when he defines ethics as (inter)human:: the 'human begins when the vitality [of my existence], innocent in appearance but potentially murderous, is curbed [by and for the sake of the other] (AV 131). Thus we have the ground for saying that ethics in Levinas' sense has primacy over ideologies of ultimacy, ontological in their embrace of Being, totalitarian in their embrace of social being.

The relevance for modern political and totalitarian thought is very close. "Levinas' opposition to contemporary ontology (and existential phenomenology— being qua being as in Heidegger and Sartre) is philosophically and politically motivated:(italics mine) 'A philosophy of power,' Levinas notes, 'ontology, as first philosophy, which does not question the Same (the binary term opposed to Other which I interpret as the collective abstract, the rule system of conformity in ethics-politics) is a philosophy of injustice. Heideggerian ontology, which subordinates the relation to the other human being [Autrui] to the relation to Being in general...persists in the obedience to the anonymous and leads, fatally, to another power, to imperialist domination, to tyranny' "(TI38, (E21)

Eskin does well to ask for his untrained reader,(E27) "What does Levinas mean by the formulaic 'reduction of the other to the same' ? ...the same or 'totality', as Levinas also calls it by way of polemic response to Hegel, refers to any structure or dynamic in which one of the constituents is subjected to inclusion, subsumption, or sublation, and thereby deprived of its singularity" (E28)[If I could simplify politically,- that is, subjected to a general collective category or group identity- with essentialized characteristics] But Eskin's answer is explicit enough.

> "From within this Greek tradition of the primacy of the 'same' in its various manifestations, Levinas reverts to the biblical, Judaic 'perspective that transcends the Greek language of intelligibility' (DwL..20) and emphasizes heteronomy and heterology (27; DL,25). Levinas' ethical evaluation of Judaism is socio-politically motivated: only if I do not reduce the other, if I realize that 'my freedom is anteceded by an obligation to the other' (ibid), can a 'fascist or totalitarian' (30) politics be prevented. In view of the socio-political disaster of National Socialism, which (for both Levinas and Celan(exacerbates the 'philosophy of the same' in all its facets by literally converting the philosophical 'reduction of the other to the same' into the factual annihilation of the other, that is, into the 'Holocaust of millions of victims under Hitler'(DL, 186), Levinas relentlessly expounds the rights of the other: only if my subjectivity is always already dependent upon the other, if my subjectiivity is constituted in response to the other's demand, if my autonomy is heteronomous,, can socio-political 'reduction', that is, domination and, ultimately, annihilation be counteracted;(DWL, 26-7) only if the 'other' orders me to serve' will I question my 'autonomy' (ibid.) and 'feed [him,]' (28) will I let the other be. ' If the moral-political order Levinas summarizes, 'totally relinquishes its ethical foundation, it must accept all forms of society, including the fascists or totalitarian, for it can no longer evaluate or discriminate between them.....This is why ethical philosophy must remain the first philosophy'"(30)(E28)

This discussion is emphatic as it can be and I would share in it, despite the relative difficulty many of my readers will have with much of both Levinas' and Eskin's philosophic vocabulary, and the rather shocking claim of anteriority for primordial, intuitive ethics. The latter requires a close sympathetic reading of Levinas's discussion of the role of *visage* or 'face' as sign and communication at a level that precedes words and concepts or makes "contact" through and beyond them. But the essential points here for me are these— that poetry is a dialogic mode of communication,—that it is primary and precedes philosophy (ontologies),—that it expresses the primordial ethical being of mankind whereas ontological modes of being tend to adhere to philosophies of power whose active expression tends to be political, that therefore cultural politics and what is called cultural poetics are disharmonious with the nature of poetry which belongs to the basic level of interhuman expression and is most expressive of that form of ethics which is "before ontology and politics." I have in my text made a gloss on the effect of democratic humanism as anti-politics, as a democratic ethic really, which is largely based on self-criticism and dissent. It conditions institutionalized debate, and is an effort to have more or less constant appeal to a level beyond ontology and politics and still have authority from secular humanity. This in turn is what is meant to be protected by the various bills of human and civil rights.

Index

"Academic Discourse at Havana" (Stevens), 151
action and desire, pathos of 130
Action Française, L,' 42, 234
"Adagia" (Stevens), 102, 111, 131, 139, 150, 151, 156, 192
Adams, Brooks, 81, and Darwinian culture theory, 50
Adams, Henry, 29-31, 48, 69; 70, 81
Adams, John, 72
adversary culture, 240-41
Against Our Vanishing (Grossman), 223
"Against the Weather" (Stevens), 135
Althusser, Louis, 220-21
"American Sublime, The" (Stevens), 149
"Angel Surrounded by Paysans" (Stevens), 127, 133, 134
"Angel Without Doctrine, The" (Stevens), 132
anthropocentric poetry, as the "poetry of the human" attacked by modernist avant-garde, 102, 150; modern poetry faced by the "pathetic fallacy" and the opposite threat of a dehumanized consciousness, 98, 168
anti-hero, in "Prufrock," 35; revenge of aristocratic criticism, 109; the loss of the noble and all categories of the sublime, 109-110; naturalist reduction, cultural leveling and the dominance of the quotidian and their effects, 109-12; the comedy of the quotidian, 112-13; as protagonist of he quotidian he survives naturalist humiliation, 113
anti-poetry, "the ordinary, the commonplace, the ugly," 110; in the poverty of existence, 111; in Williams, 115; in Stevens' verse, 110, 139-140; on behalf of moral realism, 154; anti-poetry as antidote to the false romantic and sentimental, 72, 110, 114, 156; as the spirit's cure, 114

anti-Semitism, 244-45
Antony, Mark, 31, 118, 135, 178
apocalypse, natural and cultural, 2, 39-43; and crisis and conflict in politics and culture, 2-4, 26, 37-43; and the two Great Wars, 43, 26-27, 41-43; and the political dialectic of Marx, 39; and the dread of natural entropy, 36-37; and the martyred saint 36; sacral meaning of violence 39-40; from physical void to spiritual victory, 41-42; "The Waste Land" and *Paterson*, the city and man, 78, 176; and Stevens on civilization at war, 2, 4, 26, 37-43; and the two Great Wars, 43; as the totalitarian "real" in war and political apocalypse; as sanction of force, as terror, 102,109; as in reduction to the "apotheosis of nothing" and "the mortal no," 125-128
Apollinaire, Guillaume, 150
Aristotle, 20,
Arnold, Matthew, 26,45, 48, 234
art, aristocracy of, 77; and aristocratic criticism and sensibility, 109, 120; at war against democracy, 77; as knowledge and power, 47, 56
artists, as leaders of men and races in a "higher" politics, 77, 67; at war with the world, 77, 67-78; as members of adversary culture, 240-4
"Ash Wednesday" (Eliot), 35-37, 39
author, role of the, in Foucault, 214; in Pound, 215; in Stevens, 215
auditory imagination, the, 48
"Autobiography of W.C. Williams" (Williams), 110, 138

Babbitt, Irving, 18, 234
Baudelaire, Charles, 17, 72
Beat Generation, 240
Becket, Thomas, 6, 36, 38